AUDIENCE PARTICIPATION

Essays on Inclusion in Performance

Edited by Susan Kattwinkel

Contributions in Drama and Theatre Studies, Number 101

Westport, Connecticut
London

Library of Congress Cataloging-in-Publication Data

Audience participation : essays on inclusion in performance / edited by Susan Kattwinkel.
   p. cm.—(Contributions in drama and theatre studies, ISSN 0163–3821 ; no. 101)
Includes bibliographical references and index.
ISBN 0–313–31671–6 (alk. paper)
   1. Performing arts—Audiences.   I. Kattwinkel, Susan.   II. Series.
PN1590.A9A89   2003
791—dc21   2002029893

British Library Cataloguing in Publication Data is available.

Library of Congress Catalog Card Number: 2002029893
ISBN: 0–313–31671–6
ISSN: 0163–3821

First published in 2003

Praeger Publishers, 88 Post Road West, Westport, CT 06881
An imprint of Greenwood Publishing Group, Inc.
www.praeger.com

Printed in the United States of America

The paper used in this book complies with the
Permanent Paper Standard issued by the National
Information Standards Organization (Z39.48–1984).

10 9 8 7 6 5 4 3 2

Copyright Acknowledgments

The author and the publisher gratefully acknowledge permission for use of the following
material:

Excerpts from an interview Susan Kattwinkel held with Felix Ruckert. Used with permission.

Excerpts from an interview Patrick Tuite held with Eamonn Deane. Used with permission.

Excerpts from Robert Alexander, Letter to an Actress, Living Stage Archives. Used with
permission.

Excerpts from Mark Weinberg, "Community-Based Theatre: A Participatory Model for Social
Transformation," *Theatre Symposium: A Publication of the Southeastern Theatre Conference,*
Vol. 8, pp. 22–33. Published by the Southeastern Theatre Conference and The University of
Alabama Press, 2000 © 2000 by The University of Alabama Press.

Every reasonable effort has been made to trace the owners of copyright materials in this book,
but in some instances this has proven impossible. The author and publisher will be glad to
receive information leading to more complete acknowledgments in subsequent printings of the
book and in the meantime extend their apologies for any omissions.

CONTENTS

ACKNOWLEDGMENTS

Many thanks, first of all, to the authors in this volume. They were, without exception, prompt in all replies, flexible with my editorial requests, and patient while I juggled these duties with teaching and directing projects. Thanks especially to Judith Sebesta, who stepped briefly into editorial shoes to help me with the Introduction.

The Theatre Department at the College of Charleston provided me with resources and time to work on this volume, and I am also grateful for the patience of my editors at Greenwood Press.

Finally, as always, much love to my parents, John and Phyllis Kattwinkel, and to my sister, Linda Kattwinkel, for their continuing love and support.

INTRODUCTION

We know that audiences affect performances through their reactions—laughter, sighs, restlessness—and in most traditional Western theatre, those responses are generally polite and unobtrusive. Audiences also have influence as new professional productions are tinkered with to some extent following "preview" performances. And although theatre is recognized as being incomplete until an audience witnesses it and creates it for themselves intellectually, spectators are generally relegated to "receiver" status, having little impact on the process of performance except in standard, structured response. The passive audience, of course, is a relatively new condition of theatrical experience, but nevertheless has become so prevalent that it is the status quo for most theatre in the West. The passive audience really only came into being in the nineteenth century, as theatre began its division into artistic and entertainment forms. Practitioners and theorists such as Wagner, with his "mystic chasm," and he and Henry Irving with their darkened auditoriums, took some of the many small steps in the nineteenth century that psychically separated the audience from the performance and discouraged spectatorial acts of ownership or displeasure, or even vociferous approval.[1] This expectation of the silent audience has become so accepted that in a 1991 *New York Times* article on the bad manners of theatre patrons, the columnist Alex Witchel did not even mention the history behind his demand for politeness or acknowledge that truly good theatre often inspires in its spectators just the opposite of the motionless silence he desired.[2] This polite, awed reception has come to be the norm.

But historically and in a growing variety of theatrical forms today, it has been a very different matter. For the theatre and dance performances investigated in this collection, the audience has had a direct and immediate affect on the performance. Either the performance is structured to include audience members, or the performance was created with the help of potential audience members, in concert with the artists, or greatly altered following audience response. Others of these performances were created with a very specific audience in mind, and have no purpose for existence without the spiritual and vocal presence of that specific audience.

The chapters chosen for this collection deal with artists who account for their audiences in every step of the creation and performance process. This is not a collection of essays on audience reception but on direct participation. Many of these performances simply wouldn't exist without an audience; it's not a matter of needing spectators, but of needing co-creators, that without the decisions made by audience members the product would be heavily fragmented. The reasons why artists have chosen to adapt immediately to audience response or to make their performances interactive are as varied as the styles of performance they encompass. This may explain the scarcity of previous theoretical work on direct audience participation. Audience participation may not be something that can be theorized as a whole; it may require a set of theories that can be combined to examine individual experiences. As a result, the artistic subjects covered here are highly specific—each author focuses on a distinct genre or time period, or on individual artists. The essays are therefore less theoretical and more experiential, applying a variety of methodologies to specific performance events. Therefore, I have made no attempt to organize the essays by genre or approach. Dance, personal work, historical, and theoretical approaches are all here, so, rather than being grouped in artificial categories, they are presented alphabetically by author.

Not only are the topics of inquiry widely disparate but also certainly the styles of intended audience participation vary radically. Performers include audiences by having them shout out answers to questions, they bring them on stage to become a character, they encourage vocal response and then engage in a dialogue of sorts, they choose audiences carefully and then engage them as creators, they individualize spectators and react to them personally, they leave space for audiences to provide text for the performance, they move into public spaces and create an atmosphere of "community project" rather than performance, and many more techniques discussed here and elsewhere. Whatever techniques they use, chances are the artists have the intent of engaging spectators in message-making. They aim for theatre that goes beyond entertainment and concept/message communication. They want the audience to speak the message as well as hear it.

There may be no one motivation that covers all relevant forms. But a look at all of the essays in this volume will reveal some collective themes: a desire for a Turnerian "communitas,"[3] in which the audience can feel like they are creating and expressing common sentiment along with the performers and each other; a goal of active spectatorship, with the belief that physical engagement may strengthen mental engagement; and a simple undermining of traditional theatrical expectations and behaviors along with the class structures implied by those traditions.

Performances that attempt to include their spectators in the act of creation face unique obstacles as well. An invitation for the audience to participate in some form creates a paradox in audience experience: acknowledgment of the audience, especially in direct form and requesting audience communication, distances the audience emotionally from any illusionistic happenings on stage (hence the Brechtian use of direct address to prevent the obstruction of intellectual engagement by emotional involvement); but acknowledgment of the audience by performers speaking either as themselves or through their characters with a wink connects audience members to the performers themselves and removes some of the artificiality created by the theatrical setting.[4]

Certainly the willingness of the spectators is of great import in theatre relying on audience participation. Performers in a fully illusionistic performance may experience motivational difficulties when encountering a taciturn audience, but performers in a show relying on audience input may find themselves with no play to perform when faced with the same spectators. Groups wishing to include their audience as a character cannot completely rehearse without an audience. The efficacy of their techniques can only be tested under the fire of actual performance.

The study of theatrical forms employing audience participation is also more difficult than the study of more sedentary forms. The theatrical text, although never sufficient alone as a source of information on past performance, serves even less purpose here. A play may vary greatly from performance to performance, because one of its creative forces changes nightly. Historical documents may only cover one performance, leaving the scholar in the dark about trends in audience cooperation over the lifetime of a show. One of the methodologies best suited for the study of these performances is participant observation, a technique taken from anthropology and performance studies. When dealing with contemporary performance, the scholar must be willing to take part fully as an audience member, which likely means leaving all objectivity at the door and participating herself. Dwight Conquergood has noted that this methodology "privileges the body as a site of knowing" and that the activities of speaking, listening, and acting allow the scholar to gather experiential knowledge in contrast to the solely exterior knowledge gained from detached observation.[5] In these essays, when the subject is not historical, these authors have employed participant observation to some degree. A few are writing of their own work as artists, and others write of their personal experiences as spectators.

There are several scholars that influenced the work of more than one of these authors. Certainly any work on audience is informed by the decades of scholarship on reception theory. Semioticians, particularly, have always foregrounded the communicative circuit of performer to spectator and back again.[6] Others, such as J. L. Styan and Marco de Marinis, have discussed the passive spectator in relationship to the active spectator.[7] Works that inform participation theory include Daphna Ben Chaim's *Distance in the Theatre: The Aesthetics of Audience Response*. Ben Chaim explores the relationship between the concepts of distance and fictionality in the theatre. "The deliberate manipulation of distance," she says, "is, to a great extent, the underlying factor that determines theatrical style in this century: degrees of stylization may alter from one work to another according to the specific strategies of the works."[8] Although she concentrates primarily on illusionistic theatre such as realism and expressionism, Ben Chaim's examination of distance can be applied with little adjustment to many types of participatory theatre. The chapter of my own included in this volume uses her work on distance and fictionality to look at the manipulations of the contemporary variety theatre magicians Penn and Teller.

Susan Bennett is virtually omnipresent in this volume. Many authors quote her work *Theatre Audiences: A Theory of Production and Reception*.[9] That work was groundbreaking in its practical application of theories of audience reception, but has been frustrating for many audience participation scholars because of its small attention to participatory theatre and how participation affects reception. Bennett notes that reception theory has taken over from what might be called "intention theory," putting meaning in the minds of the spectators rather than the performers, and she expands on Stanley Fish's theories of how spectators often arrive at performances as part of interpretive communities who approach the show with similar language.[10] Patrick Tuite, particularly, has used Bennett's work here as a jumping-off point for his discussion of the interpretive communities already in existence and solidified by the productions of Derry's Seige Pageants.

Another study informing the work of many of these authors is Philip Auslander's 1999 book *Liveness: Performance in a Mediatized Culture*. In the "mediatized culture," where in fact there may be little difference in "liveness" between live and recorded media, practitioners and proponents of live theatre continue, despite the regular use of recorded media in live performance events, to look for reasons to privilege the live experience over the recorded experience. This may account for the rise in participatory theatre and dance and the renewed interest among scholars in participatory genres from the past. Audience participation may be one way performance continues to define itself as "more live." Audience participation fights against the attempt of television to replace theatre. Of course, now we can "play along at home" with television game shows, but aside from beauty pageants and certain reality shows in which home viewers are able to vote via telephone or Internet, thereby directly affecting the outcome of the event, television rarely structures an event to be affected by the home audience.

The desire for a Turnerian "communitas," forever deferred by the inherent separation between performers and spectators, is confronted here by several authors, including J. Lawton Winslade, who discusses the Mystery Caravan's manipulation of belonging in their production of *The Edwardian Mysteries*. Playing on the idea that the spectator can never truly 'belong' to the production because they do not know the rules coming in, the Mystery Caravan 'initiates' audience members into various levels of belonging as they learn the language of the group. I also explore this communal atmosphere—this 'we're all in this together' sentiment—in Penn and Teller's manipulation of spectator skepticism, and David Callaghan looks at The Living Theatre's attempts to create a community of activists.

Communal desire has also been manipulated by many feminist performers, who in the modern theatre have been among the strongest advocates of the power for change to be found in the performer/spectator relationship.[11] Jill Dolan's *The Feminist Spectator as Critic* deconstructs the act of spectating in ways not previously theorized and has informed much contemporary thought on spectator agency.[12] In this volume Judith Sebesta discusses communitas and agency in the work of four feminist theatre practitioners, who manipulate "feminine" and "masculine" places in an attempt to strengthen community bonds that they believe already exist.[13] Much of this theatre is efficacious, trying not to create a community, but to mobilize for political action one that is already there.

Participatory theatre as an agent of change is a very familiar concept to practitioners of Augusto Boal's techniques. Not only do spectators control the direction of performance but also the theatrical goal is one of efficacy, in which the creation and strengthening of communities is used to change society. Mark Weinberg discusses a specific personal experience with these techniques in his own community-based theatre work. Also discussing community-based work in this volume is Susan Haedicke, who talks at length about the efficacy of the work of Living Stage in Washington, D.C. David Callaghan also reports on the use of participatory, story-guiding techniques in theatre that is not community-based per se, but that has had social change as its goal for decades. His discussion of recent work of The Living Theatre poses questions about how audiences have changed in the short time since the 1960s and how that has affected the types of audience participation that are possible. Techniques that were fascinating thirty-five years ago have taken on a weary patina of dull quaintness now.

Theorists investigating groups such as The Living Theatre, which blossomed in the 1960s and 1970s, when audience participation first began to reemerge as a strong theatrical force, have been led by Richard Schechner. A practitioner and scholar, he reconceptualized audience experience through participation in his company The Performance Group, and he continues to discuss such techniques in his writings. Schechner refers to the avant-garde theatre of the 1960s and 1970s as reflexive, drawing attention to itself as art, deferring meaning and therefore giving the spectators a voice in the creation of that performance. At that time, he says, "It was natural that reflexivity in theatre went hand in hand with audience participation."[14] He draws a continuum between efficacy and entertainment, putting most theatre somewhere in between and noting that efficacious theatre and entertainment theatre form two strands of a braid and alternate as to which type is more prevalent in Western society at any given time. At the present time, he says, efficacious theatre is on the upswing. Whereas theatre always lives somewhere between efficacy and entertainment, Schechner believes that theatre now "is a middle world where groups actually interact not only through audience participation but by subtler means of audience inclusion and environmental staging. . . . Theater people are moving into areas once occupied mostly by practitioners of religion and politics."[15]

Participation methods, like all aspects of theatre and dance, continuously evolve to meet the changing needs of performers and spectators. Some of the changes in audiences causing frustration for The Living Theatre may be the result of the "mediatized culture" of Auslander's study. He points out that live performance is no longer "a vehicle of the general code," meaning that society no longer refers to commonly viewed live events as a source of meaning.[16] A couple of the chapters in this volume refer back to a time when live performance was a significant aspect of the general code of meaning understood in the society of its inception. In fact, during the English Restoration period that Judith Fisher discusses, it wasn't a matter of spectators searching for belonging in the performance but of feeling that the theatre belonged to them. They expressed their right to judge all players and plays loudly, during performances. Performers were subjected to spectators on stage and in the audience competing for attention. Managers and performers expected and planned for this form of audience participation, choosing their selections carefully to meet with audience approval, and bowing to all wishes of the spectators, stopping performances to address the audience with pleas for patience, thanks, arguments, and so on. Dawn Lewcock looks back to the English stage of the past as well, tracing audience participation tactics through the history of English pantomime, finding in the characters and audience interactions a continuity that also betrays a feeling of ownership among audiences.

Audience participation problemitizes that line between spectator and performer, and occasionally breaches the line completely, as with the work of Boal and Grotowski. Auslander acknowledges that we desire a unity with the performers, which is an attraction of live performance. He laments, however, that live performance leads inevitably to a "sense of . . . failure."[17] Joshua Abrams confronts this "unbridgeable distinction between audience and performance"[18] in the work of Cie Felix Ruckert, who seems to see it not as a continual frustration of desire, but as an opportunity for liminal experiment. Abrams notes the possibility that in fact the separation between spectator and performer must remain clear for participatory performance to question the relationship between the two.

The boundary between spectator and performer, according to Auslander, is becoming more visible because of the blurring of genre definitions with the development and expansion of use of new technologies. He has argued that the common binary opposition set up by performance scholars of live versus recorded media in fact doesn't hold, because the two in fact overlap in so many ways. And, although his claim that he is "not yet convinced that digitality represents a cultural dominant different from the televisual,"[19] is persuasive, Nina LeNoir's chapter may help to convince some readers that cybertheatre offers a level of direct interactivity that does separate it experientially from recorded media, regardless of the perceived "liveness" society holds of television viewing.[20]

Several of these authors discuss the manipulation of performer/spectator boundaries in their own artistic work. Joanne Klein's essay problemitizes traditional passive viewership, as do the spectatorship foregrounding techniques she has used in productions such as *Weldon Rising*. Other practitioners are taking into account the responsibility of the spectator to participate bodily and spiritually in performance. Katherine Adamenko's essay, which follows the performance studies methodology of continuing the action of performance into the theorizing of it, engages the reader in what she calls Reaction Tactics to foreground the kinesthetic relationship between performer and spectator. Uttara Coorlawala delves into her experience as a performer in traditional Indian dance to examine the experience of rasa, a much-misunderstood aspect of the active spectator.

All of these chapters, but particularly those that deal first-hand with the experiential nature of participatory theatre, betray a need for further theoretical exploration. Audience participation affects theatrical style, reception theory, spatial stability, kinesthetic experience, and a host of other performance elements. Greater scrutiny is needed of current work as the use of participatory techniques expands and also of our theatrical past, in which the active audience's impact on individual performance is largely unexamined. There is considerable good work on spectators of specific theatres—on Elizabethan audiences and Shakespeare's attempts to respond to his audience,[21] the avant-garde work of the 1960s,[22] the inclusion of the spectator necessary to much Eastern theatre,[23] the spiritual efficacy of Yoruban theatre,[24] what are being called "interactive plays,"[25]—the list is endless. But there are a multitude of areas of study still open that could illuminate current and future theatrical trends and perhaps explain the rise of spectator interest in theatrical forms that include them as active creator.

One of the areas open to future theorizing is the politicization of audience participation. Scholars such as Mark Weinberg have thought of this, because Boal's methods offer an open avenue to political theorizing in his empowering of spect-actors. Certain types of participatory performance subvert traditional cultural values encoded into performative acts because they allow spectators to resist preformed reception ideals. Certainly the question of demographics is an untapped one. How many of these forms using audience participation, past and present, are reaching nontraditional performance audiences? What spectator groups are drawn to these performances, which groups are best able to enjoy them, and does that vary from group to group, just as in all genres of theatre and dance performance?

Including audience participation when discussing performance theory could add interesting challenges to many current debates, including the relationship of experience and discourse to historical understanding, as discussed by Bruce McConachie in his chapter "Doing Things with Image Schemas: The Cognitive Turn in Theatre Studies and the Problem of Experience for Historians."[26] The debate over community and changing audiences could also benefit from consideration of audience participation. Herbert Blau discusses the deferral of desire for community through representative theatre in his book *The Audience*. He claims that "the notion of a community . . . could never be satisfied in the theater as anything but a fiction."[27] If participatory theatre is truly on the rise in Western culture, we must be sure to include it in theoretical considerations of theatre and community, theatre and postmodernism, and theatre and efficacy. This collection offers several more voices to the growing study surrounding the audience as a creative agent in theatre.

NOTES

1. The examples of these "small steps" of course are numerous, as are the sources that document them. Two works dealing with the above-mentioned influences are H. M. Brown's *Leitmotiv and Drama: Wagner, Brecht, and the Limits of "Epic" Theatre* (New York: Oxford University Press, 1991) and George Rowell's *Theatre in the Age of Irving* (Totowa, N.J.: Rowman and Littlefield, 1981). A broader source is Richard Butsch's very thorough *The Making of American Audiences: From Stage to Television, 1750–1990* (Cambridge: Cambridge University Press, 2000), especially pages 57–65.

2. Alex Witchel, "Warning to Theatergoers: The Manners to Mind," *New York Times,* October 11, 1991, C1.

3. Victor Turner has explored his theory of communitas in many works, but the two that have served theatre and dance practitioners most completely are *From Ritual to Theater* (New York: Performing Arts Journal Press, 1982) and *The Anthropology of Performance* (New York: Performing Arts Journal Press, 1986).

4. Michael Kirby calls this reflexive style of performance "nonmatrixed." He theorizes a continuum from "nonmatrixed performing"—in which the performer represents no one but themselves, and makes no action not immediately personally justifiable—to "complex acting"—in which the performer is totally engrossed in character and subsumes their own personality behind the fiction they are performing. See "On Acting and Not-Acting" in *The Art of Performance: A Critical Anthology,* Gregory Battcock and Robert Nickas, eds. (New York: E.P. Dutton, Inc.,1984), 97–117.

5. See Dwight Conquergood, "Rethinking Ethnography: Towards a Critical Cultural Politics," *Communication Monographs* 58.2 (1991): 180.

6. See Keir Elam's *The Semiotics of Theatre and Drama* (New York: Methuen,

1980) and Una Chaudhuri's "The Spectator in Drama/ Drama in the Spectator" in *Modern Drama*, 27.3 [September 1984].

7. J. L. Styan, *Drama, Stage, and Audience* (London: Cambridge University Press, 1995); Marco de Marinis, "Dramaturgy of the Spectator," *The Drama Review* 31.2 (Summer 1987).

8. Daphna Ben Chaim, *Distance in the Theatre: The Aesthetics of Audience Response* (Ann Arbor: UMI Research Press, 1984) 79.

9. Susan Bennett, *Theatre Audiences: A Theory of Production and Reception* (London: Routledge, 1990).

10. For Fish's work, see particularly "Interpreting the Variorum," *Critical Inquiry* 2 (Spring 1976): 465–85.

11. One of the most complete historical accounts of these modern feminist theatres is Charlotte Canning's *Feminist Theaters in the U.S.A.: Staging Women's Experience* (London: Routledge, 1996).

12. Jill Dolan, *The Feminist Spectator as Critic* (Ann Arbor: University of Michigan Press, 1988).

13. Another influential work implied here is Marvin Carlson's *Places of Performance: The Semiotics of Theatre Architecture* (Ithaca: Cornell University Press, 1989) as well as Iain Mackintosh's *Architecture, Actor, and Audience* (New York: Routledge, 1993).

14. Richard Schechner, *Performance Theory* (New York: Routledge, 1988), 121.

15. Ibid. 146.

16. Philip Auslander, *Liveness: Performance in a Mediatized Culture* (New York: Routledge, 1999), 5.

17. Auslander 57.

18. Ibid.

19. Auslander 38, n. 22.

20. Another scholar working in this area is David Z. Saltz. See his "The Art of Interaction: Interactivity, Performativity, and Computers" in *The Journal of Aesthetics and Art Criticism*, 55.2: 117–27.

21. See Jean E. Howard's *Shakespeare's Art of Orchestration* (Urbana: University of Illinois Press, 1984), Alfred Harbage's *Shakespeare's Audience* (New York: Columbia University Press, 1941) and Ralph Berry's *Shakespeare and the Awareness of the Audience* (London: Macmillan, 1985) for some work in this area.

22. Several of the essays in the anthology *Contours of the Theatrical Avant-Garde: Performance and Textuality*, ed. James M. Harding (Ann Arbor: University of Michigan Press, 2000) touch on audience participation. See particularly Laurence Senelick's "Text and Violence: Performance Practices of the Modernist Avant-Garde," and Christopher Innes's "Text/Pre-Text/Pretext: The Language of Avant-Garde Experiment," and Mike Sell's "Bad Memory: Text, Commodity, Happenings."

23. See, for example, Jacob Srampickal's *Voice to the Voiceless: the Power of People's Theatre in India* (New York: St. Martin's Press, 1994) and Jacob Raz's *Audience and Actors: a Study of their Interaction in the Japanese Traditional Theatre* (Leiden: E.J. Brill, 1983).

24. See Margaret Thompson Drewal, *Yoruba Ritual: Performers, Play, Agency (African Systems of Thought)* Bloomington: Indiana University Press, 1992.

25. See, for example, Elinor Fuchs, *The Death of Character: Perspectives on Theatre after Modernism* (Bloomington: Indiana University Press, 1996) for references to the interactive plays *Tamara* and *Tony n' Tina's Wedding*, Gary Izzo's *The Art of Play: The*

New Genre of Interactive Theatre (Portsmouth, NH: Heinemann, 1997) and Peter Marks's "When the Audience Joins the Cast," *New York Times,* April 22, 1997, B1, 7.

26. In *Theatre Journal* 53:4 (December 2001), 569–594.

27. Herbert Blau, *The Audience* (Baltimore: Johns Hopkins University Press, 1990), 11.

1

ETHICS OF THE WITNESS: THE PARTICIPATORY DANCES OF CIE FELIX RUCKERT

Joshua Abrams

"Shall we go hunting?" the dancer invited me to join her and I trailed into the "performance space," a temporary labyrinthine construction in the top floor rehearsal space of New York's Joyce SoHo. Nymph-like, Silvia sniffed her way through the space on the balls of her feet, pausing to choose directions. Tracing her footsteps, I began to pick up her rhythms as I followed the beckoning of her trailing hand. She led me into her private space, an irregular quadrilateral walled off by tall frames stretched taut with muslin. She seated me in the single chair within the space, a tall black backed bar stool with a red velvet cushion, and she stood in front of me, beginning to move with simple elongated writhing movements. Although the concept of a private dance will often conjure up images of the seedy back room of a strip club, this piece, *Hautnah*, was performed at a fashionable New York dance space and was presented by a German postmodern dance troupe, Compagnie Felix Ruckert, and is one of two pieces choreographed by Ruckert that I will focus on here.

In this chapter, I explore two choreographic evenings developed by Ruckert, examining them through the ethical philosophy of Emmanuel Levinas. A Jewish Lithuanian philosopher who studied under Husserl and Heidegger, Levinas's particular philosophy, which blends phenomenology with a belief in the ethical relation as the primary human condition, was greatly influenced by his experiences as a prisoner of war during World War II. For Levinas, the other exists prior to the self, and it is the encounter with the other that allows for the defining of the self. He argues that I can never "know" the other but must respond to the other's existence from a position prior to knowledge. I argue within this chapter that the use of audience participation by Ruckert in his dance practices citationally performs the ethical relationship, calling the audience member into existence through the encounter with the other and asking the audience member to assume an ethical responsibility to the performer, which is prior to, and greater than, the define-ability of the dance.

Although the work done by the 1960s New York avant-garde attempted to efface many of the boundaries of Western culture, including those between performers and audiences and those between performance forms such as dance and theatre, a great deal of postmodern dance remains trapped within spaces that reinforce strict separations between dancers and viewers.[1] Concert dance remains distinct from club dance through the act of naming: although the choreography may be similar, it is differentiated through the relation between dancers and audience. The young German choreographer Felix Ruckert—a student of Jean-François Duroure, Charles Crè-Ange, Mathilde Monnier, and Pina Bausch—who founded Compagnie Felix Ruckert in 1994, continues to work to destroy these boundaries by inculcating the audience as participant in his dances. The first of his major works, *Cut*, in 1992 introduced the questions of boundaries and audience participation that he continues to explore. In Berlin in 1995, Ruckert introduced *Hautnah*, which has since been seen frequently throughout Europe and in both New York and Montreal in ever-changing permutations and combinations. Ruckert's work focuses explicitly on aesthetic appeal, although he claims that the work eschews sexuality in favor of questions of intimacy.[2] *Hautnah* derives from German and is a compound word that translates roughly as "skin-close," "closer to you even than your clothes."[3] The relationship created here reminds us that although, as Peggy Phelan has written, "Performance's only life is in the present,"[4] the audience is the locus of continued performance as the dance lives on through retelling of the event. In his corpus of work, Ruckert makes evident the importance of this testimonial transmission by foregrounding this relationship between the performer and the audience member, building a notion of performance predicated on the audience member's recognition of her/his responsibility to the performer.

The set-up for *Hautnah* is highly unusual and blurs the boundaries between club and concert dance—potential audience members pay a nightclub-like $10 cover charge, for which they receive two complementary drink tickets. *Hautnah* consists of three performance spaces. The first floor of the Joyce SoHo, generally the performance space, was here transformed into a small café. A bar sold wine, beer, sparkling water, and small baked goods, patrons mingled within the space, relaxing at small tables, reading the program, and looking at the dancers' artwork against one wall. Each of the ten dancers had designed a construction that in some way was deemed representative of her or his own dance. The basic structure of each of these visual displays was identical—a six-foot tall wooden board with a 14″ × 18″ black page mounted at eye-level—but each of the dancers had attached an object to this page: for one, a strand of uncooked linguini; for another, a packing peanut; for a third, a copy of that night's television listings (a menu of alternate options); for another, a mounted moth. The program describes this space: "Look around, relax and get ready for an evening full of encounters. The frames on the wall represent the different solos, each of which is designed to be performed for a unique spectator. You will find the name of each performer under each frame, as well as a badge/keyholder. You may take a badge as soon as you have made a choice. A missing badge means that the performer is already busy."[5] Audience members scoured the program, reading brief biographies of the performers, focusing on the performers' training to decide whom they most hope to see. As there are only ten performers and each is limited in the number of performances s/he can give each night,[6] the badges tend to be snatched up by eager audience members as soon as they appear on the boards. This occasionally becomes an ugly scene as audience members grapple over the badges. While my first thought in dealing with this was that it should have been set up in a more orderly, restricted manner—possibly a deli-counter numbering system or lines in front of each frame—as the evening progressed, the participatory nature became clear as a choreographic design: "The time you spend in the bar before, after, or between solos is part of the concept of *Hautnah*."[7] In one incarnation, the company had scheduled appointments between audience member and dancer but found that "people would simply show up about five to ten minutes prior to their dance time and leave as soon as it ended."[8]

Throughout the history of classical theatre, beginning with the Greeks and reaching its apex in seventeenth- through nineteenth-century drama, the "who's who" of the audience was a major reason for individuals' attendance. Ruckert believes that this aspect has all but vanished in the contemporary dance/theatre world, and through *Hautnah*, he attempts to choreograph a return to the creation of a theatre-going community.[9] The lobby/bar space felt much like an art opening, the audience moved fluidly within the space and, when individual members were not fighting over the plastic badges, there was a shared sense of discovery and of gratification in the evening and the performances. We introduced ourselves, commiserated over the difficulty of "winning" the plastic badges, and discussed those solos we had seen or hoped to see. At this level, the spectators become performers, taking on the task of the storyteller—probably the form of performance most antithetical (in the Western tradition) to dance. People recommended dancers whom they had just seen to people whom they had just met and eagerly awaited those people's returns to the lobby in order to share stories from the dance. The sense of community this engenders extended beyond the spatio-temporal constraints of this performance—individuals recommended other productions, discussed restaurants and art exhibits, exchanged business cards and telephone numbers. After the dancers stopped for the evening (they performed between 7 and 11 P.M. each night), people continued to chat at the Joyce; on one evening, several of the audience (who had met that night) afterwards moved down the street to continue discussing the performance and introducing ourselves over drinks and dessert until the wee hours of the morning. Despite the decentralized nature of the world of contemporary performance, the reliance on the stories of other audience members at *Hautnah* naturally extends the sense of performance-based community beyond the performance, as people run into one another at other performances. Philip Auslander responds to Herb Blau's conception of theatrical community: "Live performance inevitably yields a sense of the failure to achieve community *between* the audience and the performer. By reasserting the unbridgeable distinction between audience and performer, live performance foregrounds its own fractious nature and the unlikelihood of community . . ."[10] Ironically in *Hautnah,* the creation of community inheres through the fracturing of audience into individuals, each of whom must bear meaning for part of the "whole" performance. *Hautnah* is thus able to overcome Auslander's distinction, blurring the boundaries between where audience member ends and performer begins through the incorporation of the individual stories into the totalization of the evening. Indeed, this performance's fractious nature is so heightened and foregrounded it produces an ethically forged community, between those who entered the space as performers and those who entered as spectators.

In her discussion of "Theatre as Shopping," Elinor Fuchs proposes the "familiarization effect" that arises from the ownership that the audience is granted in performances such as *Tamara* and *Tony n' Tina's Wedding:* "the spectator is plunged bodily into the action. She is taken out of the theater . . . and invited to 'make herself at home' in a strange environment whose actual historical or cultural specificity, and thus its actual distance from her life, is almost totally obscured."[11] The participatory nature of *Hautnah* grants the spectator license, asking her to bring the individual experience to bear in encounters outside the choreographed space of the solos. In order to address the intimacy of the encounter, Ruckert effaces the boundary between actor and spectator. Through the design of the lobby space and the ratio of dancers to audience members, which implicitly asks the audience member to retransmit the performance, Ruckert creates a spectator who, unlike the spectator in "traditional" theatre, must perform a function more like that of Barthes's writerly reader—Boal's "spect-actor" is an apropos term.

When a spectator gets a plastic badge privileging him/her to a dance, s/he is taken from the communitas of the café (throughout which Ruckert wanders freely over the course of the evening) to the liminal space of the negotiation room. The program states: "You are now entering the second space of *Hautnah.* Your chosen dancer will soon introduce him/herself and will give you the price of his/her performance. You pay directly, in cash, and get a receipt. The solos vary in length from 10 to 30 minutes—and so do the prices."[12] This is a large dressing room in which there may be dancers resting between performances, patrons waiting for negotiations, or patrons putting their shoes back on after viewing a dance. The negotiation styles vary widely—my first time I was extremely unsure of the politics of the situation and found myself suddenly feeling very uncomfortable. I was purchasing a private dance—implications of prostitution, dime-dance halls, and sleazy "gentlemen's clubs" call propriety into question. Having obtained the badge for a female dancer, I began to question whether I had chosen her based on my heterosexuality, yet the politics of the situation thrust any thought or question of desire from my mind. The dancer, Silvia Freund, told me that her dance lasted about twenty minutes and asked how much I wanted to pay. Ruckert leaves the negotiation style up to the individual dancers, but the fact that the dancers directly receive the money from the transaction made me explicitly aware of my privileged status as "art patron" and yet troubled me because I was purchasing a relationship, buying the services of another person. My second negotiation, with Susanne Brian, was more relaxed—having already once been through the process, and aided by my discussions with other audience members, I was able to view this as a more traditional artist/patron relationship. Here I was the one who attempted to value the cost of the dance through relation to its duration to which Brian replied that she felt that was an inappropriate way of deciding on a price. We performed a bizarre bazaar haggling scene in which she asked for $15, I countered with $10, she suggested $12, and I offered $13 as a gesture of good will—the negotiation process is designed to shake the audience member's comfort and cause him or her to problematize and examine the relationship being established.[13]

Returning now to the first dance, after Freund and I had agreed on a price of $10, I followed her into the "performance space." She experimented (in a clearly carefully choreographed manner) with the distance between us, varying it by the full dimensions of the room—moving from an intimate closeness with my body to almost fifteen feet away from me. I didn't know where to look; frequently she was too close for me to visually acknowledge her entire body, forcing my focus to choose one bodily region over the entirety of the human figure. Although in a typical dance situation this is an accepted (and even encouraged) mode of reception, especially in much postmodern dance with a focus on individual body parts; within a charged one-on-one situation, I more strongly began to question the bounds of propriety. Frequently, in what I was self-consciously aware of as an unusual choice for most dance, I found myself focused on her eyes—the "correct" way to look at someone whom you've just met in an intimate social situation. This first dance that I viewed is one of the most explicitly sexualized pieces of the evening.[14]

The boundaries of performance were eradicated throughout the evening in instants when I became explicitly aware of the socializing control over my reception of the performance. "Do you know what I like most of all?" cooed Freund in my ear as she leaned her body over mine and suddenly the lack of comfort in my head was made flesh—should I really respond? Was I expected to respond? Was I expected to simply sit back and watch without responding?

Had I suddenly become a participant in a new "contact" improvisation? Was this still concert "dance" or had it suddenly become a more traditional partner dance? She danced very close, teasing for an answer, and I gave up—"No, I don't know," I stammered out.

"Dead animals," she told me and dropped to the floor. Writhing, caressing herself sensually, these few moments were transfixing. How does an audience member relate to movements that echo moments of intimate contact when the space is removed from the public sphere and itself presents a framing of intimacy? There is no time other than that within the room of the performance: this, too, cites the intimate nontheatrical setting of the personal sphere wherein the outside world vanishes, leaving only those who are together within the space.

Sitting up, turning away from me, Freund unzipped the top of her plum crushed velvet dress and rolled it down to her waist. Again, the rules had changed—the nudity took me entirely by surprise and I didn't know what to make of it. She hugged herself, mimicking two people in the throes of passion; "*Molto caro*," she whispered over and over in Italian. By the explicit citation of sexual contact, the audience member is forced to confront the possibility of his/her own desire and to explore the relevance of this within an event always already marked as "theatre." The audience member is interpolated as desiring subject and ethically called to explore the relationship with the performer as one dependent on a certain construction of desire—whether there is a sexual component to this the audience member is forced to address.

Putting on eyeglasses, Freund turned to face me, covering her breasts with her left arm and the tone changed yet again, "Window in I-rish means eye of the wind. Shadow in I-rish means eye of the shade . . . Grandfather had big bushy eyebrows . . . [which] he kept outside the window. I don't have bushy eyebrows." She zipped back up and lay on the ground. Four red squares of tape were peeled up and applied to her body, stigmata-like. Once again she writhed on the floor, as she had previously, only this time with resonances of the crucifixion. She held a penknife blade to her chest threatening to plunge it through her sternum and deep into her lungs—was I supposed to stop her, to join her on the floor? I sat paralyzed and she closed up the blade. She suggested that in order to be more "self-contained . . . more ecological," I wash myself with my own bodily fluids, or those of a partner—she demonstrated, spitting in her hands and "washing" her hair.

Freund opened a book and began to read a poem she had written about the seduction of Émil(e)—a man or a woman? It remains up to the viewer to decide and Freund herself remains clearly the unsaid, speaking subject and not the object of the poem. She handed me the book to hold for her and picked tape off the ground—she bound my wrists while describing the slightly sadistic seduction of Émil. For Baudrillard, seduction is predicated on the shifting locus of power and control[15]—here the control was clearly hers and yet I was the patron, without my money or presence the performance would not have taken place. By the continual change of tactics within the dance, and by the audience's interpolation as desiring subject, the dancer is able to maintain control over the performance of a seduction scene; the citational relationship begs a response controlled by both the awareness of the dance performance contract and the echoes of similar unmediated scenes. She transferred one of the stigmata to my left palm and pushed her palm to mine, a holy palmers' kiss, marking my participation and transferring her energy. This was the end of the performance. We exited as we had come in, I thanked her and we parted ways.

In several of the pieces, the viewer is given a relic: from Freund the stick-on stigmata, from Brian in the next dance, a strand of uncooked linguini. Although this is not true of all the dances, this physicalization of memory becomes a very important part of those dances of which it is a part. Something very intimate has occurred, if only for the fact that two were alone in a space charged with the political citation of desire. These mementos ritualize the performances; memories of a lost relationship—a relationship that in its only having happened within the mediated space of the theatre has always already been "missed"—they metaphorize the touch and transfer that has transpired. They serve as a call to the ethics of the witness, a reminder that the performance of the Other can only be re-membered through the testimony of the self who was there.

The second piece that I will describe felt less sexually explicit though no less intimate. I performed the role of a visitor in Brian's home. She twice offered me bouquets of pasta, the first time I looked at it and at her, querying whether to actively respond; the second time I ran my fingers through the upright strands, playing them like the strings of a cello. Both times she shattered the linguini in front of my face, allowing it to rain down on me, a ritualized welcoming and cleansing. She took me on the grand tour of her "space," showing me the window through which I could see the "Pacific Ocean" (in reality merely the shops on the East side of Mercer Street), a hallway through which was laid a buffet of "exotic foods . . . just for [me] . . . everything I like." She showed me the attic where I would sleep and the basement where she told me of a collection of rare beetles. In this dance I sat as well, although for part of this she sat in a chair facing mine, her knees straddling my legs; we danced together: having already been through one dance, I was more open, more relaxed, able to fully respond in the moment. Tactility was the central element in this piece: two props—a knife and a peacock feather were present in the space, she caressed herself with them, caressed me with them, offered them to me to do the same. I echoed but changed the movements, responding rather than imitating. She led, I followed—here the solo became a duet.

The sets and lighting for *Hautnah* are very simple: there are no external cues during the pieces, forcing the focus to remain entirely on the relationships being established. The rooms and labyrinth provide a space that is removed from the everyday world, which engenders the self-contained world of these pieces. Most important, however, they provide an environment in which the focus is entirely on the relationship between performer and performee. The "poor actor" is matched and paired with a "poor spectator" who is asked to respond and participate in the creation of the performance.

Ruckert describes the dances as solos, but within which a "safe" space opens the possibility of their becoming duet-like. In touring, the piece has become more cemented, but it remains ever-changing, depending on both the dancers involved and the audience response. Different places have received the dances very differently: "Americans take less risks, they are open but less actively . . . In North Germany the people are very controlled . . . the Italians are very playful . . . "[16] These receptions all influence the dances; while an individual reaction may simply affect the dance in the moment, the dancers have subtly shifted the individual dances over time based on the multiplicity of responses.[17] The dancers and Ruckert build the solos out of structured improvisation, enabling them to echo images throughout the various pieces. The locations of the private dances within the labyrinth are carefully worked out so that the sounds from one piece are not intrusive in those nearby: during the first piece, I could hear falling water nearby, but this was a soothing addition, rather than a complicating difference.

"If you talk, you have to listen too," says Ruckert, and this is clear within the world of the dances—they are responsive, although they exist within a prestructured choreographic frame. The participants, he adds, are hopefully "not destroying the performance, but interacting."[18] This work pushes the boundaries of not only dance and theatre but art and sex and commodity as well; forcing the audience to confront their roles not simply within this space but as the traditional passive spectator in Brecht's "culinary theatre." The blend of intimacy and community provided for one of the most exciting evenings I've spent in a dance/theatre interpolated space. Does the viewer pay for intimacy? Sensuality? Sexuality? What is the relationship between money and art? Is sex commodifiable? Is art commodifiable? Is intimacy art?

In "Diachrony and Representation," a talk Emmanuel Levinas gave in 1982, he asked: "Is language only reasonable in its *said [dit]*, in all that can be written? Is it not reasonable in the sociality of *saying [dire]*, in responsibility with regard to the Other who commands the questions and answers of the saying . . . ?"[19] Levinas's question raises the point that the importance of a message is not contained or containable solely within the text of the message itself, but that one must examine the performed act of telling. An event such as *Hautnah* is inextricably bound up with the recited or retold repetition of that event—it is only in the aftermath and the recounting that we can theorize and explicate any event that has occurred. Taking this a step further, I believe that the inseparable relationship between the "event" and the explication of the event, implies (as Lacan theorizes with respect to death in his discussion of *Antigone*) that no event is truly completed until it has been discussed and therefore recreated within the symbolic.[20] The entirety of the performance involves the audience's participatory role as conveyor of meaning.

Stepping back into the liminal space of the art gallery, from the removal of each private dance, I was immediately approached by people with whom I had earlier struck up conversations. These spectators can be grouped into three segments—those who have not yet seen any performances, those who had seen the same performer as I had, and those who had seen different performer(s). I quickly began to attempt a narration of the dance that I had witnessed. Those who had seen the same dancer often were quick to jump in to compare and contrast the performances we had seen—in broad outlines they were the same, but particular details about the dance process (from the negotiation through the return from locus to platea) would vary. Often this appeared a result of the relationship developed between the dancer and the spect-actor. Those who had seen different dancers attempted to draw parallels between the affect and effects of the different dances, those who had not yet seen any dances were fascinated to hear of particular experiences. Each performance becomes an individual story; the tales are transmitted, lore-like, second- and third-hand. At more than one point, I was told of my own dance experience, prefaced, "I heard that one of the people saw . . . "[21] This transmittal through storytelling is the Turnerian return from a rite of passage as the audience creates a performative community.

Each individual spectator reperforms the dance for which only s/he and the dancer were present by discussing it, allowing others to (re)view that dance. I draw here on Levinas's exposition of the problems created by the ontological prioritization of the traditional Western totalizing binary of "self"-"other." Levinas proposes the "Other" (*l'Autre*) as the necessary third term to destabilize this binary. Within this discussion of *Hautnah*, I propose that the "self" is the audience member, the "Other" can be read as the dancer, and the "others" are the rest of the audience. Explaining his conception of the "Other" and the distinction between the "other" and the "Other,"[22] Levinas wrote "If the same were to establish its identity by simple opposition to the Other, it would already be part of a totality encompassing the same and the Other."[23] Levinas contrasts the self to the Other, arguing that to truly do so is impossible, because in order to do so, one must subsume the Other into the self, defining the Other *only* through its relation to the self as a condition of self-knowledge. The truly ethical relationship, Levinas argues, is one in which the Other is recognized not only as not the self, but also in which the Other remains *unrecognized* because of its phenomenologically radical differentiation from the self.

I believe that an ethical viewing of this participatory performance must maintain this distinction between self/Other/others, while the self must attempt to discuss the performance of the Other within conversations with (the) others. It is by the use of language and through the accretion of testimonies that one comes to an understanding, but not a cognition, of the entirety of this performance as a representation of the impossibility of a to-talizing view. It is in the performance's extension to the social space in which the audience members interact that the question of ethical responsibility must be raised. The ethical audience member at any one particular performance *must* attempt to understand it in a way that it can be later recounted to the always-already othered potential participants. It is through one's ability to reconceptualize and reperform the story of his/her personal experience within the space of *Hautnah* that the self is reconstituted and re-formed as an ethical subject within the constructed community of the audience. Hamlet's mirror up to nature does not simply reflect nature as we understand it, but it reflects the complexities as well; we are asked to respond to not only the view of nature it presents but how it presents itself as well. In viewing and partici-pating in Ruckert's work, the audience member is made aware of Perfor-mance as a means of (re)staging the encounter between self and Other; this Performed encounter always contains both strands of behavior as it is per-ceived to be explicable and *those behaviors unable to be enunciated*. It is only through the encounter between the audience and the performer that the inarticulable can be communicated.

The other piece that I will discuss, Ruckert's *Ring*, relies on audience par-ticipation in a very different manner from *Hautnah*. Unlike the private spaces of the first piece, *Ring* takes place in a large open space with a circle of between twenty-one and thirty chairs, each facing outward.[24] Audience mem-bers make the choice of sitting in these chairs or in chairs in a second ring outside the "performance space" from where they can simply watch the ac-tion. As the piece begins, one dancer per audience member enters the circle formed by the central chairs. Each lines up behind one of the chairs, and begins to whisper, simultaneously, in the ear of one audience member. They describe something particular about the audience member, focusing on some-thing that stands out to them—it may be hair, clothing, an item of jewelry, or something else; they may merely describe it or may make inferences about the person from the choice made; they may speak in one of several languages. One of the dancers chose to focus on the rings I wore, another on the texture of my ponytail. I began to focus on these items of my constructed appear-ance—a stranger was commenting on them, always in a positive light. This clearly echoes a traditional bar encounter and yet diffuses the tension of such a situation through the performed character of this interaction. The music that underscores this performance, composed by Christian Meyer and Ulrike Haage and performed live on guitar and keyboard, creates a soundspace that is open and airy; its ethereal quality encourages nonliteral movement.

The dancers then move around the circle, as a group, each shifts to the next chair, and repeats the process with another audience member and then another. They then begin to weave through the circle, choosing audience members with whom to partner, seemingly at random. They begin to dance physically with the audience members, first dancing around the chair and the spectator, then beginning to manipulate the spectator's body—lifting a foot, caressing an arm. The dancers switch partners several times in this process, and then each dancer begins to develop an ongoing relationship with one spectator. They may sit in their laps, embrace them, rest their heads against the audience member's chest or on her shoulder. The types of movements are choreographed very generally (and Ruckert and his troupe in fact often rechoreograph *Ring* in a brief workshop with local participants who fill out the full number of dancers), but each dancer has the freedom to choose his own pattern of movement and to respond to the spectator individually. The dancers move the spectators out of their chairs, inculcating them in the dance more explicitly, by granting them the freedom that the folding chairs had restricted. I felt myself becoming a puppet, moving only to follow the cues of the dancer, and yet my process as spect-actor was always already influenced by a social understanding of those moves to which I was able to produce a response—what I read as cues and what I did not. I saw people all around the circle, some within the chairs, some outside, people lying on the floor, standing up, each of the thirty sets of partners in a different configuration relative to each other, to the chairs, to the space.

Finally, each of the audience members simultaneously is granted two minutes to control his/her partner. In this moment of shifting power and control, the audience member is confronted by an ethical responsibility, ethical both in the Levinassian sense of an acknowledgment of the Other's primacy and in the more colloquial sense of moral responsiveness. The nature of much of this contact is very intimate, and indeed here, the audience member, in the improvisatory contact that each constructs is able to take on the role of the leader in a more elaborate form of partner dance, somewhere between an understood form of contact improv and ballroom or nightclub dance.

The question of becoming, made evident in the gifting of "leadership" from dancer to spectator, and the role reversal that takes place in this moment, made me as spectator particularly aware of my lead as participation in a conversation that the dancer(s) had begun. I was not aware when the dance began that I would be granted control, although the dancer was aware of this fact, and thus I responded fully in the wake of the dancer's gestures. My awareness of the dancer's control of my body and my reflexes made me attentive to how different movements made me feel—in a way that we do not usually question the relationship between audience member and performer. Was my space invaded? Was a particular contact inappropriate?[25] Was one a freeing movement? Once I was in control, I echoed back some of the movements, the vocabulary of our ethic having been established by the dancer's initial forays. I repeated movements that had affected me in particular manners, now aware of how the dancer responded and also how I had initially responded. My response had been purely reactive, as I did not know the control would shift. Levinas writes:

The caress is a mode of the subject's being, where the subject who is in contact with another goes beyond this contact. Contact as sensation is part of the world of light. But what is caressed is not touched, properly speaking. It is not the softness or warmth of the hand given in contact that the caress seeks. The seeking of the caress constitutes its essence by the fact that the caress does not know what it seeks. This "not knowing," this fundamental disorder, is the essential. It is like a game with something slipping away, a game absolutely without project or plan, not with what can become ours or us, but with something other, always inaccessible, and always still to come [à venir]. The caress is the anticipation of the pure future [avenir], without content.[26]

This dance is comprised of caresses between dancer and spectator; the spectator becomes aware of the contact given as an attempt to broach the gap that always exists in the bilateral relationship between these two subject positions. The changing awareness of the dance and the choreographic vocabulary established by the variety of caresses that one receives, gives, and views points to the potential for change that can be produced by ethical contact in performance. This is a dance of hope: the social space created by the contact reaches toward the future that must remain unknown. It is the contact between the participants and the spect-actors that promises a future yet to come.

The dance is repeated two or three times over the course of an evening, the general shape remaining the same while the content changes because of the contributions of different participants. This allows more than thirty audience members to participate, and allows the participants in each version to view the totality created by these thirty individual points of contact in a second performance. Ruckert describes the piece: "*Ring* offers a double glance, at the intimacy progressively developing between dancers and spectators and at the esthetics of a group choreography, moving as a living organism."[27]

These two dance pieces of Cie Felix Ruckert explore the ethical effects of implicating audience members in performance. The dances as choreographed are noticeably uncompleted; they are accomplished only through the participation of the audience. The individual spaces of *Hautnah* and the individuated space within the sociality of *Ring* produce not a totality but an awareness of necessary alterity. The presence of an audience member as a suture in the gap between the more traditional role of the audience and that of performer forces the audience member to explore the creation of social meaning and the ways in which social space and subjectivity come to mean. Ruckert's imposed intimacy draws the audience into an understanding of the ethical relationship between the self and the Other, as mediated by the ever-presence of others. Within the Levinassian conception of the world, this ethical precondition is the primary situation of existence. Through the work of Felix Ruckert, we can explore ethics as the precondition of performance, not relying on the ontological appropriateness of Heideggerian *Dasein* in the traditional theatre wherein the character **is** and all relation devolves from this being.[28] Rather, this is a shift back to a first philosophy of *mitandersein*—

being with others in the world—and it generates a model of performance that is broader and more open to alteration through the performance of the audience. The primacy of the performer extends a caressing hand to call me, as audience member, into being, necessitating my return of the caress—physical or not—and my extension of the caress into the world of the others, outside the private moment I share with the performer on stage.

NOTES

1. Many performers and choreographers such as Yvonne Rainer and Steve Paxton created "pedestrian" dances in which all could participate and the Happenings, under the eyes of people such as Allan Kaprow and Claes Oldenburg, experimented with participatory dance movements, but most of the highly recognizable postmodern choreographers, including such people as Trisha Brown, Pina Bausch, Bill T. Jones, and Merce Cunningham continue to largely retain the formality of concert dance. The boundaries between dance and theatre remained clearly marked in works such as *The Brig* by The Living Theatre and *Dionysus in 69* by the Performance Group, although these did challenge questions of audience propriety.

2. Felix Ruckert, personal interview with the author, New York, October 25, 1999.

3. Ibid.

4. Peggy Phelan, *Unmarked: The Politics of Performance* (New York: Routledge, 1993), 146.

5. Program for *Hautnah,* Joyce Soho Theatre, October 1999.

6. Ruckert estimates that there are generally about eighty individual dances per night. Ruckert, interview.

7. Program for *Hautnah.*

8. Ruckert, interview.

9. Ibid.

10. Philip Auslander, *Liveness: Performance in a Mediatized Culture* (New York: Routledge, 1999), 57.

11. Elinor Fuchs, *The Death of Character: Perspectives on Theatre after Modernism* (Bloomington: Indiana University Press, 1996), 138–139.

12. Program for *Hautnah.*

13. Ruckert, interview.

14. Ibid.

15. For a detailed discussion of Baudrillard's notion of seduction, see Jean Baudrillard, *Seduction,* ed. Arthur and Marilouise Kroker (New York: St. Martin's Press, 1991).

16. Ruckert, interview.

17. Ibid.

18. Ibid.

19. Emmanuel Levinas, *Time and the Other [and Additional Essays],* trans. Richard A. Cohen (Pittsburgh, Penn.: Duquesne University Press, 1987), 103.

20. For Lacan's discussion of the social death vis-à-vis *Antigone,* see Jacques Lacan, *The Ethics of Psychoanalysis 1959–1960 (Seminar of Jacques Lacan, Book 7),* trans. Dennis Porter, ed. Jacques Alain-Miller (New York: W.W. Norton & Company, 1997).

21. Although a great deal of importance must be placed on the specifics of these

retellings within the world of the evening, I believe that given the nature of this essay, it is the structure of the retelling that matters rather than the details.

22. In this chapter, I use the terms "Other" and "other" following from the distinctions developed by Levinas.

23. Emmanuel Levinas, *Totality and Infinity,* trans. Alphonso Lingis (Pittsburgh, Penn.: Duquesne University Press, 1969), 38.

24. In New York, this piece was presented in Judson Memorial Church.

25. Certainly this is a similar response to that evoked by much of the late-1960s and 1970s generation of theatrical performance.

26. Levinas, *Time and the Other,* 89.

27. Ruckert, interview.

28. Although an exploration of Heidegger's philosophy is beyond the scope of this chapter, the recent translation of *Sein und Zeit* explores the notion of *Dasein* in a very accessible manner. Martin Heidegger, *Being and Time*. trans. Joan Stambaugh (New York: NYU Press, 1997).

2

REACTION TACTICS: REDEFINING POSTMODERN SPECTATOR RESPONSE AND EXPECTATIONS

Katherine Adamenko

We are at a critical time in performance studies where we need to view post-modern performance outside of the very same boundaries from which it is itself escaping. I do not believe that it is entirely possible to watch and study postmodern performance while still situated in the framework as the conventional spectator. Not only do we need to continue to develop and explore new performance strategies, but also we need to shift our focus to what I like to call Reaction Tactics, to directly redefine the role of the audience member as a postmodern spectator. As an experimental performance practitioner, I have afforded myself the opportunity to push the traditional performance boundaries not only in content but in context as well. In the process, I have become particularly fascinated with the affect this has on the visceral audience/spectator relationship.

I ask the postmodern spectator to enter a new kind of contract with the makers of new performance. I ask this new postmodern spectator for three things: investment, to engage in an interaction the performer is asking you to do; complicity, to act without self-consciousness in that activity; and discipline, to commit to opening yourself to new forms of audience interaction. I ask performance creators to rekindle the primal essence of the body and to disengage themselves from the overriding (and often physically limiting) psychology of the theatre. I ask practitioners to become even more aware of, and responsible for, creating new expectations for their prospective audiences. First and foremost I ask for an embodied relationship. Perhaps it is because I engaged with the world as a dancer first that I see the intense potential of the kinesthetic relationship of bodies in performance, especially in the performer-spectator relationship.

It's all about the body, babes
It's all about the bod

As part of my study into this relationship, I chose to experiment within another traditional setting: the academic conference. The following article originated as a performative paper presented at the Performance Studies International (PSi) 6th Annual Conference, The Visceral and Virtual at Arizona State University, March 2000, using the very same tactics I was speaking about. Throughout the conference paper, I used a number of overt tactics as a way of demonstrating these points. First, and the most obvious, was the way in which I greeted fellow colleagues at the door, dressed in a bra and figure-slimming slip. The second, after I begin my initial introduction, I engage the audience members in a series of warm-ups, similar to those given in an acting class. The third is the presentation of further ideas in the form of an interactive performance poem, in the form kinesthetic talking, in what I like to call *Kinespeak*.

THE STAGE IS SET

The conference room is set up for the panel of performative paper presentations. At the head of a long table there is a tray of about fifteen peaches and a burning incense stick standing straight out from the mound. In front of the table is a music stand from where I present my paper.

I am quite presentable; my hair is clipped back and I have on foundation, powder, blush, mascara, lip liner, and lipstick. I am wearing only what is colloquially known as "foundation garments," an extra supportive bra and body-shaping white slip (otherwise known by our mothers as a girdle). I greet the conference attendees as they enter the room, ignoring the fact that I am in my underwear. The attendees are asked to sit around the table for the panel to begin.

I began to question seriously the role of the spectator in postmodern performance at PSi's Here Be Dragons conference in Aberystwyth, in 1999. During the conference weekend, I was struck by the ways in which we were all passively watching and listening to presentations about unconventional performances and then, later in the evening, passively watching some more unconventional performances. Everything was too polite for me. Only Guillermo Gomez Peña's multimedia work, *La Pocha Nostra*, had an immediate and lasting effect. There, the audience was asked to respond to Gomez-Peña's obvious Brechtian characterizations and calls for the audience to respond and interact within the performance. A day later, I heard on more than one occasion that it was too unstructured to be considered "good enough." It was the only show I thought was not too heady and disconnected from the body. *La Pocha Nostra* worked, specifically because it asked to engage us beyond nonvisceral intellectualism and encourage us to challenge the piece directly.

Peña repeatedly asked the audience for an immediate and direct response to what was happening on stage. Bold and embodied moves were taken physically as we also were bombarded with loud music and an ongoing streaming screen of images. Yet, no matter how hard Peña and cast tried, the audience remained predominately unresponsive.

I began to think of ways in which feelings could be expressed, to return to the idea of a more ancient communal experience, and away from the isolation of passive silence, a kind of post–Living Theatre, especially in the advent of technology-driven performances. I envisioned ways for audience members to use items to make noise to symbolize or signify a more immediate visceral, emotional, and mental reaction *throughout* a performance. For example, why not use candy wrappers to be crinkled if you were bored, bells to be rung if you disliked something, and rattles to shake if you liked it, even sounds, lights, and voices could be incorporated; the possibilities are endless. These types of audience contributions can create an underlying and ongoing orchestra of reactions—impulse, instinct, and expression—before intellectual processing in which both the performer and the spectator each have the potential to become more invested by the end of the night. Perhaps I am just not polite and I would like to see our audiences take Artaud to heart in the age of technology.

However, something spectacular happened to me immediately after *La Pocha Nostra*, as a fellow colleague and I were walking along the boardwalk to see Forced Entertainment's *Quizoola* at the Bandstand, by the seaside. As we approached the performance space, we saw a woman emerge from the ocean and collapse on the sand. For one instant, as we ran over to her, turned her over onto her back and tried to rouse her before carrying her onto dry land, I honestly thought that her "performance" was part of Forced Entertainment's show. Yet, instead of witnessing a performance, we had just saved this woman's life. It became the most critical moment in my life where the boundaries of life and art had completely merged. In honestly believing that this *could* be part of the performance, I found myself to be a complicit spectator on the beach, willing to go "along with the act" if indeed it had really been part of the performance. Thus, I realized an even greater performer/audience potential than I had ever envisioned before. I believe that if we raise the level of what is expected, we also can raise the level of response.

From Broadway to store fronts, whether watching a performer roll around naked in honey or cook rice and beans on stage, I cherish the opportunities not only to see experimental performances but also very much look forward to experiencing new and exciting forms of audience engagement. I have been asked to sit, stand, walk, sing, speak, eat, drink, dance, conga, and use my cell phone—all as part of the performance. In my own work, I have asked my audiences to eat, pile into tiny rooms, sit, stand, turn around their chairs, stand outside in the freezing cold, cheer, clap, recite ridiculous text, play strip poker, arm wrestle, and make confessions. Yet there are still other ways to goad and guide spectators into complicity beyond ingenuity, shock tactics, or simply engaging the audience within a performance. For me, it begins before a performance commences.

AUDIENCE WARM-UPS

Audience members are now asked to actively participate in the following exercise: (I am also asking the reader of this chapter to partake in these exercises)

- Sit up straight and take a big yawn, stretch up and exhale with a loud "ahhhh."
- Reach down, bend over between your knees, and roll up,
- Roll your neck from side to side and then all the way around.
- Lift shoulders up, hold, and then drop (2 × s), roll shoulders backward and forward (2 × s).
- Open up your face and hands up wide like a lion, stick out your tongue, and make a nice big sound—"blahhhh." Then make a fist with your hands and tighten up your whole face like a tiny mouse—make a small sound—"mimimimimimi." (2 × s)
- Massage your face, temples, cheekbones, eyebrows, nose, above the lips, the chin, the jaw, the scalp, the back of the neck, the traps, the shoulders, the top of the back.
- Give your hands a good shake—stop—shake again.
- Close your eyes, inhale and exhale slowly and deeply through your mouth, keeping eyes closed.
- Take a deep breath in through the nose and exhale with an OM. . . . MA. Go at your own pace and focus on the way the sound resonates through your body. Let go of your self-consciousness and keep your eyes closed . . . OM. . . . MA. OM . . . MA.
- Sit silently for a moment with your eyes closed. Be aware of your body—that it is relaxed and alert. Be aware of the space and people all around you. Gently open your eyes.

I pause to take the audience in—which in turn makes the audience take in the moment and myself.

KINESPEAK

It's all about the body, babes
It's all about the bod

Repeat after me, all together (I am also asking readers to partake in speaking aloud)

It's all about the body, babes
It's all about the bod

Don't forget this dimension
Up yours, with apprehension
Your mommy ain't here
To scold you for dissentin'
From synapses' snitch
To the twitches from brain
To stain cellular longings
These words live on my muscles
Housed in my flesh
The road to goad
From me to you
Supped-up sinew
Not bothered or bored
With passivity's activity
Of "let me watch in peace"
Instead, you get upstarts like me

Hey it's called, ki or chi
In English it's named energy

I send out some chi

Now send some back to me (*pause*)

I take in a deep breath

exhale

all together

It's all about the body, babes
It's all about the bod

The Audience, the bawdience
Has slept through these years
Returned through the modernist maze,
To be as passive as their gaze

Politeness as standard
Moneyed middle classes the asses
On the new street
No ribald events
Hairless responses to Dusa's laments

Meyerhold broke with the mold, proposing complicity's duplicity
While making movement the key to unlock naturalism's door

Artaud appealed to the senses, not pretenses
To fill his stage with the militant cruelty of impolite sentiments

Brecht me some delicious form of distance
Empathy's antithesis to bring us closer to social's organs
Grotowski's gift of sifting the seas of ritual and splendor
More than mere hearts beat as one when gestures gist us along

The actor the living link, the food chain of performance
Between the stage and those seated in front of the doors
Physically arranged to socially change
Ask more of your audience and we have a play to put on

(all together)

It's all about the body, babes
It's all about the bod

Ask any dancer, any prancer on the stage
And the answer will always be the same
I strut my stuff to move you in some way
Beyond the seats and into your senses
Or else I did not succeed
Can my gestures convey what I did not say?
I move to the groove to move you out of your seats!

I suppose, I propose
Speaking is no different
Words can be as kinesthetic as lightning
Else we do not leave the space to say
"Oh, Henry, the show really moved me!"
My body is the text
Next to blood and crotch
"I can move this audience to tears, darling," the diva confidently exclaims

Words bounce off my body
Across the stage, turn the page
To hit your heart, head and shoulder
Even bolder, to goose-pimpled flesh
The mesh of muscles and loin-looped arousal
Backed up by bones clinking in action
Each an imaged reaction
Behind a tear, a laugh or somber reflection
The injection is real
I call this transaction,

This moving, grooving reality of words
Dialogue's twin disciple
Artaud's theatre of poetry
Moving, talking, kinesthetic walking
Words for the street, feet, meet me on stage
The lightning streak I call
KINESPEAK

(all together)

It's all about the body, babes
It's all about the bod

Kinetic talking
Faster than walking along thoughts
Into the bed of the heads
But the senses much faster, ever after
Into moving words
Those are now yours
To dance home
When the lights go out
To reconnect our hearts beyond our heads
Too much psychology has been the death of us all
Let's take the text beyond the syllable and into the flesh
Kinespeak me Shakespeare's shades
The knaves are still sitting quietly in their seats
Critically exclaiming "I didn't get that at all!"

Cross-discipline this day
Technology's astrology
Prediction's predilection
To pump up new perception
The reflection of my gaze
From the screen
I scream for some new way to react
Under trenchcoats
Cloaked in desire
The fire is real
Stroke the joke the jig is up
Sup up virtual visceral
Multi-media medicinal

Let's take what I've said as tools
To teach the new peaches in the grove to groove
Ripe with juices flowing

Bitten to feed the seed of innovation
It tastes so delicious
Like lip-smacked kisses of delight
When the flight of a performance is beyond clapping
And snapping because new expectations were made.

As I say this last line, I pick up one of the peaches on the tray and squeeze it and let the juices run down my arm and then take a large bite of it.

(all together)

It's all about the body, babes
It's all about the bod

I pass out the rest of the peaches to the members of the audience and we all eat together.

3

STILL SIGNALING THROUGH THE FLAMES: THE LIVING THEATRE'S USE OF AUDIENCE PARTICIPATION IN THE 1990s

David Callaghan

To discuss the work of The Living Theatre in relation to the topic of theatre and audience participation is quite appropriate, in that this dynamic has helped define the historic avant-garde group for over forty years. Founded by Julian Beck and Judith Malina in 1947, the company is still struggling to promote its anarchic vision of world peace through productions in America and Europe. Since Beck's untimely death from cancer in 1985, Malina and her current husband Hanon Reznikov, who first saw their work while a student at Yale in 1968, have led the troupe. Reznikov also has written or adapted many of their recent productions, including most of the plays presented in the early 1990s at their now-defunct theatre on East 3rd Street in New York City.

Since 1990, The Living Theatre has produced a number of new works, all the while maintaining their reliance on the active role of the spectator in performance. Although much of their work before 1989 has been extensively documented, less has been written about their more recent plays and ongoing mission. I myself worked with them as an assistant director on their 1991 production of *The Rules of Civility and Decent Behavior in Company and Conversation*, which Reznikov adapted from the writings of the young George Washington. One consistent factor in the ongoing work of The Living, as they are best known in Europe, remains their interaction with their spectators. My essay will explore and evaluate how an ongoing "existential encounter with the audience"[1] has played a role in The Living's recent work, and how their theory of theatre and audience participation has evolved over the years.

The Living Theatre's early productions explored a poetic drama as part of the Off-Broadway movement, but their exposure to the theories of Antonin Artaud in the 1950s led to a shift away from literary based text and language. Artaud wanted the spectator "placed in the middle of the action . . . filling all four corners of the room,"[2] so it was perhaps inevitable for The Living to experiment with the actor-spectator relationship in productions such as *The Connection* (1958) and *The Brig* (1963). Their goal was to achieve a visceral audience response that could hit people "in their bellies as well as their minds,"[3] but for the purpose of promoting their own newly emerging anarchist-pacifist political agenda.

During the1960s, The Living Theatre staged a series of collectively created works that received a good deal of public attention during a 1968–1969 U.S. tour. At the end of the 1960s era, the company traveled to far-flung terrain such as Brazil, Paris, and Rome to further explore the interactive element of theatre in hospitals, prisons, and on the streets. When they returned to America to showcase their latest work at the Joyce Theatre in 1984, press releases heralded a new, friendlier Living Theatre. As Beck himself stressed, "in the Sixties, our theatre became more outspoken. . . . We used shock techniques to make people sit up and listen . . . Today, that closes people up."[4] Their productions at the Joyce received a harsh critical reception, with most reviewers arguing that their performance style seemed dated. Allan Wallach's comments in *Newsday* about Beck's *The Archeology of Sleep* are representative of the critical response: " . . . [the piece] is filled with the same played-out devices that dotted past performances: company members slithering around the stage or indulging in orgiastic rituals, shouting meaningless phrases, prowling the aisles, touching and talking to members of the audience and sometimes leading them onstage. The theater has moved on: the troupe has stayed behind. . . . At one point, performers walk up asking, 'are you afraid if I touch you like this?' . . . I was touched lightly on the back of the hand by Beck. Afraid? No. Bored? Yes. . . . "The Living," as it's called, isn't very lively these days."[5] Never a group to be defeated by setbacks, the company regrouped and established a home base for itself on the Lower East Side of Manhattan by 1989. Wallach's quote was prescient, however, in illuminating the issues that The Living and their critics would grapple with during the 1990s. Namely, was their brand of political theatre still relevant for a contemporary audience, and could those spectators be reached through methods that the company had pioneered during the 1960s—particularly audience interaction? In the period after Beck's death, *Theater Week* interviewer Renfreu Neff suggested to Malina that such devices had become "shop-worn cliché" given that Broadway musicals such as *Cats* had performers "in the aisles molesting the audience."[6] Malina defended her "aesthetic" as follows: "my interest is in the unification of the performers and those who have worked on the play with the spectator, to find some key to the horrible alienation of people sitting there listening. I think there is something horribly wrong in ignoring one or two hundred people and asking them to sit there quietly and listen to us, the actors. . . . I haven't spent the last twenty years of my life trying to get the audience to get up and dance and sing in the aisle. Anybody can sing, and dancing is dancing. It's of no interest to me. What I'm talking about is creating for the audience a true role in which choices must be made that will reveal to them their own decision making processes."[7]

For me, herein lies the problem with The Living's productions in recent years: although I agree with Malina's views in the abstract, I would contend that much of their work that I saw during the 1990s did engage the audience in a way that often seemed obligatory and even cliché. Philip Auslander sees this as representing a tension between the politically minded artists of the 1960s and the impact of postmodernism on the interaction between performers, spectators, and the larger societal framework.[8] Auslander labels postmodern culture as one that is mass-mediatized, and therefore aware of its own role, and potential complicity, within the larger cultural apparatus. In contrast, experimental theatre companies of the 1960s such as The Living Theatre saw their participation within a "commodity economy" as unacceptable. By emphasizing the potentially ecstatic presence of the actor, they hoped to bring a greater level of personal and communal integrity to the theatre by providing the audience with direct access to the actors. This sense of a forged community also sought to give the spectators a participatory role that could theoretically offer them potential status as co-creators of the artistic event.[9] Postmodern theatre and performance artists—and, by extension, audiences—essentially have rejected these models. High-profile experimental artists of the 1980s such as the Wooster Group, Richard Foreman, Laurie Anderson, and so on, critiqued and deconstructed postmodern culture from *within,* suggesting the possibility of an avant-garde that could conceive politics and political theatre itself in more implicit or "resistant" terms. These larger cultural shifts and their impact on the NYC performance community during this era undoubtedly affected the potential audience response to The Living Theatre's work in terms of content and style.[10]

At this point in my chapter, I would like to discuss several specific productions as a means to further examine the evolution of The Living's commitment to audience participation in the context of shifting cultural paradigms throughout the 1980s and 1990s. In the first year of their long-hoped-for "permanent" theatre (it was closed in 1993 for fire code violations),[11] the company actively produced a repertory of plays, a European tour, and a street theatre project. They also hosted various local political, artistic, and social gatherings and exchanges.[12] Although this neighborhood was generally considered dangerous and difficult to reach, the choice of location was intentional for Malina and the company. The Living's commitment to the disenfranchised of the local community was perhaps best reflected in their 1990 production *The Body of God.* This play was collectively created with homeless people from a nearby shelter who made a commitment to attend rehearsals and performances. In return, the company provided them with a

daily meal and a forum to express their voices in a production that directly
engaged the spectators in a dialogue about the growing homeless problem
in New York City. The mainstream theatre trade paper *Back Stage* called it
an "electric celebration of the style of ritualistic performance for which the
Living Theatre has become duly renowned. It would take a heart of stone to
be engulfed in one of these performances and not be moved."[13]

I reacted similarly to *Tablets*, the first Living Theatre production I attended
at the East 3rd Street theatre. In this piece, Reznikov explored the metaphysical implications of several Sumerian texts through a fusion of narrative
language, highly stylized choreography, and ensemble choral work. It was
polished and compelling in a way that clearly represented years of experi-
mentation and practice with these forms in an effort to affect the audience
"through the skin." Although audience involvement was not an intrinsic part
of this production, when it did occur at the play's end it captured Beck's
hopes for a theatre experience "halfway between dreams and rituals."[14] Indeed, as one of the actors held my hand and gazed into my eyes while participating in a group choral response, I viscerally experienced the potentially
transcendent power of the "presence of the actor" in a shared live performance space.[15]

This reaction in part led to my later involvement as assistant director with
The Rules of Civility, where audience interaction *was* vital to the intent of the
production. The play sought to deconstruct the young George Washington's
prescribed system of rules for "decent" personal and social behavior through
a series of scenes that were choreographed to an original score. At times, the
action would break for the actors to consult the audience as "doctors" or
move among them as an "expeditionary force," and so on. While sometimes
providing a level of comic relief or creating striking visual imagery, Brian Parks
of the *Village Voice* observed that, "despite forays off the stage to directly
confront audience members, the piece works best when kept at an ironic, and
sometimes hilarious, distance."[16]

In contrast, the play's conclusion sought to abandon irony and create a
searing, visceral response from its spectators. The Gulf War had broken out
during our rehearsals, and consequently both Reznikov and the ensemble
hoped to find some way to incorporate a pacifist-based criticism of America's
military involvement into the production. The play's ending was rewritten
for the ensemble to don camouflage cloth as they moved into the audience
to confront the atavistic image of the elder (Tom Walker) and younger (Isha
Beck) "George Washington" on stage. Singing a refrain of "no more war"
that built to a dramatic climax, the actors tore the "Desert Storm"-like material in collective protest as the "two Washingtons" cowered in fear on stage.
Afterward, the audience was invited to partake in a silent, candlelight vigil
held outside the theatre in protest of the war. This postproduction event took
place beyond the formal boundaries of the performance site, but was perhaps

most successful in bringing the cast and lingering audience members together to consider the play's premise in relation to current world affairs.[17]

The company's 1994 revival of their heralded 1960s play *Mysteries and Smaller Pieces* offered another good opportunity to examine the interplay between form and political content in their work during this period. Co-directed by Malina and Steven Ben-Israel (a member of the original *Mysteries* cast), the production, like most of their work during the 1990s, featured a predominantly youthful ensemble supplemented by several company veterans such as Malina, Reznikov, Tom Walker, and Rain House. The revival was particularly noteworthy because of interest in the 1960s created by media coverage of the Woodstock II concert at that time. Consequently, a new production of *Mysteries* perhaps offered the post-1960s generation a rare opportunity to encounter a more authentic representation of that era's counterculture sensibility.

Based on Saul Gottlieb's description of *Mysteries* in the Summer, 1966 *TDR*,[18] the company chose to recreate literally the original structure of the piece. The revival thus opened on a bare stage with a solitary actor standing at attention, holding the position without expression or movement for approximately ten minutes. The audience sat politely for several minutes, then began to shift restlessly, and eventually started to chat among themselves. Most people seemed neither angry nor particularly interested, and no one called out for the actor to move or get on with the evening.

The production then proceeded to recreate the seven other scenes outlined in Gottlieb's article. What was most striking to me at the outset of the production was the failure of the opening image to provoke a verbalized audience response. As the evening progressed, a similar pattern emerged as the viewers responded to the production with responses that ranged from disinterest to outright laughter. For me, its most captivating moments drew on the company's strength in creating striking visual images and sensory experiences (e.g., the actors' moving into the house as they lit incense sticks in tandem with Joni Fritz's haunting, improvisational raga). These sections engaged the spectators on a more poetic, metaphysical level of response that, as with *Tablets*, brought the collective whole together in a celebration of presence and community that has always been a major goal of The Living Theatre. In this case, the result was achieved not through direct engagement, but rather a more implicit altering of the actor-spectator relationship.

Other scenes seemed to exclude the audience, as when the company gathered in a circle to perform its well-known "chord" exercise. Gottlieb noted that some audience members were "moved" to join the humming circle of actors at various performances in the 1960s.[19] This time around, the only non-cast members who left their seats were Ben-Israel and an audience member whom I recognized as another Living Theatre actor. Later, when the cast engaged in a sound-and-movement exercise that dragged on for well over thirty minutes, some onlookers actually left the performance. The result of this repetitious scene seemed to be an unintentional estrangement of the audience, which carried over into their enactment of Artaud's legendary essay "The Theatre and the Plague." In this penultimate scene, the actors exhibited all sorts of horrific plague symptoms as they slowly, painfully died. As performed in the 1960s (especially in the context of the Vietnam War), Gottlieb characterized the scene as having a "most violent effect" on the spectators, with many of them rushing to help or hinder the final, gasping moments of the actors.[20] Ironically, the audience response I witnessed in 1994 seemed to find the scene amusing, with many spectators laughing at the performers or once again choosing to ignore them. The cast did manage to win them back in the final section, where several actors rose from the dead to ritualistically gather the "corpses" in a macabre yet visually striking "body pile." Unlike the 1960s, no one volunteered to join the procession in solidarity, but the remaining spectators were appropriately contemplative during this moving section.

This striking and disturbing lack of viewer response also signaled a shift in the nature and expectations of their audience. In a critique of the late director Reza Abdoh's 1993 production of *Tight, Right, White,* Marvin Carlson noted Abdoh's generational uniqueness in his commitment to an Artaudian inspired theatre that redefined actor-spectator relationships and spatial configurations. Carlson contended that much recent experimental theatre in America had seemed "more intellectually abstract, more technological,"[21] in contrast to the highly "exhilarating theatre" of the 1960s. He also argued that Abdoh's work almost assaulted the audience through its use of multiple layers of stimuli, frequently involving a complex synthesis of actors; shifting locations; numerous and simultaneous focal points, and the use of video and film. Thus, he was more akin stylistically to postmodern performers such as The Wooster Group or Laurie Anderson, although his plays engaged a variety of social, sexual, and racial "politics and phantoms" that were more overtly political than the typical work of those artists.[22]

Richard Schechner's 1982 essay entitled "The Decline and Fall of the American Avant-Garde" also evaluated what he called the abrupt "disappearance" of politically oriented subject matter from experimental theatre during the 1970s. Describing the post-1960s experimental artists' work as "privatized," Schechner found much of it visually stunning and technically impressive, but also lacking the capacity to "be in a rage for/against, the life of the people."[23] In tandem with the pursuit of financial profit that marked American culture during the Republican-dominated 1980s, such a climate created a reactionary backlash against the perceived hedonism and radicalism of the 1960s. Thus, The Living Theatre, which continued to promote its anarchist-pacifist agenda in this self-obsessed period and beyond, was "often characterized as an incense burning, mantra-chanting dinosaur, a hangover from the Winter of Discontent and the Summer of Love."[24]

Given the political numbing of audiences in recent years, perhaps it was impossible for them to participate in the direct form of engagement and active response required by a Living Theatre production. The few younger artists such as Abdoh who were able to engage successfully a contemporary audience with political content also employed a more technologically sophisticated and multi-layered palette of production signifiers, almost holding the audience captive through a sensory overload of sorts. In contrast, The Living Theatre's "low-tech" reliance on the human connection between the audience member and the "presence of the actor" in service of political theatre might have been perceived as almost quaint by more jaded, post-1960s spectators. In an article on postmodern psychology, Steiner Kvale described the recent cultural climate as one where "an attitude of tolerant indifference has replaced the involvement and engagement in the social movements and the inner journeys of the 1960s and 1970s. What is left is a liberating nihilism, a living with the here and now, a weariness and playful irony."[25] If so, the frequently polemical activism of The Living Theatre worked against the dominant cultural current, and surely contributed to the varying degrees of audience resistance they have encountered in recent years. Overall, the problem here might lie as much with the make-up and cultural conditioning of The Living's current audience as opposed to the company's tactics, but nonetheless such responses remain troublesome for the historic troupe.

Although a sense of the company taking itself too seriously was a major drawback of the *Mysteries* revival, some of their other plays during the 1990s clearly expressed a sly sense of self-referential humor. I have found this dynamic to represent the biggest leap forward in their efforts to find new ways to "change" the audience, which I think was best captured in their somewhat self-exploratory 1993 production, *Anarchia*. Adapted from the 1890s essay by Italian anarchist Errico Malatesta, the episodic play was full of self-reflexive humor, as when one actor joked that Malina "speaks with the weight of history—it's also a burden to her."

The play involved a group of Living Theatre actors preparing for their new work, *Anarchia*. As they debated the validity of assuming fictitious roles to examine Malatesta's views on anarchy, the action cut to the offices of Flash magazine in New York City, where the editors of the once vital, politically active magazine are considering whether or not to pursue a more commercial direction. The company cleverly used this construct to mirror and analyze its own past and declining popularity in recent years (and how their conclusions might impact on the future direction of The Living Theatre). This willingness to examine what Reznikov called their own "political baggage" (warts and all), in the hopes of "inspiring the audience to do the same in its own terms,"[26] further reflected a subtle shift in their perception of the nature of audience involvement. Indeed, the most successful section of the play reflected this desire to posit change through example and dialogue as opposed to didacticism or crude political rhetoric. It involved each of the performers addressing the spectators directly to explain why they had committed their lives to anarchist principles, and climaxed with the still charismatic Judith Malina taking center stage. She confessed to the audience how the company has often struggled with its exploration of anarchist-pacifist principles over the years, including attempts (often messy) at nonhierarchical collective collaboration and communal living. Malina ended by politely asking the onlookers to discover the meaning of anarchy for themselves, and thanking them for attending the performance. When recalling images of a wild-eyed Malina shouting slogans at angry-looking conservative spectators during the 1960s, such work indicated that times had indeed changed for The Living on at least a cosmetic level.

As with *Rules of Civility*, other sections involved the actors intermingling with the audience, or even requiring spectators to leave their seats and directly participate in the action. In one Pirandello-like construction, the viewers were given the opportunity to "save" the fictional characters from a bomb set by a violent anarchist group. On the night I saw the play, two characters "died" because of passive spectators who failed to respond to "message rocks" given them by the cast. While reinforcing The Living's message of fostering anarchy through peaceful change, the play ended on a less optimistic note than many previous Living Theatre productions. This ambivalence was underscored when Malina herself cried out "they won't listen" in the general direction of the audience, a scolding comment that abruptly recalled the older, more didactic Living Theatre of the 1960s.[27]

All of the facets involved with their various efforts to engage the audience in the past decade or so were best realized in their 1996 production of *Utopia*. Written by Reznikov and directed by Malina, the play used their signature techniques in ways that dynamically explored the company's desire for utopia. *Utopia* began with the cast's hypnotic, slow motion entrance through the aisles of the theatre. They then seized hanging incandescent globes and dispersed throughout the performance space to address spectators in a whispered, ritualistic chant. One of the longest and most memorable of the subsequent etudes was entitled "The Lagoon," in which the ensemble undulated on stage in an almost trance-like state, while actor Martin Reckhaus approached three individual audience members regarding their perceptions of utopia. "What do you most desire?" he asked, receiving successive answers of "nothing," "chocolate," and "peace" after various degrees of probing for a response. After this dialogue, a prancing Reckhaus led each spectator on stage into the arms of the waiting company, which gleefully shouted the stated desire while enveloping one after the other in an affectionate and actually quite humorous body pile.

The play continued with the company engaging the audience in their exploration of the ever-elusive notion of utopia. Periodically, the actors would cry out "reality check" and puncture the soothing atmosphere (aided by the distribution of wine, bread, and grapes at one point during Act One) with commentary such as "What happens in Utopia when a loved one dies?" Thus, the company strove to simultaneously create a model utopia over the course of the evening, while also acknowledging the intrusion of real world dilemmas on that construction. *Utopia* ultimately ended on an upbeat mood after a mournful funeral procession involving a "dead" audience participant who volunteered for this mission at intermission (along with several other spectators, all of whom received direction from Malina regarding their participation in Act II). While interjecting a somber note into the generally lyrical proceedings, the ritualistic march eventually ended with the symbolic "loved one" being resurrected by the company and two other audience participants, reinforcing The Living Theatre's emphasis on the need for resilience in the face of life's inevitable obstacles and suffering.

Malina acknowledged that poverty, disease, hunger, hatred, and so on, flourished outside the cocoon of the theatre space, but stated in her director's notes that, "if we are not yet ready to create utopia, we can at least enact it. . . . Our intention in working on a play about utopia is to overcome the spectator's disbelief in her own desires."[28] Unlike some of their more polemical earlier works, the ensemble's production of *Utopia* offered no concrete statement as to how utopia could be achieved. Instead, as with the most penetrating aspects of *Anarchia*, the company engaged each other, and the audience, in an open-ended dialogue as to how each of us can stay open to the possibilities of our "deepest desires," and within that exploration perhaps find the basis of our own personal utopias. Both works received a generally more positive reception in the New York City theatre community than previously discussed Living Theatre productions, which can be explained, perhaps, by their absorption of some of the postmodern currents that affected various realms of avant-garde performance after the 1960s. While still pursuing a distinctly political agenda in both productions, The Living no longer seemed to deny its own implicit, or explicit, role within the socio-political process (as when they playfully acknowledged their status as a "registered corporation" in the state of New York during *Rules of Civility*). In his book *Breaking The Rules*, David Savran contends that Wooster Group productions such as *L.S.D.* and *Route 1 and 9* can be construed as political theatre in the sense that they examine our cultural memory[29] and can "force confrontation, both inside and outside the theater," through the use of emotionally charged signifiers such as blackface routines as a form of social deconstruction.[30] However, they ultimately provide no answers but, rather, lead the spectators to engage a variety of questions regarding aspects of our personal lives in the context of larger cultural and political frameworks. Although I am not contending that The Living Theatre should emulate The Wooster Group, they did at times successfully utilize such strategies in *Anarchia* and *Utopia*.

Utopia also represented their first performance venture outside of The Theater for the New City since losing their home theatre in 1993. The spatial configuration of The Vineyard, in which the audience sat on two sides of the stage surrounded by several aisles, was well suited to their penchant for breaking the fourth wall and communicating directly with the audience. Consequently, the interconnectedness between spectator and actor in *Utopia* seemed organic to the play's structure, as opposed to a heavy-handed stylistic imposition. This need for a kind of "breathing room" that effectively serves their interactive, kinetic theatre is perhaps one reason why they have continued to perform in the streets of New York City and Europe. Indeed, one of their most recent and ongoing American productions, *Not in My Name*, is a street theatre piece involving a protest of the death penalty on days where condemned prisoners are scheduled for execution.[31]

Where does this leave us regarding an assessment of The Living Theatre's ongoing mission to create an active role for its audience members that will lead to radical personal, and social, change? While the company's current work is still very much reliant on a physical engagement of the audience, the tone of that interaction has definitely changed since the 1960s and early 1970s. They have tried to reinvent themselves in order to reflect changes in the larger postmodern culture and avant-garde artistic community, but have relied too heavily on a performance style that, although fresh and highly influential in the 1960s, now seems dated. All too often their actors seem to break the fourth wall simply because they feel that is what The Living Theatre is expected to do, rather than out of any vital purpose or necessity. Although historically interesting and at times entertaining, I would generally agree with critics such as Ed Morales of the *Village Voice* in their contention that this approach has become static: "The actors . . . were actually quite good. I've been piqued by that wild and crazy '60s gimmick of breaking the boundary between actor and audience. . . . The point, I guess, was the jolt one gets from actors' continual engagement of the audience, challenging our idea of sitting comfortably and being entertained. But this is a revelation that must be as old as this company's 45-year old history. I was hoping to be challenged by the text . . . but instead there were touchy-feely exercises about feeling the limits of one's aura. As much as I sympathized with the troupe. . . . "Utopia," or anything like it, seemed extremely anachronistic to me, and after a while I felt like I was humoring the actors."[32]

Another problem lies within the decidedly political nature of their mission. Despite their flurry of activity from 1989 to 1995, they still have performed primarily for a rather limited audience of avant-garde theatre artists, aging kindred 1960s spirits, and younger students who have typically studied the company in theatre history classes. Their refusal to work in venues that might be more economically viable or geographically accessible is admirable on an idealistic level and was aptly expressed by Malina and Reznikov in a 1994 fund-raising letter: "We have always wanted to work, not necessarily where we are most popular, but rather where we are most needed."[33] For a company whose identity and history is predicated on changing the consciousness of an entire society, however, playing to small houses, regardless of the degree of positive reception, is problematic. Although undoubtedly some viewers have responded with enthusiasm to their idiosyncratic brand of theatre, the make-up of their typical audience reflects a troubling degree of "preaching to the converted." I would contend that other spectators, critics, and the larger theatregoing public generally regard them and their zealous reliance on "touchy feely" audience participation as no longer in touch with contemporary sensibilities.

In conclusion, it is clear that they face an undeniably strong challenge in achieving Malina's aim to enlighten a new generation of theatregoers. Like it or not, however, the audience participation techniques that they helped pioneer have been co-opted by the larger mainstream theatre, with highly commercial offerings such as *Tony n' Tina's Wedding* now utilizing these once avant-garde practices. While The Living Theatre uses them for more serious purposes, they are still no longer experimental in nature but rather commonplace theatrical conventions. This is not to say that performer-spectator interactivity no longer has validity as a potentially fresh, dynamic way of provoking, if not altering, the consciousness of an audience. In my estimation, the aforementioned Reza Abdoh and New York's site-specific company En Garde Arts offer two examples of artists whose work successfully engaged their audiences through well-conceived theatrical interactivity during the 1990s.

In 1984, Malina stated that "the word that sums us up is 'commitment.' We have something to do and say. We want to change the world as much as possible and want to do it through theatre art."[34] They have indeed remained admirably committed to their mission, although their efforts to forge a theatrical playing space where the spectator can abandon a passive role, become empowered, and take "significant action"[35] have led to mixed results in the last decade. For Richard Schechner, one result or gain of the intense political and theatrical activity of the 1960s era was a personal rethinking of "political theatre" in a more anthropological and less postmodern context. In his words: "I don't think this expanded awareness will lead to political theatre in the Brechtian or Living Theatre sense. Theatre doesn't do politics as Beck and Malina think; it doesn't do ordinary behavior as Stanislavski and Strasberg thought; it doesn't do ritual as Grotowski believed . . . the same event can be political, ordinary, ritualized, and theatrical."[36]

Schechner's comments reveal a willingness to redefine the kind of direct political engagement that so vigorously characterized the theatre and performer-audience dynamic of the 1960s. He has embraced and praised the continual changes and interplay between how audiences and artists locate theatre in recent performance styles (e.g., the fusion of theatre, dance, and music among artists such as Anne Bogart and Robert Lepage; or the rise of activist, "community based theatre" groups). Unfortunately, I don't believe that The Living Theatre has been similarly capable of absorbing recent, or post-1960s, aesthetic currents into their productions in a significant way. Given that the company's entire mission and identity rests on their exchange with the spectators in the nexus of the performance space, this problem particularly affects an assessment of the role of audience participation in their most recent theatrical work. The critic Richard Gilman once argued that "to grow out of the sixties may mean to begin working again toward the reality of the theater, which cannot save us but which may provide us with the images we need in order to know we aren't saved."[37] I would contend that The Living Theatre's unalterable faith in the power of the individual's capacity for "commitment" and action is admirable and important, but perhaps also reductive to a degree given the complexities of society and life in the twenty-first century. Certainly the construction of political theatre and the operation of performer and spectator within that discourse can take many forms. The Living Theatre's ongoing advocacy of a theatre of direct action that typically eschews textual, political, and aesthetic ambiguity, however, has refused to adapt to the ever-shifting boundaries of an audience, and larger artistic community, that has left them behind in many ways. As the new century progresses, time will tell if their style of audience engagement can hold any further currency as our individual, and collective, notions of performance continue to change.

NOTES

1. Program notes, Joyce Theatre Repertory, 1984 ("Living Theatre Collection," Papers 1945-Present, Series XIII, Boxes 43–47, Billy Rose Theatre Collection, Lincoln Center, New York City).

2. Antonin Artaud, *The Theater and its Double.* trans. Mary Caroline Richards (New York: Grove Press, 1958), 56.

3. Malina; quoted in Karen Goldfarb, "Carrying On." *Dramatics.* (March 1991), 17.

4. Peter Wynne, "Living Theatre Cultivates Sense of Commitment," *Bergen Record,* January 29, 1984 ("Living Theatre Collection"), 3.

5. Allan Wallach, "'Sleep' Approaches a Night of the Living Dead," Review of *Archaeology of Sleep. Newsday,* January 20, 1984 ("Living Theatre Collection").

6. Renfreu Neff, "Judith Malina: Living Tradition, Living Theater," *Theater Week.* January 25–31, 1988: 26.

7. Ibid., 26–27.

8. Philip Auslander, *Presence and Resistance: Postmodernism and Cultural Politics in Contemporary American Performance* (Ann Arbor: University of Michigan Press, 1994), 22.

9. Ibid., 26, 39, and 37.

10. Ibid., 52–55.

11. Alisa Solomon, "Paradise Lost: Once again, the Living Theatre Loses Its Home," *Village Voice,* January 10, 1993, 88.

12. Malina and Reznikov, "Dear Friends" letter, 1989 ("Living Theatre Collection"); 1990–91 season brochure (personal collection of the author).

13. *The Body of God.* Review, as performed by The Living Theatre, New York. *Back Stage,* July 13, 1990 ("Living Theatre Collection").

14. *Uptown Dispatch,* October 1985, ("Living Theatre Collection"), 11.

15. *Tablets.* By Hanon Reznikov. The Living Theatre, E. 3rd Street Theatre, New York. December 1989.

16. Brian Parks, "Let's Not Let George Do It," Review of *Rules of Civility*, by Hanon Reznikov, as performed by The Living Theatre, New York. *Village Voice*, February 26, 1991.

17. *The Rules of Civility and Decent Behavior in Company and Conversation.* By Hanon Reznikov. The Living Theatre, E. 3rd Street Theatre, New York. November 1990—February 1991; Unpublished script with production staging notes (personal collection of the author).

18. Saul Gottlieb, "The Living Theatre in Exile," *Tulane Drama Review* 10 (Summer 1966): 140–45.

19. Ibid., 141.

20. Ibid., 145.

21. Marvin Carlson, Review of *Tight, Right, White*, by Reza Abdoh, as performed by Dar A Luz, New York, *Journal of Dramatic Theory and Criticism* 8 (Spring 1994): 187.

22. Ibid., 189–90.

23. Richard Schechner, *The End of Humanism* (New York: Performing Arts Journal Publications, 1982), 27, 53.

24. Mark Gevisser, Review of *Tablets*, by Armand Schwerner, as performed by The Living Theatre, New York. *Village Voice*, June 13, 1989, ("Living Theatre Collection"), 1.

25. Steiner Kvale, "Postmodern Psychology: a Contradiction in Terms?" in *Psychology and Postmodernity*. London: SAGE Publications. Quoted in Walter Truett Anderson, ed. *The Truth About The Truth: De-confusing and Re-constructing the Postmodern World* (New York: G.P. Putnam's Sons: 1995), 24–25.

26. Program notes, *Anarchia*, 1993 (personal collection of the author).

27. *Anarchia*, By Hanon Reznikov. The Living Theatre, Theatre for the New City, New York. December 1993.

28. Program Notes, *Utopia*, 1996 (personal collection of the author).

29. David Savran, *Breaking the Rules: The Wooster Group* (New York: TCG, 1988), 173.

30. David Savran, "Revolution . . . History . . . Theater . . . The Politics of The Wooster Group's Second Trilogy," in Sue-Ellen Case and Janelle Reinelt, eds., *The Performance of Power: Theatrical Discourse and Politics* (Iowa City: University of Iowa Press, 1991), 52. In this essay Savran focuses on a later play, *Frank Dell's The Temptation of Saint Anthony*, in the context of the group's earlier and sometimes more controversial productions. He claims that the piece "reduces its politics almost to the point of invisibility" (52) and, as with earlier works, "produces a dazzling and perplexing double text that eludes any conclusive meaning." Interestingly, though, he concludes by reversing some of his praise for the company in *Breaking the Rules.* Given the range of domestic and international concerns facing American society, Savran confesses an increasing sense of feeling uncomfortable with artists and critics whose "cultural critique" is so ambiguous as to do "little else than deconstruct itself" (53). Although published in 1991, I think Savran's position is still an atypical one in promoting the return of a 60s-like, humanist and activist stance in American avant-garde theatre. The lack of support for such a mission, of course, had been a major issue in

the decline in popularity among audiences and lack of critical support for The Living Theatre's work here since 1984.

31. *Not in My Name: A Protest Play Against the Death Penalty.* The Living Theatre. Times Square, New York, Spring 1998; flyer, 1994 (personal collection of the author).

32. Ed Morales, "Strange Daze," Review of *Utopia,* by Hanon Reznikov, as performed by The Living Theatre, New York. *Village Voice,* January 30, 1996, 69.

33. Judith Malina and Hanon Reznikov. Living Theatre "Dear Friends" letter, August 25, 1994 (personal collection of the author).

34. Wynne, "Living Theatre," 3.

35. Larry Myers, "An Interview with Eric Bentley and Judith Malina of the Living Theater," *Theater Week.* October 2–8, 1989: 33.

36. Schechner, *End of Humanism,* 73.

37. Richard Gilman, "Growing Out of the Sixties," *Performance* 1 (December 1972): 30.

4

IT MATTERS FOR WHOM YOU DANCE: AUDIENCE PARTICIPATION IN RASA THEORY

Uttara Asha Coorlawala

The reign of the Emperor Akbar, the Mughal ruler, is celebrated in tales as a period when Hindus and Muslims went beyond respect and tolerance to explore the arts, concepts, and lifestyles of the other. In this story, Akbar's court was graced by the musical genius of singer Tansen, whose renditions of raga were so accurate on the subtle realms of sound, that they could induce rain or fire. One day Tansen sang a song, composed by the blind seer and poet Surdas, that deeply touched Akbar's heart. The Emperor Akbar summoned Surdas to the royal court but his messengers dallied in Surdas's presence. Eventually, when they returned, they were transformed, but arrived without the singing sage. Noticing their state, Akbar decided to visit Surdas in his forest hermitage. After returning to his court in Agra, Akbar began to needle Tansen: "O Tansen, I always thought you were the most amazing and wonderful singer alive, but now I have heard Surdas. Tell me, how is it, that the impact of his singing is exceedingly more profound than yours?" Tansen replied "O my liege, undoubtedly Tansen sings for the Greatest Emperor on Earth, (Jahanpanah) but Surdas—he sings for God." The implication could not be stated more effectively that a performer is only as great as her/his audience.[1]

Despite its tit-for-tat humor, this legend propels us straight to the core of the interactive aspect of ancient Indian aesthetic theory of rasa. The performer-audience relationship that it exemplifies informs current praxis, aesthetic structures, grammars, and conventions of traditional performance. This legend illuminated my own experience as a performer in India in the seventies, when television, internationally convertible currency, and globalism had not yet inflected the lives of most urban persons. Performing the same solo concert in major Indian cities and for not-so-metropolitan audiences taught me that performance is an ongoing dialogue between performer and audience.

Audience members indicated their performance preferences by the way that they attended to the event, drawing closer, becoming restive, still, or discussing the dance even as it was occurring. Some audiences gave love and support, others drained energy into a consuming black hole. Some bore witness to an inner journey adding their intensity and experience into the mix of my body memories. Others withdrew in resistance.

Finally, in the early 1980s, I had the great joy of performing on three separate occasions for the *rasikā* (ideal spectator) of my innermost desires,— my spiritual guru Swāmi Muktananda Paramahamsa or "Baba."[2] As I continued to travel and perform internationally, I realized that my ideal spectator had transformed my awareness of performance; that each performance subtly and profoundly clarified and intensified my awareness of audiences and of dancing. In seeking to understand more on this mysterious and wonderful dialogue between performer-audience, I found it exemplified in live performances, in stories about performers and most profoundly in the theoretical expositions of *bhavā* and in the ways that dances can be deliberately structured so as to ensure that viewers remain active and alert.

THE IDEAL SPECTATOR OR *RASIKĀ*

In Indian dance, the performer-audience relationship has historically been considered crucial in determining the quality of performances. If a performance is to be deemed successful, there must be rasa. But it is not the performer's responsibility to evoke rasa. The performer's role is to represent the prescribed emotional moods or *bhavā* with sustained clear focus.[3] *Sattva,* or the luminous communicative energy (presence serves as a partial synonym) that results from the performer's bodily activities and mental focus becomes flavored, as it were, with the appropriate emotion—*bhavā*. The sympathetic (*sa-hridaya*) but critically discerning viewer (*rasikā*) apprehends this emotion not as a cathartic experience, but as rasa.[4] "Rasa" literally translates as that which is tasted, relished. Rasa is a reflective experience of tasting, rather than of devouring or being devoured by emotions. Rasa involves seeing with an inner eye, hearing resonances, and touching inner spaces.[5] Until the poem is read, it has no existence. Unless the spatial aesthetic and symbolic characteristics of a sculpture are apprehended, it is no more than inert stone. An image of a deity in the temple, a *moorti,* remains just another icon, until the worshipper is transformed in its presence. Without at least one viewer to taste (even when that viewer is The Unseen Witness), there cannot be a performance.

This leisurely inner savoring of a performance or a work of art is not only a mental practice assiduously cultivated by those educated in traditional Indian arts and literary forms. The intensity of this experience of rasa is the

measure by which success is evaluated. Rasa may involve a spontaneous experience of insight (*pratyaksha*). Very often, a performer in Indian dance will
attribute a spontaneous flash of creative improvisation to the presence of
rasikā(s). Accomplished and master performers build audience dialogue into
their presentations:

After performing a few items Birju Maharaj said he was very uncomfortable and requested that the overhead nontheatrical lighting be turned on, so that he could see
the faces of the audience. He spoke in English (which he rarely speaks) for his invited
guests who were unfamiliar with Kathak. Once the lights were turned on, he appeared
to be more at ease, structuring his presentation according to the responses of the
audience and playing off their moods. At the end of the performance, when he was
being showered with applause he said in wonder, that it was the heart of the audience
that had inspired him, that he had found himself performing with insights and subtle-
ties that surprised him; he did not know from where they came, but that it had to do
with 'the heart of the audience.' He said that the rasa of this performance would surely
remain with him for a week.[6]

And the reverse unfortunately holds true, too. At one of Balasaraswati's appearances at the Jacob's Pillow theatre, she is said to have cut short her performance. When asked about this she is said to have felt that the audience
had been insensitive to her art. However, she declared that she would not be
averse to performing for the students and faculty on that same evening after
the paying public went home. Apparently she did just that and held them
enthralled. So goes this story told by Ted Shawn in one of his "curtain
speeches"[7] to educate American dancegoers to performer-audience conventions of other cultures.

In Bombay, I was attending a concert featuring the well-known singer
Bhimsen Joshi. Beside me a gentleman slouched back in his chair, his eyes
half-closed. About forty-five minutes into the performance he suddenly sat
up alert and beaming. Noting my interest in his changed demeanor, he bub-
bled over, "Now—now he has warmed up! Now [music] begins." How I had
misperceived this person! Now clearly his patience, stamina, generosity, and
discerning expectations all signaled "*rasikā!*"

RASA THEORY

In order for the reader to better follow how rasa theory informs the
performer-audience relationship, I need to make a brief digression to sum-
marize how rasa is currently generated in performances of Indian dance that
may be new but in accordance with historic prescriptions. The concept of
rasa itself has generated two kinds of written texts, the philosophical inquiry
that involves dialogue between various scholars (Bharata, Bhhatta Lollatta,
Shri Shankuka, Bhatta Naayaka, Abhinavagupta,[8] etc.) down the ages, and

practical manuals of instruction (*Natyashastra, Abhinayadarpana, Kamā Sūtra, Sangītaratnākar, Vishnudharmottara Purāna*, etc.). In addition, there
are numerous references to dance in various regional languages, and to aspects of rasa in the Indian arts from poetry and drama to sculpture and music.[9]

Currently, lineages of concepts of dance as performance, an arsenal of pro-
scriptions, appear and reappear side by side as a palimpsest of received knowledges. Practitioners are not always meticulous about the sources of praxis,
although historic manuals (*shāstra*) still are being invoked as evidence of the
early origins of multiple lineages of dance. Whereas scholars agree that praxis
preceded the writing of these historic manuals, today performers often assume
the reverse, that is, that practice followed the writings, as this more accurately
reflects not only their own relationships with these movement texts but also
the recent processes of recovering and reconstructing Indian dances as classical
forms. In this time of global diasporic movement, it is hard to hold on to the
slippery meta-narrative spanning two millenniums of geoculturally specific performance practice. Accumulating traces from previous models of rasa in performance, philosophic inquiry, and imaginative play continuously layer and
transform each act of interpretation, each performance. Understanding and
conceiving rasa is an intertextual game of reading/interpreting written and
performed texts as their changing contexts continue to change their meanings.

The following description summarizes conventional processes of generat-
ing rasa that are based on praxis and the principles listed in aesthetic texts
and manuals. A poet, director, performer, or playwright will first determine
a thematic mood or *sthāyi bhavā* whose flavor will permeate the entire performance from nine generic emotional states as delight, laughter, sorrow,
anger, heroism, fear, disgust, wonder, and peace. Different dance forms prefer
different *bhavā*. For example, Kathakali dance dramas may dwell on heroism
and martial accomplishments, whereas Bharatanatyam dancers might focus
on the theme of delighting in love of the eternal. Buddhist dance dramas
choose peace (*shānti*) as their generic *bhavā*. Then proceeds the task of developing complex, multi-layered narratives that digress, return, interconnect
with, and intensify the dominant mood or the *sthāyi bhavā* as it is termed.

Productions may involve several characters played by different performers
or a solo performer of either gender who will play all the roles including that
of narrator. Building narrative calls for imagination in developing differentiated and plausible situations to which the protagonists will respond each
according to their assigned natures. The causes (*kārana*) of visible behaviors
(*kārya*) in daily life are aestheticized in performance. Thus motivating factors,
vibhavā, are recognized by the behaviors (*anubhavā*) they engender. A dancer's gestures may indicate heat emanating from her body. Then she might
sigh as the back of her hand wipes off drops of perspiration. The indication
of perspiration is recognized as *anubhavā* and the heat as its *vibhavā*. Whether
her actions signal climatic heat, the heat of her passion, or both, will unfold.
As she continues to wait for her Beloved, the dancer may transit though

various emotions (*vyabhichāri bhavā* or transient emotions)—anxiety, joyful anticipation of his arrival, anger at the time he is taking, fear lest he may have been harmed. Because all these passing emotions arise from her being in love, the thematic *bhavā* (dominant emotional state) of this dance remains love (*śringāra*). The NatyaSastra lists thirty-three of these complementary states (*vyabhichāribhavā*) that might be so used to build one of eight durable states (*sthāyi bhavā*). It also lists eight extreme emotional states called *sāttvika bhavā*, which in real life would be inferred from involuntary symptoms as perspiration, trembling, change of color, and so on.

It has puzzled some readers that although characters are types and emotions are generic, the NatyaSastra lists numerous synonyms for the same category of emotional state to co-relate shades of interpretative activity with character types ("superior," "middling," and "inferior") as they are hierarchically named in the NatyaSastra. It is said that while each human being functions according to a mix of three *guna* or qualitative characteristics, the one that predominates endows his or her personality with its categorized characteristic. In god-like heroes, *sattva*, or luminous clarity predominate. Villains (often more theatrically rewarding roles) are usually characterized as *rājasa*, or passionately infatuated. Comic foils often are characterized as *tāmasika* or lethargic and slow-witted. King Rama (God and *sāttvika*) would show his anger in a much calmer way than perhaps King Ravana (*rājasika*) the demon king who steals Rama's wife.[10]

In solo dances, the lines of the accompanying song might be repeated several times, allowing the dancer space to improvise transitional states.[11] A dancer may develop a dominant *bhavā* by narrating several exploits of the addressed Beloved and collapse different narratives, times and places into one. Or she will infer an entire episode by a mere gestural reference, assuming that her audience is familiar with the story, and that the association itself will trigger devotion. Kalanidhi Narayan, a leading exponent of the art of *abhinaya* (performing narratives) in classical solo dance forms, believes that the convention of stringing episodes together (sometimes called monodrama) are a practical but unimaginative response to demands that erotic implications should be minimized or erased; that to focus exclusively on the spiritual aspect of the dance restricts possibilities for excavating interior landscapes and for developing a rich and complex layering of resonances. Thus, each performer, each dance, each play, might orchestrate differently, a pyramid of emotional states, with a broad base of many passing emotions that accumulate as one (*sthāyi bhavā*) generic emotional state. When these resonate for the viewer as a lingering aftertaste, then there is said to be *rasa*.

Abhinavagupta compares rasa to *ananda*, or the spiritual ecstasy of the yogi. But, he argues, whereas the accomplished yogi (*siddha*) is able to achieve and maintain steady continuous objectless focus,[12] the average person needs something to contemplate that will call forth this ongoing stream of attentive energy, and performance offers just this. Emotions must be performed so that they compel engagement. At the same time, what is performed must be clearly unreal so that the viewer remains detached and does not identify his or her self with the protagonists, their circumstances or drift into a nondiscriminating sentimental haze. For this, Abhinavagupta lists various presentational conventions that he calls "obstacles" to identification.[13] Abhinavagupta's detailed, practical directions for performance presage many postmodern and feminist concerns and are rarely given their due.

First, Abhinavagupta secures the hook. As it is the purpose of all performance to teach and enlighten those who do not have direct access to the written literatures[14] Abhinavagupta suggests that performances, especially those with moralistic narratives, need to ensure the spectators' involvement. He suggests narratives that include familiar characters of mythic status, characters that have inhabited the consciousness of the viewers extensively over time. This would partially suggest why so many stories link into iconic figures such as Rama, Krishna, Radha, and Satyabhāma. Today, a similar strategy appears in popular television characters, such as the Simpsons, Tarzan, Hercules—characters disassociated from real life by their two-dimensional representations as cartoons who regularly invite us to contemplate moral dilemmas.

What prevents the spectator's consciousness from being seduced into fascination with the presence of the live performers? Abhinavagupta suggests stylization (*nātyadharmī*),[15] and the use of plural subject positions. Fantastic costumes, make-up, and jewelry separate performers from individualized personality and everyday life and endow each role with a "typical" look that signals a generic socially constructed identity for each character and for the aesthetic form. What will ensure that the spectator's active flow of attention does not become subsumed in pleasant or unpleasant emotions and associations? Abhinavagupta prescribes judiciously alternating modalities of experience. Dances and songs not only divert the spectator from wallowing in a particular emotion, they also call on varied abilities for processing experience. Thus to ensure both psychic engagement and critical distance, he recommends theatrical use of visual pleasure (*āharyā*), spatial, linguistic (*bhāsā*), musical (*sangīta*), verbal (*vāchika*), and bodily conventions (*āngika abhinaya*) to attract and sustain attention,[16] very much in the mode of performance art today.

Abhinavagupta's arguments and suggestions so far might seem reminiscent of Brecht's concept of the Alienation Effect advocating that the spectator be distanced from narrative in order to assess its veracity and relevance objectively. But the two systems differ vastly in practice and performance. Here, I am indebted to Cara Gargano for her observation that this disparity lies in Abhinavagupta's prescription for overcoming the "fourth obstacle."[17] Abhinavagupta recommends that visual information be encoded to ensure that reception will engage the mind and not appeal only to the senses. Sensual communication needs to be routed via social constructions, aesthetic conventions and literary associations, all of which continually call on the viewer to minutely observe and actively decode what is presented. For example, lovemaking might be shown through hand gestures enacting the metaphor of the vibrating (male) bee seeking honey, or the female protagonist drinking the soma of ecstatic union. Sets and realism are not part of this aesthetic. Locations are inferred by poetic text, descriptive movements (such as going up and down hill, entering or leaving an abode), symbolic gestures (the temple of Tillai), by conventions that consistently allocate spatial zones, and by focus.[18] Abhinavagupta's proposal that performance should direct the movement of the senses inward toward contemplating subjective experience rather than toward external and discrete sense objects is consistent with concepts of consciousness mapped out by Kashmir Shaivism and in Patanjali's *Yoga Sūtra*.

In solo forms particularly, gender is performed as a location rather than as a bodily given. Women or men performers may perform in the third person as narrator, in the first person as the leading female character (*nāyika*), and also as persons addressed or encountered. The staging of both subject and object positions by the same person not only allows the performer to construct his or her bodily text in accordance with her or his own gaze, it can be orchestrated such that the viewer must access the work via alternating gazes.[19] The performance of gender removes the necessity for both sexes to engage on stage separating performer from the role. While this strategy enables the dancer to delve into sensual and sexual imagery and experience without resorting to an "in-your-face" kind of performance of sexuality, it layers on yet another set of visual codes. The viewer must now also actively decode gender locations in order to follow the narrative.[20]

At Krishna Gana Sabha (an annual festival in Chennai) in 1995, the focus was on Purush or the Male as dancer. A kudiyattam performer (Margi Madhu) was about to reenvision, through Ravana's desiring but worshipful perspective, the exquisite beauty of Sita's entire anatomy, part by part, from her head down to her toes. Kudiyattam, perhaps the sole surviving form today of classical Sanskrit theatre, has historically been the exclusive preserve of Chakyar and Nambiar caste and subcastes and continues to be so. The archaic and pristine quality of the performance heightens my awareness of how it calls for a different kind of spectatorship.

The passage revisited the fifth act of the Ramayana where Ravana enters his garden after kidnapping Sita. Contemplating her exquisite beauty, Ravana recalls how Brahma was called on to judge between the beauty of a strand of Sita's hair and a peacock feather. This becomes the frame launching Margi Madhu's performance where he first takes on the roles of Brahma, then the peacock and continues on to reenvision through Ravana's desiring but worshipful perspective, the exquisite beauty of Sita's entire anatomy, part by part, from her head down to her toes.

As a spectator, my first response was alarm at being invited to participate in the patriarchal and voyeuristic act of undressing Sita, but curiosity prevailed, and I stayed for one and half-hours watching this scenario unfold through eye, face, and hand gestures to the sound of three different percussive instruments.

In Kudiyattam, the performer's face is painted into a fantastic mask as in Kathakali, but unlike Kathakali, the performer simply sits on a chair and "narrates" with hand gestures and eye movements. We were invited to focus our attention on the performer's eyes, to observe how the eyelids would quiver in synchrony with the percussive rhythms of the accompanying orchestra. Actually, it was not only the lower lids of the eyes but also, at different times, the eyebrows and lips also "danced" in this rhythmic way.

In order to follow the narrative, I had to stay closely observant to not only the performed actions but also to the way they connected to either make puns, metaphors, or other poetic conceits. Occasionally I would lose the narrative and look over to my *rasikā* friend the dance critic and Sanskrit scholar Sunil Kothari. Sunil would oblige with a running commentary just like a sports commentator on television, "translating" for me. Here at Chennai, instead of being disturbed by this, members of the audience around us would lean over to listen in and join in the commentary. I was very grateful for this, for surely I would have missed so many wonderful finer points of the performance but for their participation. Disturbing the performer's delicate concentration was not an issue here as in many traditional performance venues in rural India where performers include the audience in their focus, acknowledging latecomers, and ignoring the crying child. We were intent on accessing Margi Madhu's every nuance.

The peacock would appear from time to time on Brahma's left as Margi Madhu would stand up and move to the left of the chair. Then to show Brahma's response he would return to the chair. Each transition was undertaken casually but precisely and unhurriedly, as he would unfold his foot off his thigh, stand up, adjust his costume, turn around, and move into place. Each of these transitions allowed us all to relax our attention a bit, so as to return and refocus afresh. "Am I not more beautiful than the hair?" the peacock kept insisting. Initially, Brahma responded with consideration, "Indeed you are beautiful." But as the peacock became insistent, Brahma became increasingly absentminded in his responses, until finally he pushed the peacock out of the door and bolted it tight. Then he returned to his seat to contemplate the exquisite hair.

When Margi Madhu performs Sita, he has a demure slightly downcast head, but at the same time the corners of his mouth turn up in a very slight smile. His Sita has an ineffable "I-am-beautiful" look. As Ravana, he contemplates Sita's thick and beautiful hair, her eyebrows, eyes, the snake-like hairline that rises from navel to chest and hides trembling under her full breasts, on and on, until the final moment of climax. Here his two hands, palms facing down, with the thumbs wiggling excitedly, move together one on the other to form the gesture of swimming fish, but its meaning is clear. Then he simply sits, showing contemplation for about five minutes continuously and holds our attention throughout. The representation of this "thinking" stays alive by changing in minute gestures, as the eyeball, for example, moves very slowly around the upper circumference of the iris. His head drops ever so slightly, as if lost in a recollection, and then lifts. There is a mere indication of a headshake, a wondering nod, and so on.

To conclude, the actor returns from first person representation to his role as narrator and sums up the event with danced and formal gestures. It is at this point that I realize that we have been watching intently for nearly two hours, that despite the excessively erotic content, I am not titillated or angry, but in a gentle, quiet inner space—rasa. By appealing to the senses via the mind,[21] by calling for minute observation and continuous interpretation of signs, the performance generated an idealized dream-like state thereby demonstrating the effectiveness of Abhinavagupta's "obstacles" while also showing how they are embedded in the form.

SUBTLE DIMENSIONS OF PERFORMANCE— A DISCOURSE OF EMOTIONS

A discourse of emotions informs the reception of traditional Indian performance. Rather than perceiving emotions as passive, irrational, natural, universal, and female, they are culturally viewed as appraisals, as judgments of situations based on learned beliefs and values that are valued in male and female experience.[22] Discussions of the horizontal and vertical relationships among emotions, perception, body, and meaning form a major part of historical commentaries of rasa theory and include psychological, social, aesthetic, and theological perspectives. Key words (for example, names of Krishna) locate within networks of associations and resonate differently for speakers of the various indigenous languages. For example, wherever Krishna appears in a narrative with his consort Radha, the two names together signal *bhakti* or devotion in religious contexts (usually associated with the Odissi and Manipuri forms) or amorous dalliance in secular contexts (Kathak). Narratives, as in the Mahabharata or in the Bhagavad Gita, that focus on Krishna with his warrior disciple Arjuna, however, signal karmic concepts of action without personal motives, war, martial arts. These tend to be performed in Kathakali.

This shared discourse of emotions enables shared communion between performer and audience. Malavika Sarrukkai, an exquisite performer of Bharatanatyam, resident in Chennai, is constantly extending her own research in the dance tradition she performs internationally. Sarrukkai's best performances occurred when she felt that the audience was with her simultaneously, with no time lag between transmission and reception. She noted that this experience involved simultaneity of images, emotions, and ideas. Malavika Sarrukkai recalled for me a performance in which she had experienced *anukirtana,* a moment of communion between her metropolitan self and women in a rural Gujerat. She had performed out of doors on a makeshift stage, at a village festival. It was Choolaband, she said; in other words, on this day no one cooked so that all could participate in the celebration. She had selected what she would dance carefully, choosing the language and dialect of the text accompanying the dance because of its local genesis (selected from Tulsidas's Ramayana) so that it would resonate with this particular audience in Gujerat: "In *janatavam* Kunti asks Yashoda 'what deed must you have done that He calls you mother?' There was a moment when I was holding Krishna here (gestures to her lap), I looked at Krishna—isn't he beautiful? Then I looked towards the audience. They were nodding! Yes, nodding! We were seeing Krishna together! It was as we say *anukirtanam* (a re-creation, making anew.) The moment with Krishna, it is a presence at *that point* of time. It is not always there, nor is it a presence for which you have rehearsed. It is a presence *in that moment,* a *kind of first time.*"[23] Sarukkai went on to distinguish between this kind of audience and the *rasikā*. When she dances for a conservative audience of classical dance lovers in Madras, where esoteric references and complex renderings are expected of a performer of her experience and stature, Sarukkai feels that the audience is so knowledgeable that "They *know* that here she is going to take off and do this little *sanchari,* (elaboration) and they are waiting for it. They *know how* you will structure it. There is an excitement in that too." Sarukkai is now in the enviable position of being able to choose her audiences, and always performs in Chennai, at least once during the performance season, although she eschews comparable *sabha* (local cultural organization) performances in most cities of India.

Just as secular and sacred discourses of emotion simultaneously inform the dance today, so too a discourse informs the reception of emotion and idea. Both are said to be received in body-mindscapes, in accordance with Ayurvedic and yogic theories of the body, its functions, and of perception. Such theories identify two to several systems (also called bodies) through which the individual navigates the world. Starting with mastery of the material body (*sthula sharira*) the evolved person develops in more subtle abstracted and interior ways. The culminating attainment is the *turya* state of the supracausal or transcendent body (*turya* or *neelbindu*) translated according to various philosophical perspectives as soul, Self, Brahman, or Blue Pearl. In between the material and the transcendent "bodies" is the subtle body (*sukshma sharira*), consisting of energy centers (*chakra*), "subtle organs of perception," and mind (*manasa*), a center of reason, judgment, and emotions, all said to be located in the heart. Also, a range of sheaths function as intermediary systems involving both physiological and psychological functions.[24] This physical-emotive-cognitive configuration of the senses seems to inform Sarukkai's own practice: "dance is a yoga. This morning someone commented 'You must practice so much' but I do not. At first, you practice and practice. Then your body intentions take over and move you in a particular way. These days, I internalize a lot more. Now I spend hours internalizing."[25]

Revisiting Abhinavagupta's prescription that the physical and the erotic should be transmitted via mental processes bypassing the senses, one realizes that eroticism and spiritual ecstasy need not be mutually exclusive;[26] dance itself is discourse when it depends on the presence of the *rasikā* for its consummation,[27] when it involves cognizing movements, melodies, rhythm patterns, sculptural, historical, and mythic texts. It involves images, movement grammars, and vocabularies. But what happens to rasa when there is no *rasikā* to share the meanings of the highly symbolic gestures and to illuminate the finer points of performance? What happens when a highly stylized and subtle, performance of say, Kudiyattam, is performed abroad? Or any Indian traditional dance for that matter? Vatsyayan, recalling Kathakali performances of Ramana Krishna Kutty in the Soviet Union, said, "We need to address what has been done by this overexposing of dance to uninitiated audiences. It is the presented surface body that we are looking at, not the experienced body. The attitude of 'how I will be seen by you' makes for a completely different aesthetic experience than a concern with experience and communication."[28]

How are traditionally trained artists to present this culture-specific yet transcendent art abroad where criteria for excellence are different than their own? I recall such yawning differences being negotiated in the performances across the United States during the early 1970s, of the sitarist Ravi Shankar and his tabla playing partner Allah Rakha. Watching them make their music visually accessible, I noticed that each was his partner's best listener; that, in fact, they were performing for each other. Ravi Shankar might look over to his percussionist with a questioning or challenging glance, as if to say "And how did you like that?" Allah Rakha might respond, "Vah! Vah!" or tilt his head from side to side with enthusiastic approval. Each supported, challenged his colleague, so eliciting better performances.

Roshan Jagatrai Shahani, a music and dance critic in Mumbai, explained that this camaraderie was not unusual. In fact, it was a performance convention—*sangati dena*. For example, she explained, a vocalist like Kishori Amonkar[29] sings with her palm laid over her ear. Not only does this custom have an acoustical effect for the singer, but it also announces that the singer is listening and so should you. In this moment of getting everyone to focus, her accompanist Shree Purshottam Walavalker (harmonium) may cue listeners as to the notes that she may sing or harmonize with by playing these suitably in advance on his harmonium. Conventions such as this one heighten expectations. When Amonkar completes an exquisite climactic moment, Walavalker and the tabla player may respond by taking their hands off their instruments in delighted acknowledgment. Or one of them might twist his shoulder, leaning his head on it in a gesture of ecstatic listening. Thus, physical responses make visual the musical dynamics, educate listeners, and demand their continued attention. Kathak dancers involve similar processes to cue their audiences and ensure their active participation.

In India, dancers will explain the import of each dance before they perform it. In the United States, this approach is seen as didactic and not compatible with the American vision of art as phenomenologically accessible to all. Most dancers in Euro-American situations resort to program notes. Kritika Rajagopalan, who lives in Chicago, introduced bilingual narrations to accompany her dance and builds the "explanation" into body of the both the dance and its accompaniment. In doing this she is actually extending the traditional convention of performing a summary of the narrative before beginning to elaborate upon its nuances.

Chandralekha, a dancer-choreographer living in Madras (now Chennai), has successfully extended the performer-audience dialogue beyond culture specific locations to the extent that her work is seen as a model for diaspora dancers. In Chennai, an astounding proportion of the population either dances or sings in the demanding traditions of Carnatic music and its dance Bharatanatyam. Chandralekha, responding to what she perceived as the loss of physicality and integrity of the dance, resorted to modernism and its conventions of simplicity and pared down form to readdress Bharatanatyam. In *Angika* (1985), she incorporated into the choreography Kalaripayattu training exercises and a demonstration of the elements of Bharatanatyam technique as taught in Kalakshetra. For many in India and abroad who had not known of the existence of this martial movement tradition, it was an exciting work. But those already steeped in these traditions were offended by its didactic mode of address, which reduced active educated role of the *rasikā* to that of passive receiver of a simplistic message. Chandralekha opted for didactic minimalism over layered complexity at the same time as her works began challenging conventional patriarchal representations of women. Those who would resist her unconventional representations of gender roles also had to resist her reorientation of conventional audience-performer relationships. Furthermore, *Angika* even deliberately conflated the two relationships.

At a recent diaspora Bharatanatyam dance conference in Chicago,[30] it was as if Chandralekha's challenge to *rasikās* of Indian dance had completed a cycle. Although the movement vocabulary of her work *Sharira-Fire/Desire* did not even reference bharatanatyam, *rasikās* from Chennai, imported to Chicago for this conference, agreed that their appreciation of her work had evolved to new levels of understanding. In *Sharira-Fire/Desire,* slowed down abstract movement served to aestheticize a steamy duet. The singers, the Gundecha brothers, layered secular eroticism with spiritual associations as they sang about the union of Shiva and Parvati, in Dhrupad, a style of singing that tends to be meditative and focuses on subtle transitions of tone and tempo.

Responding to Chandralekha's new work *Sharira-Fire/Desire,* U.S.-educated dance critics noted precision of movement, attention to minute detail, containment, the detached cool presence of performers, and how the choreography challenged traditional spatial hierarchies by maintaining continuous horizontality. However, the dancers, and *rasikā(s)* educated predominantly on Indian dance traditions focused on how they had been transported by this mating ritual to several levels of inner experience—simultaneously seeing self in union with a perfect mate, seeing desire and its mechanisms, and also seeing the transcendent aspects in not only content but also in its exceeding of culture-specific boundaries. The two categorically different kinds of responses within the same situation to the same work exemplify how two sets of aesthetic criteria (the rasa of inner touching versus the marking of what is observed as materially verifiable) informed perception differently and how Chandralekha's work holds interest for both sets of perceptions. In the global market, performers today ideally seek out both kinds of audiences. The affirmation or criticism of the local audiences educate the performer, and provide a kind of authenticating history, which is then useful in marketing the performer internationally. Performing abroad endows the performer with yet more (or less) authority when s/he returns to his or her local culture.

Within the Indian performance tradition are embedded at least two more *rasikā* gazes that have intercultural applicability. By offering a performance inwardly, privately or publicly to a personal Loved One,[31] the performer develops a permeable independence from her actual audience, for her mental practice has forged another eye, another *rasikā*, who will always "see" the dancers' state and intent. Who is this Loved Other for whom dancers dance?[32] A meta-*rasikā* bearing an archetypal Gaze? The Shiva Sūtras[33] say that, for the accomplished yogi, the inner senses are the spectators of the dance on the innermost stage, the Self. So here is the gaze of the dancer herself watching her material body participate in her performance of designated emotions. Both detached and involved in her performance, her inner seeing-while-doing would generate the blissful rasa of value-free witness consciousness. This gaze of the inner spectator is closest to but not necessarily experienced as identical with the meta-gaze of the Loved One.

In keeping with the Indian narrative tradition of frames within frames, this chapter has included three kinds of stories: I have offered here socio-cultural frame of traditional Indian dance within its present day multi-cultural urban environment in the global performance scene. I have offered a synopsis of rasa theory as it is read and utilized in constructing and reading performance within a worldview in which thought is action with all the karmic consequences of action. And I started from my personal autobiographic experience, which led to the awareness that IT MATTERS FOR WHOM YOU DANCE.

It matters for whom one dances because each audience writes on the dancer's interpretative body of dances its own reading of those dances. Each audience writes anew on the dancer's body[34] its own collective narrative. That imprinting will season the way that each performer will inflect her next performance and consequent audience reading.[35] So each body performing Indian dance today bears on its surface a history of audience readings,[36] while the (structure) body of the dance carries its aesthetic equivalents of that same history. The audience itself can be read as history, from those who supported secular dancing (as represented in Shilappadikaram in second century A.D.),[37] theological dancing (Abhinavagupta), erotic devotional dances (Kshetrayya,[38] Jayadeva[39]), twentieth-century Victorianized sanitized dances, to dances that decolonize and in the process unpack and reconstruct identity through representing cultural bodies.[40] This writing back and forth continues with intercultural interaction. An immediate history of audience responses becomes the history of each individual dancer. This history is embedded in the representations of the classical Indian dance. And that brings me full circle back to the story of Tansen, Surdas, and Akbar. A dancer is as good as her audiences.

PRONUNCIATION AND TRANSLITERATION KEY

a as in but or cup

a or *aa* as in calm, father

s as in shine or shower

N.B. Words commonly used without diacritical marks reflect the way they are used at source, which in turn marks the political and practical perspective of writers.

NOTES

1. The music historian Dr. Thakur Jaideva Singh posits that Surdas, the blind poet and singer, lived for 103 years from 1478 to 1583 and sang of his love for Krishna "in matchless music" in the Shreenath (Śrīnātha) temple of Govardhana. Singh notes that this incident is recorded in a book called *Caurāsï Vaiṣṇavana Kī Vārtā* written in the seventeenth-century in Braja-bhasa, a regional language associated with devotional literature. Jaideva Singh also cites the *Akbarnāmah*, in which the traveling Arab historian, Abul Fazl, has noted that Tanasena was enrolled in Akbar's service in 1562 and died in 1589. In the *Ain-I-Akbari*, the same Fazl comments on Tansen's musicianship. See Thakur Jaideva Singh, *Indian Music* (Calcutta: Sangeet Research Academy, 1995), 170–173. This version of the Akbar-Surdas relationship is informed in part by a recent production, "The Life of Surdas" by SYDA Foundation in August 2000.

2. All these three performances were at the Siddha Yoga Dham in South Fallsburg, New York, July and August 1982.

3. Patanjali describes contemplation as the mental ability to maintain a steady uninterrupted focus on a single object of contemplation in his *Yoga Sutras* Book III, sutra 2 (hereafter written as *YS*, III, 2). See Swāmi Hariharānanda Āranya, *Yoga Philosophy of Patanjali* (Albany: State University of New York Press, 1983).

4. See Bharata, *The NatyaŚastra Vol. I*. Edited and translated by Manmohan Ghosh (Calcutta: Manisha Granthalaya Private Limited, 1956–67), Chapter 27, verses 49–58. Hereafter written as *NS*.

5. The following aphorism from the *Abhinayadarpanam* (Verse 249), an injunction for performing abstract dance movement, summarizes the process:

Where the hand goes, the eye goes.
Where the eye goes, the mind goes.

Where the mind goes, there is rasa.

Translation is mine. For the Sanskrit text, see Nandikeśvara, Abhinayadarpanam or *The Mirror of Gesture*. Edited and translated by Mahmohan Ghosh (Calcutta: Manisha Granthalaya, 1975), 105.

6. Uttara Asha Coorlawala, "An Evening with Kathak Master Birju Maharaj," *News India,* March 8, 1991: 36.

7. Conversation with Ted Shawn in 1967 at Jacob's Pillow, Massachusetts.

8. Walimbe presents the theoretical arguments of various thinkers as re-presented by Abhinavgupta in his Abhinavabhāratī. See Y. S. Walimbe, *Abhinavagupta on Indian Aesthetics* (New Delhi: Ajanta Publications, 1980), 15.

9. Kapila Vatsyayan has enumerated numerous sources of information about dance in historic literature, legends, myth, and in art, sculpture, and music. See *Classical Indian Dance in Literature and the Arts* (New Delhi: Sangeet Natak Akademi, 1968).

10. This is not to justify the obvious patriarchal bias of scribes who delineated characteristics of the woman, rarely as superior. The "superior' type of female character (e.g., Sita) was always expected to display an abundance of submissive traits, as attentiveness to superiors, shyness, and so on.

11. See V. Subramaniam's article "Rasa, Bhava and Sanchari: Textual Prescription and Changing Practices" in *Sruti,* December 1998: 71–79.

12. See Patanjali's *YS*, III, 2 in Swāmi Hariharānanda.

13. In *Abhinavabhāratī*, Abhinavagupta's commentary on the Sixth Adhyaya (or chapter) of the NatyaŚastra, Abhinavagupta lists seven such obstacles and proposes theatrical ways to overcome them. See Raniero Gnoli, *The Aesthetic Experience According to Abhinavagupta* (Varanasi: Chowkhamba Sanskrit Series Office, 1985) 62–78, and Y. S. Walimbe, *Abhinavagupta on Indian Aesthetics* (New Delhi: Ajanta Publications, 1980), 48–61.

14. See Bharata, *The NatyaŚastra Vol. I.* Edited and translated by Manmohan Ghosh (Calcutta: Manisha Granthalaya Private Limited, 1956–67), 1, 7–12.

15. See *NS* 4, 25, and 8, 70, and V. Raghavan, *The Number of Rasas* (Adyar, Madras: The Theosophical Publishing House, 1940).

16. The four modes of performing listed in *NS* 6, 23, and *NS* 10, 14 that lead to rasa, are *āngikābhinaya* or bodily expression, *vāchikabhinaya,* the oral-aural mode, *āhāryābhinaya,* the connotations of costume, make-up, and so on, and *satva* or clear focused performance.

17. Dr. Cara Gargano is the director of the Program of Theater, Film, and Dance at Long Island University, New York, and president of The Congress of Research in Dance.

18. For baby Krishna, the gaze is focused at knee or thigh level; for the lover Krishna, one focuses at or slightly above one's own face level; for God Krishna, the eyes turn upward and inward as the eyelids half close.

19. See Coorlawala, "*Darshan* and *Abhinaya:* An Alternative to the Male Gaze," *Dance Research Journal* 28:1 (Spring 1996). Kelucharan Mohapatra's representations of Krishna and an active initiating Radha combine with the custom of *darshan* to offer spectators an alternative to the inevitable male gaze postulated in Feminist film theory.

20. Abhinavagupta's prescription for theatrical representation of the collective subject and the transpersonal protagonist presages the concerns of recent feminist performers. See Sue Ellen Case, "From Split Subject to Split Britches" in *Feminine Focus:*

The New Women Playwrights, ed. Enoch Brater (New York: Oxford University Press, 1989).

21. See Walimbe 49–61.

22. Owen M. Lynch, ed., *Divine Passions: The Social Construction of Emotion in India* (Berkeley: University of California Press, 1990), 3–17.

23. Personal communication, September 8, 2001, Chicago.

24. This body construct particularly informs the practice of yoga, martial arts (ka-laripayattu), and the performing arts. See Muktananda Paramahansa, *The Play of Consciousness* (San Francisco: Harper and Row, 1978), 85–86; Uttara Coorlawala, "Classical and Contemporary Indian Dance: Overview, Criteria and a Choreographic Analysis," Ph.D. dissertation, New York University, (Ann Arbor: UMI Dissertation Services, 1994), 59–65; and Phillip Zarilli, *When The Body Becomes All Eyes: Paradigms, Discourses and Practices of Power in Kalaripayattu, a South Indian Martial Art* (New Delhi: Oxford University Press, 1998).

25. Interview with Malavika Sarukkai on September 8, 2001, at Columbia College, Chicago.

26. See Frédérique Apffel Marglin, "Refining The Body: Transformative Emotion in Ritual Dance," in *Divine Passions: The Social Construction of Emotion in India,* ed. Owen M. Lynch (Berkeley: University of California Press, 1990), 220–223; Owen Lynch, "The Social Construction of Emotion in India" in *Divine Passions* 4–6. Owen Lynch has drawn attention to the social constructs of emotion and Frédérique Apffel Marglin has pointed out how ballet is structured for visual viewing, whereas Indian ritual dance involves language, linguistic structures, and the senses.

27. See Janet O'Shea's article, "Technique and Theory in the Work of Kapila Vat-syayan—the Kapila Vatsyayan Honorary Papers," in *Dance Research Journal 32/1* (Summer 2000), edited by Julie Malnig, guest editor Uttara Coorlawala.

28. Uttara Asha Coorlawala, "Kapila Vatsyayan—Formative Influences: An Interview," *Dance Research Journal,* 32/1 (Summer 2000).

29. Kishori Amonkar is a leading exponent of the Jaipur *Atrauli gharana* tradition of singing. Interview with Roshan Jagatrai-Shahani, Mumbai, June 26, 2001.

30. The performance took place on Saturday, September 8, 2001, at Columbia College, Chicago, and was followed by a discussion the next morning as part of the Natya Dance Theatre's Conference on "Bharatanatyam in the Diaspora."

31. See Swāmi Hariharānanda, Patanjali's *YS,* II, 45. The practice of *Īśvara-pranidhāna* consists in bringing the individual will into alignment with the cosmic Will by mentally dedicating actions to *Īśvara* or God.

32. Most Indian philosophic systems maintain that the purpose of all effort is to "know" that the Loved Other is actually one's own self.

33. *The Śiva Sutras,* a ninth-century text, was said to have been revealed by Shiva to Vasugupta. This text, along with a commentary on it by Ksemaraja, are considered authoritative on the perspective of Kashmir Shaivism. See the English translation and commentaries by Swāmi Muktananda Paramahamsa in *Siddha Meditation: Commentaries on The Śiva Sutras and other Sacred Texts* (Ganeshpuri, India: Shree Gurudev Ashram, 1977), 51–53, and by Thakur Jaideva Singh in *The Śiva Sutras The Yoga of Supreme Identity* (Delhi: Motilal Banarsidass, 1979), 152–157. The sutras are: 3/9 *Nartakatman* (the inner self is the blissful dancer, Shiva); 3/10 *rango'sntaratma* (the inner self is the stage); and 3/11 *Prekshakāni indryāni* (the senses are the spectators).

34. This idea resonates with the perception of the performer as *patra* or leaf on which is written the techniques and rule structures of the dance form.

35. Susan Leigh Foster elaborates on this concept of the body on which is inscribed the characteristic and particular movements prevalent in one's environment in *Choreographing History* (Bloomington: Indiana University Press, 1995), 3–19.

36. Randy Martin theorizes that an audience's evanescent presence and responses offer a way of marking performative histories and the profound interactive consequences of the audience's gaze. See "Agency and History: The Demands of Dance Ethnography," in *Choreographing History* (Bloomington: Indian University Press, 1995), 105–115; and "Dance Ethnography and the Limits of Representation" in *Meaning in Motion,* ed. Jane Desmond (Durham, N.C.: Duke University Press, 1997), 325–341.

37. See V. Subramaniam, "Rasa Bhava and Sanchari: Textual Prescription and Changing Practices," in *Sruti 171,* December 1998; V. Subramaniam, "The Sacred and the Secular: Symbiosis and Synthesis," in *The Sacred and the Secular in India's Performing Arts,* ed. V. Subramaniam (New Delhi: Ashish Publishing House, 1980). V. Subramaniam argues that, before the sixth century, love poetry, music, and dance were secular arts.

38. Kshetrayya's padams are danced in most performances by seasoned Bharatanatyam dancers. A. K. Ramanujan et al. list the three major poets of the *padam* tradition as Tallapaka Annamacarya (1224–1503), Kṣetrayya, and Sārangapāni (mid-seventeenth century). See A. K. Ramanujan, Velcheri Narayana Rao, and David Schulman, eds. and trans., *When God is a Customer* (Berkeley: University of California Press, 1994), 2–5.

39. Barbara Stoler Miller places Jayadeva's literary activity at 1205, and his *Gītagovinda* was known throughout India by the fifteenth and sixteenth centuries and is the subject of many dances today, particularly in the form called Odissi. See Barbara Stoler Miller, ed. and trans., *Love Song of the Dark Lord, Jayadeva's Gītagovinda* (New York: Columbia University Press, 1977).

40. The idea that the history of Indian dance is embedded in the current dancer image was earlier proposed in my dissertation (Coorlawala, "Classical and Contemporary Indian Dance").

5

AUDIENCE PARTICIPATION IN THE EIGHTEENTH-CENTURY LONDON THEATRE

Judith W. Fisher

When the monarchy of England was restored in 1660, the theatres in London had been closed for about twenty years, and visits to the playhouse were no longer common practice among the capital's citizenry. The Restoration audience was more closely allied to the court than its predecessor was; its members were more accustomed to being the center of attention. By the beginning of, and increasingly throughout, the eighteenth century, more "middling sort" of people attended the theatre, along with a vociferous servant class. This more diverse audience was determined, however, to continue the role it had inherited from its courtly predecessor: to participate actively in each and every performance. The eighteenth-century London theatre was a purely commercial venture where the actors worked for salary rather than for shares, and where playwrights and players vied for favor and attention from their outspoken and demanding public. Although written in 1747, for the opening season of David Garrick's management of the Theatre Royal, Drury Lane, the line from Samuel Johnson's "Prologue"—"The drama's laws, the drama's patrons give"—has become a maxim for the entire century with regard to the audience and its involvement in stage matters. The eighteenth-century theatre patrons not only influenced what was written for the stage but also determined "laws" for the practitioners, who, for the most part, capitulated to the public's wishes, declaring, again in Johnson's words, "For we that live to please, must please to live." No longer were players protected under letters patent as household servants of the nobility, as those in the prestigious London companies had been during the late sixteenth and early seventeenth centuries; they now had a new master—the "town." In his book *The Drama's Patrons*, Leo Hughes explains that, even after the Licensing Act of 1737

vested the right to censor plays with the Lord Chamberlain, "[t]he power
and right to approve or disapprove a licensed play was reserved to the audience, almost without limit."[1] How what James Boswell called the "many-
headed monster"[2] executed its "power and right," and the practitioners dealt
with such execution, is the subject of this chapter.

The documentary evidence, compiled from contemporary reviews, commentary, letters, pamphlets, and plays, suggests that the participation of the
audience did as much as, perhaps even more than, that of the "star" players
and powerful managers to direct the course of theatre throughout the eighteenth century. James Lynch, in *Box, Pit, and Gallery*, agrees that the audience "had great influence on the regulation of the repertory, and in various
ways helped to determine the dramatic fare of the eighteenth century."[3] The
audience's active role in performances undoubtedly produced a vibrancy that
is rarely apparent in the dramatic literature of the period, except as hinted at
in the plays containing the various participants as dramatic characters. The
town's displeasure with a manager's decision, or a dramatist's script, or a
player's performance or nonappearance, could result in varying degrees of
disruptive behavior, from full-scale rioting and pelting the stage with fruit
and other objects to hissing players and demanding apologies. The theatre-
goers' pleasure could be equally disruptive: they might call for several encores
of a particular speech or song, or cheer so loudly that, even if a performance
were not brought to a halt, the actors could not be heard. During such action
spectators and players often reversed roles, producing a situation that invariably changed the nature of the evening's presentation, one in which, as the
Welshman in Frederick Reynolds's play *Fortune's Fool* (1796) declares, "The
audience are the performers . . . "[4] Against reports of the London audience's
consistently loud and exuberant behavior should be measured the following
comment by a German visitor in 1775, one of many similar accounts recorded
by foreign spectators: "When the play begins, all noise and bombardment
ceases, unless some especial provocation gives rise to further disturbances;
and one is bound to admire the quiet attentiveness of such an estimable
folk."[5] It did not, however, take much to provoke those "estimable folk" into
action.

During the eighteenth century, nearly all members of the London public,
whatever their social class, became increasingly confident about taking com-
mand of the entertainment offered at the theatres, partly because of the increased political power and critical freedom granted them in the 1689 Bill of
Rights,[6] and partly because of the master/servant relationship between theatre
patrons and practitioners that had developed since the late seventeenth century.
As the anonymous author of the Preface to *A Dialogue in the Green-room*
(1763) asserts: "Whatever notions modern performers may have imbibed, by
inflated applause and profuse recompense, actors are neither more or [*sic*] less
than the servants of the public."[7] The audience's awareness of their own
importance as theatre participants was, James Lynch suggests, also based on

the fact that they were "constant theatergoers."[8] It was often the rivalries between various parties in the audience that instigated action in the house, whether on behalf of a favorite player, in support or opposition of a playwright's work or a manager's decision, or because of status or class differences amongst themselves. Everybody expected the audience to participate, whether physically, vocally, or emotionally. Indeed, writers, managers, and performers were so used to the audience ensuring that they were involved that their participation was taken more for granted than recorded as an unusual event. Major riots are well documented, so I shall not examine them here, except to point out that it was at the Haymarket Theatre riot in 1738 that the audience determined, in response to Justice Deveil's plea from the stage that "the Play should be acted," that they "had a legal Right to shew their Dislike to any Play or Actor."[9] A right, whether legal or not, they did not hesitate to demonstrate.

On busy nights, when the crowd would have waited many hours to get into the house, and the crush in the passageway leading to the pit and on the stairs to the galleries would have been almost unendurable, it is not surprising to find spectators in a state of agitation and lively expectation.[10] Although riots did not occur with regularity, enough disturbances took place, especially those during which audience members attempted to climb onto the stage and wreak havoc with stage properties, to prompt the management of the London theatres by mid-century to install iron railings or "spikes" along the front of the stage.[11] But even though such preventative measures increased the physical separation between the players and their patrons, and possibly, thereby, the ferocity of the latter's participation, they did not always deter the most determined of those in the auditorium. On the third night of Henry Bate's *The Blackamoor Wash'd White* in 1776, some audience members' anger at the play reached fever-pitch, which, as the *Chester Chronicle* in February of that year records, was "resented by the rest of the house." The battle that ensued became so violent that "numbers of the audience . . . got upon the stage; several persons were knocked down, and many turned out of the house. A man was thrown from the gallery, but saved himself from hurt by hanging on the chandelier . . . "[12] Rarely, on occasions such as these, did the players stay to watch the patrons' performance.

Managers, understandably, tended to choose plays that they knew or hoped would please or be popular with the audience. Theophilus Cibber recorded the following early eighteenth-century encounter in a coffee house between the actor Barton Booth and a group of gentlemen complaining about the entertainment being offered at Drury Lane: "He [Booth] begged them to consider there were many more spectators than men of taste and judgment; and if, by the artifice of a Pantomime, they could entice a greater number to partake of the *Utile Dulci* of a good play than could be drawn without it, he could not see any great harm in it."[13] Although a few patrons might have been able to disturb a performance, it was obviously the wishes of the majority that determined the dramatic fare.

The lower-class audience members in the upper galleries were frequently the instigators of disturbances, but the critical "town," seated usually in the pit, also was keen to make its judgment of an evening's entertainment known. In his preface to *Medea* (1731), Charles Johnson condemns the behavior of these "noisy Criticks": "who . . . give their Judgment, in a Manner not easily to be opposed; not only in feeble Hisses, but in Hootings, horse Laughs, squalings, Catcalls, and other mechanical Criticisms pointed at any Passages in the Play . . . to prevent the Attention of the Audience, to disturb the Action, and to condemn the Play, without hearing or suffering others to hear it."[14] The higher-class members of the audience in the boxes created another kind of disturbance. The *Theatrical Monitor* in 1768 complained that "[d]uring the time of the representation of a play, the quality in the boxes are totally employed in finding out, and beckoning to their acquaintances, male and female; they criticize on fashions, whisper cross the benches, make significant nods, and give hints of this and that, and t'other body."[15] With the boxes on the sidelines, both figuratively and literally, battles of opinion were usually waged between pit and gallery. However, in 1763, "angry theatre-goers prevented Garrick and his rivals at Covent Garden from stopping the half-price concession after the third act or at nine o'clock, a practice which had first been introduced in the 1690s."[16] This particular riot was successful because all classes in the house joined together to oppose the theatre managers.

The managers' frequent deferrals to the patrons' wishes were undoubtedly connected to box-office receipts. The noisiest of receptions appear to have been reserved for new plays, up to and including the third night, which was usually for the author's benefit, because the members of the audience were determined to have their judgment of each new work heard and acted on. For instance, at the opening of *The World As It Goes* by Mrs. Cowley at Covent Garden in 1781, "The comedy was interrupted in the last act. [The actress] Miss YOUNG . . . came forward, and said that as several alterations would be made in the piece by the ensuing Tuesday, it would then, by permission, be offered the public in its altered state; but the proposal was disapproved of . . . "[17] James Boswell was even ready to condemn David Mallet's *Elvira* because it "would probably be bad," the playwright being, in his opinion, an "arrant puppy."[18] He sat in the pit on January 19, 1763, alongside two friends, with "oaken cudgels in [their] hands and shrill-sounding catcalls in [their] pockets"; but, although they "hissed it and had several to join [them]," the majority "were disposed to let it pass" and they "were obliged to lay aside [their] laudable undertaking . . . "[19] Boswell's experience suggests that a few patrons could not always rouse the many into action; nor could cajoling by managers or actors dissuade the "multitude" from demanding, or making a fuss until they received, what they found most pleasurable, hence the plethora of farcical afterpieces and pantomimes by mid-century and the increase in spectacle.[20] Although, as Lynch observes, "[t]he repertory . . . often reflected the propensities of the players, and trivial and unrecorded motives must often have determined whether *King Lear* or *The Rover* would be 'given out' for the following night[,] . . . the theater and its company could not thrive on thin houses. No matter how much power the actors exerted, that power was ultimately circumscribed by the audience."[21] The limits the patrons defined had more to do with their own immediate satisfaction as participants and their sense of ownership, as Brewer suggests, than with the quality of the material performed: "Less conscious of being in the presence of 'culture' and more mindful of being part of the theatrical experience, [the audience] . . . looked on drama as their property."[22]

There is no evidence to suggest that the players found the audience's active participation in the on-stage entertainment extraordinary, but that did not mean they were unaffected by it. One of the players' greatest fears was that the audience might shout "Off! Off!," hiss, or catcall. Such outbursts could bring players and plays to an abrupt halt. As the audiences flexed their muscles in their growing role as critics during the century, the "*mob*," as John Harold Wilson calls them, "became the supporter and the destroyer of the actor."[23] Subsequent to Garrick's return to Drury Lane, after he and Charles Macklin had led the failed actors' secession in 1743 in protest against unpaid wages and unfair treatment, a feud was initiated between the former friends and colleagues, fuelled by letters to the press. When Garrick reappeared on stage, Macklin's supporters were waiting in the auditorium: "On Mr. Garrick's appearance in Bayes, on the 6th of December 1743, he was saluted with the usual cries of 'Off! off!' sounds so unusual to him, and entreated to be heard in vain. The rioters and their leaders seemed more bent upon battle than explanation. . . . [T]hey showered *peas* upon the stage, to prevent any walking on to trouble them with addresses, and for two nights together enjoyed all 'the current of a heady fight.' "[24] Needless to say, Garrick was not destroyed by the crowd's action, but the experience made him realize how careful he had to be in his dealings with the audience. Mrs. Montague was not so perspicacious when cast to play in *Henry II* for Mrs. Hudson's benefit. She liked neither Mrs. Hudson nor the part and refused to study the role. On the night of the performance, after the audience had been told that "Illness had prevented [her] from studying the part of Queen Elenor, and she begged to read it," they sent for her. They told her that "if she did not do the part, as was her duty, and of which she had had timely notice, she must depart that instant; for rather than submit to such intentional insult and effrontery, they would desire the *cook-wench* from the first ale-house to read it."[25] Accounts of what the actress did next vary. Janet Dunbar says that "Mrs Montague saw the point, and made an effort—but . . . was 'hissed heartily'"[26] while Wilkinson says that she "threw the book into the pit, and made her exit amidst shouts of disgrace."[27] Whatever actually happened, the audience fully participated in the outcome.

One of the most frequent and dangerous activities, mainly practiced by the gallery spectators, was pelting. The anonymous play *The Author on the Wheel* offers an amusing insight into the players' understandable fear of being pelted. Having gathered in the green room to receive cuts to Vainwit's play, the premiere of which the audience had damned, the player characters exchange stories about their opening-night experiences, the fruit thrown, and the consequent embarrassment of one of the actresses:

SOCK . . . some pleasant gentleman upstairs, not satisfied with what she was saying threw a Windsor pear with such vehemence against her head-dress, that it unfortunately gave way and expos'd her bald pate and a few hairs of a side ha! ha! *(all laugh)*

THESPIS The Gods saluted me with a few apples and oranges, but having a large wig on they did me no other damage than making the powder fly about.[28]

The tall head-dresses worn by the actresses on top of their wigs were an obvious liability; and yet such fashionable adornments were known to have protected members of the audience. In *The Garrick Stage,* Nicoll mentions an occasion when "a keg full of liquor" was thrown from the gallery: "it luckily fell on a woman attired in the latest mode, so that, as the paper announced, her head-gear prevented 'the mischief that otherwise might have been occasioned.' "[29] Pelting and other such violent measures were ways in which the audience exercised its "legal Right" in the theatre, and the other participants had little choice but to tolerate such expression of freedom. As a socially conscious Joseph Palmer mentioned in 1775, with reference to the dangers pedestrians faced from hackney-coachmen and lamp-lighters in the street, " . . . such is the off-spring of glorious liberty, and these *wild dogs* must not be muzzled, lest in curbing licence, we should touch their sacred birth-right, English freedom."[30]

However, the "freedom" granted the audience, which enhanced their status and separation from the performers in the theatrical hierarchy, also was limited in a way that led to an increased intimacy between them. After the Licensing Act of 1737, when players and play-goers had only two patent theatres—Drury Lane and Covent Garden—in which to disport themselves, the membership of the London companies changed infrequently for each generation of the theatre-going public. Even after Samuel Foote was granted, some thirty years later, a license for summer productions at the Haymarket theatre, the pool of principal players remained fairly constant between the three theatres. The public, therefore, came to know the performers well and developed an insatiable appetite for gossip about their private lives. Such familiarity possibly made the eighteenth-century theatre patrons more possessive and authoritative than they were legally entitled to be; but practitioners and public alike assumed and played within the established master/servant relationship, one that, as Charles Macklin found to his cost, was fixed in the patrons' favor. In 1773, Macklin offered a new interpretation of Macbeth at

Covent Garden, as he had done with his Shylock at Drury Lane thirty-two years earlier. But this time the audience disapproved and Macklin, believing there was a conspiracy against him, reacted strongly and contrarily. Later, to appease them, he returned to playing Shylock, but the public had lost interest in him and the veteran actor was dismissed from the company. Macklin took his case to the King's Bench, where his motion against the audience "for hissing and otherwise insulting him" was rejected, as the *Annual Register* (1774) records, on the grounds that "the audience had a right to applaud, condemn, nay, reject, what performers they thought proper."[31] The public's right to hiss a play or player if either displeased had become so entrenched in the cultural tradition of London theatre that it had acquired a legal force long before Macklin contested it.[32]

Indeed, so accustomed were players to audience participation, that any lack of or tardiness in response was an unusual theatrical event. In 1750, adhering to the patrons' laws, Peg Woffington appeared on stage to ask the audience for permission to substitute for an indisposed Susanna Cibber: "The spectators, instead of meeting her address with approbation, seemed to be entirely lost in surprise. This unexpected reaction so embarrassed her, that she was preparing to retire, when Ryan . . . asked them bluntly if they would give Mrs. Woffington leave to act *Lady Constance*. The audience, as if at once awakened from a fit of lethargy, by repeated plaudits strove to make amends for their inattention to the most beautiful woman that ever adorned a theatre."[33] But woe betide playwrights, managers, or players who tried to outwit the audience. Mary Robinson relates her experience on February 24, 1777, with an audience who "expressed a considerable degree of disapprobation" when they discovered that the play *A Trip to Scarborough* was not new, as they had supposed, but an altered version of Vanbrugh's *The Relapse*. It was, according to the actress, the Duke of Cumberland, in the stage box, who "bade [her] take courage": "'It is not you, but the play, they hiss,' said his Royal Highness. I curtsied; and that curtsey seemed to electrify the whole house, for a thundering appeal of encouraging applause followed."[34] One wonders whether it was her courage or her act of obeisance that altered the audience's reaction. Dialogue between actors and audience was, Brewer explains, "considered distinctively English. Foreign tourists visiting London went to the theatre as much to observe play-goers as the players. And, though they knew what to expect, they were repeatedly surprised. A French visitor to Covent Garden in 1763 was shocked that 'the gallery controlled the acting and thanked the players.' "[35] But, as we have seen, the gallery could be equally unforgiving, even when the players gave pleasure, as Sophie Von la Roche read in the daily paper of September 7, 1786: "Miss Farren reprimanded for having been ashamed to repeat an epilogue for the fourth time."[36] The performers, understandably, did not always enjoy having to deal with the spectators' demonstrations of their power, despite the tradition "that the Judicature of the Pit had been acknowledged and acquiesced to, Time immemorial . . ."[37]

The anonymous piece, *A Dialogue in the Green-Room, upon a Disturbance in the Pit* (printed in 1763 at the time of the half-price riots but never performed), alludes to some of the difficulties managers faced when forced to acquiesce to patrons' demands. The Coadjutor complains about the lack of justice against riotous audiences who stop performances and destroy theatrical property: "If a fellow picks my pocket of a handkerchief, I may transport him; if a rogue takes a shilling from me upon the highway, I may hang him; but here, if I am injured to the amount of threescore, or a hundred pounds, there's no relief, I must sit quietly down with the loss;—not only that, but I must fawn and court these very perturbators of the peace not to do so again. . . ."[38] The Manager (an unflattering portrait of Garrick) joins the Coadjutor in bemoaning the harsh economics of running a theatre and their treatment at the hands of the public. But their lamentations take place off-stage in the green room, out of the audience's hearing; on-stage, costumed as an actor, the Manager, we discover later in the play, surrenders unhesitatingly to his auditors' demands. Garrick's position as both actor and manager placed him in the unenviable position of trying to appease and simultaneously retain authority over his company members as well as his patrons. If, however, the audience chose to uphold a manager's decision, the performers faced a most formidable foe. In 1796, the actress Elizabeth Farren, acutely conscious of recent successful performances, refused to wear the costume provided by the management for her role as Lady Townley in a forthcoming production of *The Provoked Husband*. As a result, "the play was suddenly advertised to be withdrawn":

But on the night when the play should have been acted there was a riot in the theatre, with loud calls for Miss Farren. Fortunately for her she was not there; and some sort of apology was made for her absence. But . . . they would not be quiet until a promise was made to produce *The Provoked Husband* on an early specified night. When that night arrived the theatre was crowded, everybody being anxious to see who had conquered in the green-room. But Miss Farren had been unable to stand out against the management when it was evidently backed up by the public, and she not only appeared in the despised old satin dress, but was then compelled to make an apologetic curtsy to the angry audience before they would allow the play to go on.[39]

Writers, on opening nights, were at the mercy of patrons and players alike, waiting to see what the players did with their material if, in fact, the audience allowed their play to be performed. It is interesting to speculate whether dramatists such as Henry Fielding and John Gay would have satirized Robert Walpole's government quite so overtly in the 1720s and 1730s if the audience's approval had not carried such social and cultural weight.

Until Garrick banished spectators from sitting on the stage at Drury Lane in 1762 (Covent Garden management soon followed suit), the players also endured the presence of patrons alongside them, a situation that often altered the look as well as the nature of the performance. "Building," that is, the placing of tiers of benches to the side and behind the actors on stage on benefit nights to increase the seating capacity, certainly interfered with the work of players and playwrights alike. Hogarth's painting of John Gay's *The Beggar's Opera,* for example, illustrates how the audience members on stage appear to be characters in the play; such an effect in the performance of a tragedy could significantly alter the work's genre. "[W]hat a play [*Romeo and Juliet*] must have been," declares Tate Wilkinson, "whenever Romeo was breaking open the supposed tomb, which was no more than a screen . . . and Mrs. Cibber prostrating herself on an old couch, covered with black cloth, as the tomb of the Capulets, with at least (on a great benefit night) two hundred persons behind her, which formed the back ground, as an unfrequented hallowed place of *chapless* skulls. . . . I do not think at present any allowance but peals of laughter could attend such a truly ridiculous spectacle."[40] Wilkinson also records, or rather embellishes, the story of Charles Holland's performance of Hamlet on his benefit night in April 1756, when his hat came off as he started on seeing the Ghost. A lady, who, "hearing Hamlet complain the air bit shrewdly, and was very cold, with infinite composure crossed the stage, took up the hat, and with the greatest care placed it fast on Hamlet's head, who on the occasion was as much alarmed in *reality* as he had just then been feigning." Apparently, both the Ghost and Hamlet quickly left the stage amidst "incessant peals of laughter."[41] The story as recorded by the prompter that evening merely refers to an "ignorant man" who, not realizing that the hat was a piece of stage business by the actor, picked it up and "clapt it upon his head."[42] The actors wanted as many people as possible to attend the theatre on their benefit nights and so agreed to share the stage with their patrons, but, at times, they must have felt as if they were dealing with an obstacle course rather than a dramatic presentation. Imagine an actor having to push "his way through the people sitting in front of [the balcony over which he had to make an escape] and apologise as he went along,"[43] while attempting to retain character, or James Quin, "aged sixty-five, with the heavy dress of Falstaff," trying to make an entrance "through the numbers that wedged and hemmed him in . . . "[44] The evidence suggests players generally suffered such on-stage participation as part of their job, but their eventual agreement to the patrons' relegation solely to the auditorium hints at unrecorded dissatisfaction.

We have seen the audience's power over the players: how easily they could disrupt a performance, how quickly their hostile mood could become one of approbation. The players, however, could also disturb or alter performances by wielding the power they had over their patrons' emotions. An audience might become so absorbed in a player's performance that they would leave the theatre after his or her character's last appearance, as happened when Sarah Siddons performed Lady Macbeth's sleepwalking scene for the last time. Mrs. Bellamy, later in her career, so thoroughly engaged both herself and her audience in the tragedy she was playing that she passed out and had to be carried off stage; "[a]nd the audience, too, unable to endure the strain, departed, so that the piece had to be finished without the leading lady, before a handful of unusually hard-boiled spectators."[45] But the audience, as Samuel Johnson declared, never forgot they were watching actors perform. Indeed, the public's knowledge of the players' private lives often affected their reaction, especially when the roles in which the players appeared ironically emphasized what their patrons knew about them. What are usually referred to today as "in jokes"—circumstances in which information is humorously shared only among the performers on stage—were in the eighteenth century more like "out jokes"; the members of the audience were well aware of the players' particular circumstance or reputation and usually began the laughter triggered by its connection to the drama. Chetwood remembers how

a virtuous Actress (or one reputed so) repeating two Lines in *King Lear*, at her Exit in the Third Act,

> Arm'd in my Virgin Innocence I'll fly,
> My Royal Father to relieve, or die,

receive[d] a Plaudit from the Audience, more as a Reward for her reputable Character, than, perhaps, her Acting claim'd; when a different *Actress* in the same Part, more fam'd for her Stage-Performance than the other, at the Words *Virgin Innocence*, . . . created a Horse-laugh . . . and the Scene of generous Pity and Compassion at the Close turn'd to Ridicule.[46]

Thus the actresses' varied reputations rather than their performances caused the different reactions. Players would sometimes pointedly make a connection between their lines and their lives for the audience's enjoyment. The "adventure" the actress-singer Ann Catley had with a "Lord R—," when he was "found in her apartments with a basting ladle in his hand," was soon after lampooned in the newspapers: "At a performance of *Comus* as Euphrosyne, . . . [as] she was singing "The wanton god that pierces hearts," she turned to look at Lord R—in the stage box— . . . [and] when she came to the line 'No squeamish fop shall spoil my rest,' she turned full upon his lordship with a look of archness, so pointed and so marked with contempt, that the mortified nobleman rose from his seat and left her to enjoy the thundering plaudits of the audience, which were . . . accompanied by bursts of laughter."[47] Obviously most of the audience had read the papers and knew both the man and the incident.

The way in which the press reported players' off-stage activities or hostilities, as well as green-room squabbles, often invited audience participation in performance. But the medium also was used by players enlisting public support against managers, by managers explaining their points of view, by members of the public criticizing the behavior of both managers and players, and by players forced to defend themselves against misinformed public accusations. Mrs. Jordan, for instance, being unwell, had excused herself from performing in *Richard Coeur de Lion* on November 26, 1791. Mrs. Crouch played in her place, but paragraphs in the press suggested Mrs. Jordan was not actually indisposed and that she "betrayed a want of respect to the Public."[48] Mrs. Jordan immediately wrote a letter to the press defending herself, because she thought "it my duty" to respond "to an attack on my conduct in my profession, and the charge of want of respect and gratitude to the public," even though the "unprovoked and unmanly abuse" directed against her was "related to subjects about which the public could not be interested."[49] Despite this letter, which also explained her particular indisposition on that night, the audience would not let her play when she next appeared until she had addressed them directly. Her "apology," in which she declared that "the slightest mark of public disapprobation . . . affect[s] me very sensibly . . . [and] it has been my constant endeavour, my unremitting assiduity, to merit your approbation," was, records Oulton, "received with bursts of applause, and the disturbance ceased."[50] Whatever the players might have felt about such subjection, they accepted it as part of their business; they knew that if the audience were unwilling to participate in a manner that allowed performances to go forward, there would be no business.

That is not to say that players were always submissive or apologetic. They also were capable of standing up to their patrons and commanding due respect. But, in all cases, in whatever manner sought, pleaded for, or demanded, the public's participation was integral. In 1725, Mrs. Horton took over the part of Phillis in *The Conscious Lovers* when Mrs. Younger left Drury Lane; but because the audience had enjoyed Mrs. Younger's portrayal so much, they hissed Mrs. Horton when she first played the role. Thomas Davies tells us that "Mrs Horton bore the treatment patiently for awhile and finally made an appeal to the audience: 'What displeases you; my acting or my person?' This show of spirit won over the partisans of Mrs Younger and the audience told her, 'Go on, go on.'"[51] On another occasion, Peg Woffington refused to be dictated to by an audience who wanted an apology for what she considered was no fault on her part. She had continuously substituted for indisposed actresses during the season of 1750–51 with no acknowledgment in the playbills and had warned John Rich, the manager, that the next time he wanted her to play her popular role of Sir Harry Wildair in *The Constant Couple* she would refuse. She kept her word, but when she next appeared the audience shouted "Off! Off!": "[They] treated her very rudely, bade her ask pardon, and threw orange peels on the stage. She behaved with great resolution, and treated their rudeness with contempt. She left the stage, was called for, and with infinite persuasion was prevailed on to return. [She] . . . walked forward to the footlights, and told them she was ready and willing to perform the character if they chose to permit her—that the decision was theirs—on or off, just as they pleased—a matter of indifference to her. The ayes had it, and all went smoothly afterwards. . . ."[52] The preceding examples demonstrate how noisy the audience could be, but, as Pedicord reiterates, "For the most part the performance evenings were relatively quiet, and, given a good series of entertainments and performance, most spectators behaved themselves once the first music sounded."[53]

Eighteenth-century players, as we have seen, could be as alarmed by the quietness as by the loudness of their audience's reaction; they might leave the stage in fear, confusion, anger, even unconscious; they might try to placate rowdy audiences or pretend amid a tumult that nothing was amiss; but they always expected the audience to participate in the proceedings. Even at the beginning of the nineteenth century, as Paul Ranger explains, "[t]he plays were [still] written in the expectation that the audience would respond overtly to the emotive flights of oratory."[54] Theatre audiences' perception of their role in a performance has changed since the eighteenth century. They still recognize and acknowledge the players' "technical proficiency," but, Ranger points out, audiences today are less likely to greet it with "a mixture of applause, shouts, sobbing or cheers"; such vociferous participation "today is lacking in the responses that an audience makes, for its members no longer consider themselves an integral part of the action of the play."[55] The darkened auditorium has completely separated the players from their patrons and overt public displays of emotion in the theatre are no longer commonplace. Human emotions have not changed, but theatrical tradition regarding audience behavior and dramatic presentation has. Although most practitioners are undoubtedly pleased that today's audiences are usually quiet and polite, the theatre is in danger of becoming culturally exclusive. Noisy patrons who create a disturbance, for whatever reason, will more likely be removed from the theatre than be applauded, joined, or shouted at by those around them. I am certainly not advocating a return to the earlier master/servant relationship between patron and player, to pelting or rioting, but I do, nevertheless, regret the loss of proactive and uninvited audience participation. Perhaps the passing of the critic's baton to media representatives limits not only current audiences' sense of ownership, which eighteenth-century patrons considered was theirs to exert in any way they chose, but also the degree of responsibility and accountability required of all participants in the delivery and reception of a theatrical performance.

NOTES

1. Leo Hughes, *The Drama's Patrons: a Study of the Eighteenth-Century London Audience* (Austin and London: University of Texas Press, 1971), 10.

2. James Boswell, *Boswell's London Journal 1762–1763,* Intro. and notes Frederick A. Pottle (London: The Reprint Society, 1952), 156.

3. James J. Lynch, *Box Pit and Gallery: Stage and Society in Johnson's London* (Berkeley and Los Angeles: University of California Press, 1953), 206.

4. Quoted in Dane Farnsworth Smith, and M. L. Lawhon, *Plays about the Theatre in England, 1737–1800* (London: Associated University Presses, 1979), 177.

5. von Archenholz, qtd. in Harry William Pedicord, *The Theatrical Public in the Time of Garrick* (Carbondale and Edwardsville: Southern Illinois University Press, 1954), 63.

6. Hughes, *Drama's Patrons*, 9, 15.

7. *A Dialogue in the Green-Room, upon a Disturbance in the Pit* (London, 1763), vii.

8. Lynch, *Box Pit and Gallery*, 304.

9. Benjamin Victor, *The History of the Theatres of London and Dublin*, 3 vols. 1761. (New York: Benjamin Blom, 1969), 1: 55. For further specific instances of audiences' disruptive behavior, see *The Diary of Sylas Neville 1767–1788*, ed. Basil Cozens-Hardy (London: Oxford University Press, 1950), 27, 120–21; W.R. Chetwood, *A General History of the Stage, from its Origin in Greece down to the present Time* (London: Printed for W. Owen, 1749), 43; Allardyce Nicoll, *The Garrick Stage: Theatres and Audience in the Eighteenth Century.* ed. Sybil Rosenfeld (Manchester: Manchester University Press, 1981), 87–91; and Nicoll, *A History of Early Eighteenth-Century Drama 1700–1750* (Cambridge: Cambridge University Press, 1925), 12–13; Edward A. Langhans on the Chinese Festival riots, "The Children of Terpsichore," ed. Shirley Strum Kenny, *British Theatre and the Other Arts 1660–1800* (London and Toronto: Associated University Presses, 1984), 133–45; and Harry William Pedicord, "The Changing Audience," ed. John Hume, *The London Theatre World 1660–1800* (Carbondale and Edwardsville: Southern Illinois University Press, 1980), 236–52. For more general information on audience behavior, see *London Stage 1660–1800: A Calendar of Plays, Entertainments and Afterpieces Together with Casts, Box-receipts and Contemporary Comment Compiled from the Playbills, Newspapers and Theatrical Diaries of the Period* (Carbondale: Southern Illinois University Press), Part 2: *1700–29*, ed. Emmett L. Avery. 2 vols. 1960, 2.1: clx–clxix; Part 3: *1729–47*, ed. Arthur H. Scouten. 2 vols. 1961, 3.1: clxviii–clxxv; Part 4: *1747–76*, ed. George Winchester Stone, Jr. 3 vols. 1962, 4.1: clxxxiv–cxcviii; Part 5: *1776–1800*, ed. Charles Beecher Hogan, 3 vols. 1968, 5.1: cxcv–cxcix; Hughes's *The Drama's Patrons*, and Pedicord's *The Theatrical Public.*

10. Samuel Rodgers described what it was like getting into the theatre to see Garrick act: when the doors were opened, "a dangerous trial of skill ensues; every person endeavours to enter first; the space is clogged; and pushing, screams, and execrations follow" (qtd. in Pedicord, *Theatrical Public*, 48). It was also possible, however, to find the house almost empty and audience members sleeping, as William Byrd records he did in 1718 (Hughes, *Drama's Patrons*, 69).

11. Nicoll, *Garrick Stage*, 26.

12. Qtd. in Cecil Price, *Theatre in the Age of Garrick* (Oxford: Basil Blackwell, 1973), 99.

13. Qtd. in Hughes, *Drama's Patrons*, 105–6.

14. Qtd. in *London Stage* 2.1: clxvi.

15. Qtd. in John Brewer, *The Pleasures of the Imagination: English Culture in the Eighteenth Century* (London: Harper Collins Publishers, 1997), 353.

16. Ibid., 351. Half-price concessions were given to patrons who arrived during the third act of the main piece or at the start of the afterpiece. See Thomas Davies on the price riots (*Memoirs of David Garrick* [London, 1808], 2: 2–6).

17. Walley Chamberlain Oulton, *The History of the Theatres of London: containing*

an annual register of all the new and revived tragedies, comedies, operas, farces, panto-mimes, &c. that have been performed at the Theatres-Royal, in London, from the year 1771 to 1795, 2 vols. (London: Martin and Bain, 1796), 1: 100–1.

18. Boswell, *Boswell's London Journal,* 154.

19. Ibid., 156.

20. For a full account of the audience's and critics' influence on the changing tastes in the dramatic literature of the century, see Leo Hughes's *The Drama's Patrons,* particularly chapters 3 and 4.

21. Lynch, *Box Pit and Gallery,* 302.

22. Brewer, *The Pleasures of the Imagination,* 351.

23. John Harold Wilson, *All the King's Ladies* (Chicago: University of Chicago Press, 1958), 90.

24. James Boaden, ed., *The Private Correspondence of David Garrick with the Most Celebrated Persons of His Time; now first published from the originals, and illustrated with notes. And a New Biographical Memoir of Garrick.* 2 vols. (London: Henry Colburn and Richard Bentley, MDCCCXXXI [1831]), I: xii.

25. Tate Wilkinson, *The Wandering Patentee.* 4 vols. York, 1795. Reprinted. (London: Scholar Press Ltd.), 1: 245.

26. Janet Dunbar, *Peg Woffington and her World* (London: Heinemann, 1968), 232.

27. Wilkinson, *Wandering Patentee,* 1: 245.

28. *The Author on the Wheel, or a Piece cut in the Green Room* (1785. In *Three Centuries of Drama: English 1751–1800.* Readex Microprint. New York, 1956. Courtesy Henry E. Huntington Library. Larpent Collection. #695), scene 2.

29. Nicoll, *Garrick Stage,* 87.

30. *Four Months Tour through France,* qtd. in Hughes, *The Drama's Patrons,* 65.

31. Qtd. in Price, *Age of Garrick,* 100.

32. See Hughes, *Drama's Patrons,* 29; *London Stage* 5.1: cxcix.

33. Thomas Davies, qtd. in Brander Matthews, and Laurence Hutton, eds., *Actors and Actresses of Great Britain and the United States from the Days of David Garrick to the Present Time.* 5 vols. Vol. 1: *Garrick and his Contemporaries* (New York: Cassell & Co, Ltd., 1886), 1: 117.

34. [Mary Robinson], *Memoirs of Mary Robinson "Perdita" from the edition edited by her daughter.* Introduction and notes J. Fitzgerald Molloy (London: Gibbings & Co. Ltd. and Philadelphia: J. B. Lippincott Co, 1895), 132.

35. Brewer, *The Pleasures of the Imagination,* 352.

36. Sophie Von la Roche, *Sophie in London 1786 being the Diary of Sophie v. la Roche,* trans. from the German with an Introductory Essay by Clare Williams (London: Jonathan Cape, 1933), 98.

37. Victor, *Theatres of London and Dublin,* 1: 55–6.

38. *A Dialogue,* 39.

39. John Fyvie, *Comedy Queens of the Georgian Era* (London: Archibald Constable & Co. Ltd., 1906), 269–70.

40. Tate Wilkinson, *Memoirs of His Own Life.* 4 vols. (York, 1790), 4: 111.

41. Ibid., 4: 114–15.

42. Qtd. in *London Stage* 4.2: 539.

43. Price, *Age of Garrick,* 96.

44. Wilkinson, *Memoirs* 4: 115.

45. John A. Kelly, *German Visitors to English Theatres in the Eighteenth Century* (Princeton, N.J.: Princeton University Press, 1936), 55.

46. Chetwood, *A General History,* 28.

47. *Life of Miss Anne Catley celebrated singing performer of the last century* (London, 1888), 62–3.

48. Oulton, *Theatres of London,* 2: 103.

49. Qtd. in Ibid., 2: 103–4.

50. Ibid., 2: 105–6.

51. Qtd. in *London Stage* 2.1: clxiv–clxv.

52. Wilkinson, qtd. in Philip H. Highfill, Jr., Kalman A. Burnim, and Edward A. Langhans, *A Biographical Dictionary of Actors, Actresses, Musicians, Dancers, Managers & Other Stage Personnel in London, 1660–1800.* 16 vols. (Carbondale and Edwardsville: Southern Illinois University Press, 1973–93), 16: 210.

53. Pedicord, "Changing Audience," 246.

54. Paul Ranger, '*Terror and Pity Reign in Every Breast's: Gothic Drama in the London Patent Theatres, 1750–1820* (London: Society for Theatre Research, 1991), 23.

55. Ibid.

6

THE CHALLENGE OF PARTICIPATION: AUDIENCES AT LIVING STAGE THEATRE COMPANY

Susan C. Haedicke

A poem by Federico Garcia Lorca, written in large, colorfully illustrated lettering, adorns the wall of the performance space at Living Stage Theatre Company, the community-outreach venture of Arena Stage in Washington, D.C.

> the poem
> the song
> the picture
> is only water
> drawn from the well
> of the people
> and it should be given back
> to them in a cup of beauty
> so that they may drink
> and in drinking
> understand
> themselves.

The beautiful poem-poster is not simply decoration for this unique theatre: it also reflects the core of their work. Here, the company of professional actors seeks to empower the audiences, usually poor and underserved, through their participation in the artistic process.

Founded in 1966 by Robert Alexander, the Living Stage is now located in a renovated jazz club on Fourteenth Street in Washington, D.C. This community-based theatre rarely gives public performances and instead creates theatre not *for* but *with* special populations: those Alexander calls the "forgotten" people—mainly children, especially those from the inner city and the disabled, but also the elderly and inmates of D.C. prisons. Sometimes, Living Stage offers a single workshop for a particular group, but the company prefers working with the same audience members on a weekly basis for a year or more. The program for teen mothers requires a three-year commitment from the teens, whereas programs at area schools last the academic year. In some cases, Living Stage has long-term relationships of a decade or more with institutions such as Lorton Prison (until its closure in the mid-1990s) and Sharpe Health School. Here some of the audience members participate for several years, whereas others do so for only a few months. In each program, the spectators work with the Living Stage actors to create characters and improvise scenes exploring issues that are of particular importance to the participating group. The scenes are not rehearsed and developed into a public performance for an outside audience, but instead are used to understand, analyze, and explore solutions to a specific problem that the members of the group face in their daily lives. Thus, the significance of the theatre work is in the process, not in the product. These participatory performances grow out of and speak to the needs and hopes of a particular community and strive to engage the hearts and minds of the audience participants, empowering them through their involvement in art production. A noble mission certainly, yet various questions arise: (1) how does audience participation contribute to empowerment, (2) what does that empowerment actually mean to the audience-participant at a workshop, and (3) does this theatrical work contribute in any way to social change.

The success of Living Stage is not tied to ticket sales or rave reviews, but to an increase in a participant's self-esteem, self-determination, and practical skills (individual empowerment) and to the ability to translate that improvement in one's personal life into some form of social transformation. This transformation represents the efficacy of the theatrical event–what Baz Kershaw defines as "the potential that theatre may have to make the immediate effects of performance influence, however minutely, the general historical evolution of wider social and political realities."[1] In order to begin to measure the success of such ventures, distinguishing between concepts of individual empowerment and performance efficacy is crucial because it offers a way through the tangle of claims of community-based theatre, claims like 'individuals are empowered when they recognize their own creativity' or 'audience participation can change lives and contribute to social change.' Current research in empowerment theory for use in both psychology and in development (organizational and community) stresses the importance of a parallel differentiation. M.A. Zimmerman, who has made significant contributions to empowerment theory and community psychology explains: "A distinction between empowering processes [individual empowerment] and outcomes [efficacy] is critical in order to clearly define empowerment theory. Empowerment processes are ones in which attempts to gain control, obtain needed resources, and critically understand one's social environment are fundamental. The process is empowering if it helps people develop skills so that they can become independent problem solvers and decision makers. . . . Empowered outcomes refer to operationalization of empowerment so we can study the consequences of citizen attempts to gain greater control in their community or the effects of interventions designed to empower participants."[2] For Zimmerman, successful grassroots approaches to development balance the specific strategies to promote individual and community participation and empowerment with wider strategies to promote economic, social, and cultural transformations that represent equal opportunities and social justice. Zimmerman's distinction between empowering processes and outcomes parallels concepts of individual empowerment achieved within the theatrical event and performance efficacy, and it provides a framework from which to examine Living Stage's use of participation and decision-making within the artistic process as a model or rehearsal for the struggle for equity, human rights, and democracy outside the walls of the theatre. As Gramsci points out, people are often dominated more by coercion and consent than by laws that limit actions.[3] By demystifying the production of art (culture), Living Stage helps participants to recognize the constructed nature not only of artistic, but also of social, political, and economic structures (the dominant hegemony), which appear legitimate and non-contestable. This knowledge, in turn, encourages participants to resist these structures. Thus the role of the audience at Living Stage is radically altered from that of mainstream theatres in this process of participation to empowerment to efficacy. Before the claims of empowerment and efficacy can be assessed, however, it is essential to understand the nature of the theatrical activity at Living Stage.

AUDIENCE PARTICIPATION AT LIVING STAGE

A clearly articulated philosophy that valorizes art and its power to make life more comprehensible and meaningful underlies all the theatrical activities at Living Stage. Robert Alexander claims that, "If you don't value art, then you don't value life. Art is the foundation of culture . . . art is the inner landscape of humanity. Art is our birthright. It is who we are."[4] When he speaks of art as a birthright, he means that everyone is an artist; everyone has the potential to make art and culture. When people experience their artistry, he continues, "they will be able to articulate their needs, articulate their hopes, and feel that they do make a difference. Transforming spectators into artists validates their creativity which, in turn, empowers them to change things for the better."[5] Brazilian director, Augusto Boal, who is internationally recognized for his work in community-based theatre, calls these techniques "poetics of the oppressed" where "the main objective [is] to change people—'spectators,' . . . into actors, transformers of the dramatic action"[6] which, in turn, trains them for real action. In spite of the differences between

the work of Boal and Living Stage, both aim "to help the spect-actor transform himself into a protagonist of the dramatic action and rehearse alterna-
tives for his situation, so that he may then be able to extrapolate into his real
life the actions he has rehearsed in the practice of theatre."[7]

At one Living Stage performance at the D.C. Jail, an inmate suggested an
ending full of hope and happiness for a scene about a mother and her addic-
tive teen-aged daughter. When Alexander later asked her about her choice,
she responded that if the character could do it, then she could do it herself.
Alexander explains, "Audience members become creators when they talk
about the experiences of the characters. If you can make choices in the imagination, you can make choices in life."[8] Boal agrees when he writes, "The
liberated spectator, as a whole person, launches into action. No matter that
the action is fictional; what matters is that it is action!"[9] This type of performance allows the spectator to "understand the situation better, to try to see
the possibilities of action in a given situation, and to train . . . for action."[10]
The concept of participation used here rejects the traditional theatrical relationship of passive spectator (object) and active actor (subject)—an asym-
metrical power dynamic—in favor of a more equal subject/subject relationship
where spectator becomes actor and so works alongside the professional actor
to determine the theatrical event.

At the beginning of each theatre workshop, the Living Stage performers
welcome a small audience into a large room that looks more like a child's
playroom than a theatre. A coat tree covered with hats and pieces of brightly
colored cloth, a ladder, an arch, and a few large red, blue, and yellow cubes
are scattered around the room. The musician plays the keyboard as the performers sing and invite the audience to join the improvised jam by handing
them instruments as they enter and by encouraging them to sing and make
up their own lyrics. Rhyme, rhythm, or even logic is not necessary; what
matters is the will to express oneself. The jam flows into a scene (sometimes
improvised, sometimes scripted and rehearsed in advance), which is performed by the company; thus the role of the audience momentarily shifts
from participant to observer. This shift draws attention to the act of spectatorship by making the audience aware that they are now "watching" and thus
fosters a Brechtian *verfremdungseffekt* in order to politicize the audience so
that they begin to question what they had before accepted as "the way
things are." Fredric Jameson points out: "The purpose of the Brechtian
estrangement-effect is . . . a political one in the most thoroughgoing sense
of the word; it is, as Brecht insisted over and over, to make you aware that
the objects and institutions you thought to be natural were really only historical: the result of change, they themselves henceforth become in their turn
changeable."[11] This shift from participant to spectator enables the audience
to get an overview of the situation and, consequently, to bring a very different
perspective to the decision-making process than if they had remained participants in the action.

The characters in the scene, performed by the Living Stage actors, are usually the same age as audience members and face the same crises and dilemmas; they also make choices that get them into trouble. As the story enacted by Living Stage performers reaches a climax, a moment of decision for one of the characters, the action is frozen so that the audience can create the ending. Empowered to change the events, the spectators offer several endings and become actors as they don hats and scarves and take over some of the roles. Actors and spectators work together to find solutions to the difficulties faced by the characters—difficulties and decisions that audience members experience in their own lives.

This principle is taken one step further in another performance strategy that Living Stage calls "environments." Here the spectator-participants create characters that would inhabit a specific locale: a crime scene, a courtroom, a hospital, a lab doing experiments on human behavior, an African village one thousand years ago, a farm run by the vegetables, a space station for outcasts. The actors suggest an event to start the "action," which then develops according to the participants' needs. Often multiple "scenes" occur simultaneously, and time, place, identities, and relationships are fluid as audience members are encouraged to "try on" a wide range of roles. In an environment with young children, which begins at the dinner table, a Living Stage actor might pair up with a young girl and adopt the role of the child while encouraging the young spectator into the role of parent by saying to her, "Mommy, I hate spinach and I refuse to eat it." The child thus occupies the position of authority or must relinquish that position by denying parentage and sending the scene in a different direction. Oran Sandel, actor in the company for over twenty years and director from 1995–2001, explains that the Living Stage actors develop the character roles they play in an environment from the character choices made by the spectators so that they can "wedge themselves firmly into the fabric of the situation" where they can intensify the environment and push participants beyond familiar responses and stereotypes.[12] Exploring a situation from the other side of the power dynamic than the participant usually occupies allows him or her to see an issue from a different perspective or to create an authority figure who responds to the imagined need.

Sometimes environments go beyond play-acting to address the practical needs of the audience participants. During the teen mother program, Living Stage discovered that these young women, aged twelve to seventeen, needed diapers, cribs, toys, strollers, and other tangible objects necessary for child-rearing. Alexander appealed to the Board and friends of the Living Stage who donated a roomful of items, and at the next workshop, each young mother received a bag of beans and entered a bazaar set up in the theatre. There she bargained with the Living Stage actors/merchants for the purchase of things she needed for her child—things she then owned and took home. Sometimes she shifted her role to that of merchant to sell what she had bought to obtain enough beans to buy something else. Performative event/real life skills—here the boundaries between art and life, artist and community, blur.

The audiences who participate in Living Stage's performances are not just passive recipients of a finished text or even co-producers of the meaning of the text in their imaginations. Instead they are active artists who create, together with the performers, the complete performance text. In this participatory theatre, "stories" are not just something observed safely from one's seat, but actually "lived" as the participants move from one cluster of activities to another, from one personality to another. And the participants experience the consequences of their choices and the choices of others. Harry Elam, in his book on Valdez and Baraka, argues that participation is "an act of symbolic rebellion," which does not imply "total social commitment," but which acts like the "foot-in-the-door" technique explained in advertising and persuasion theory. Here research has shown that the key step in persuading someone to take additional action after a persuasive appeal is to get him to do a simple act, like signing his name, during the appeal. Participation during a performance acts in the same way.[13] For Living Stage, the act of participation is synonymous with the act of creation, and because there is no public performance by the participants, the act of creation is more like a rehearsal for real-life action than an end in itself. This ownership of the theatrical event allows the participants to focus on the event itself and their personal responses to it, rather than on preparation of the event for external reactions and approval. Thus the work is determined by the self-defined needs of the participants instead of by the imagined needs of an outside audience.

This creative participation in the production of theatre intended to lead to empowerment and action raises several questions however. Are the participants being falsely taught that they can change their circumstances? Does the work preserve the status quo by defusing the participants' anger and frustration, offering them a temporary "feel-good" solution while robbing them of the impetus toward real action? Or does it, as activist and scholar Muhammad Anisur Rahman warns, divide the poor into relatively privileged participating groups and even further disempowered others, thus "making it more difficult for the poor to challenge wider power structures"?[14] How does participation lead to empowerment?

THE RELATIONSHIP OF PARTICIPATION AND EMPOWERMENT

Empowerment is a term that is very difficult to define, but it is closely tied to notions of self-esteem and self-reliance, to the belief that one has worth and that one can make things happen, either on the individual or the community level. Thus empowerment implies action.[15] As Zimmerman claims, it "suggests a distinct approach for developing interventions and creating social change."[16] Rahman, writing on people's self-development, contrasts two opposing views of empowerment: the "consumerist" view, which looks at empowerment as increasing the flow of consumption of goods and services to those segments of the population who are traditionally under-served versus the more recent "creativist" view, which argues that satisfying the five "basic needs" (food, clothing, shelter, medical care, and education) advocated by the consumerist view is inadequate. What distinguishes human beings, these scientists argue, is the urge "to fulfill our creative potential in ever newer ways."[17] And while satisfying that urge to create, human beings discover ways to fulfill other needs. Thus, rather than increasing access to consumer items, the creativist approach encourages individuals to take the initiative to produce needed goods and services and thus to redistribute opportunity and power. Living Stage promotes a creativist strategy of empowerment by establishing a democratic and safe place where participants can reappropriate and construct knowledge and where they can learn real life skills.

The theatrical signals of place at Living Stage alert the audience to the nature of the performative event as democratized and accessible. The theatre building is in the heart of the community that it serves and, as mentioned earlier, it does not resemble a traditional theatre space. The large windows in each of the two performance spaces are never masked and thus reinforce the connection with the community outside as they short circuit any impulse to create a self-contained space. No separation between stage and auditorium exists; the entire room is a performance space, and no chairs for observers are available. The only places to sit are the large colorful blocks scattered around the room that become the set in various scenes. The building also has a large kitchen with a big table, couches, and books, where actors and audiences can share a meal or talk, thus developing a personal connection that undermines the hierarchical divisions between artist and spectator. No backstage area or dressing rooms, off limits to the public, exist at Living Stage. The pictures, poems, speeches, and songs, often the words and images of people fighting for freedom and justice, which cover the walls in the performance space, the bathrooms, and the halls invite anyone who is in the building to linger, to read aloud, to share, to gain insight and inspiration. All the signals indicate a place to work together rather than to be entertained as a passive observer. In a 1986 interview on National Public Radio, Jennifer Nelson, then a member of the company, explained: "If you think of what a traditional theatre is like, and how usually when you come into a theatre, it's like going into a church, . . . you're ushered in, and there's this atmosphere of 'we have to whisper,' and there's this great sacred act that's going to take place up on the stage that you really don't have anything to do with, you're only there to observe it. So what we create is just the opposite: an atmosphere where you come in, and the lights are up in the whole room, and the performers are right on the same level as the audience, and they're invited to participate. It's like coming into somebody's house instead of coming into somebody's sanctuary."[18] This idea of "home" goes beyond the physical space, however, as Living Stage strives to create a safe place, a family-like community where each participant feels like he or she "belongs." According to Margaret Beyer, a psychologist who evaluated the work of Living Stage on numerous occasions for social service organizations, the psychological process that fosters a sense of belonging is called "holding." Beyer found that Living Stage "designed holding into all aspects" of the programs creating a "loving, safe and supportive context" that allowed the participants to grow and increase self-confidence and self-worth which, in turn, improved their chances for accomplishing their goals.[19] Nelson explains, "The creative process is in no way limited or diminished by one's economic, educational, or social status and so it *ipso facto* carries no possibility of failure, which is the motivating factor for opting out of the mainstream. Living Stage creates an atmosphere in which everyone participating is successful; in which each person can be recognized for the gifts that she/he has; and in which whatever opinion one has about the world can be expressed freely."[20]

In this creative process, participants never play themselves, but instead always assume a character. While the improvised scene may parallel their actual lives, it never represents an enactment of their own story. This technique frees them from aspects of the actual event that blocked creative solutions the first time. "When you create a character," insists Alexander, "the character can do anything because it is not you. When you create a character, the imagination sets you free from your worldly body, your specific situation, your life. The creation of stories allows you to tap into areas that have remained hidden because you're afraid or ignorant."[21] This fictional action can transform lives. Two drawings by Ted, a teen participant in one of the Living Stage programs, provide a striking visual testimony of "before" and "after" Living Stage. The teens were asked to create an image of themselves in the world on the first day and the last day of the year-long program. Ted's first drawing shows him imprisoned in a cage on the top of a building in a city either on fire or bleeding. Reds and blacks dominate the drawing. In his second drawing, Ted is on the top of a mountain with his arms outstretched to the sun. Another group of inner city teens gained enough confidence in their own paintings and collages after their visit to "Free Within Ourselves" at the Smithsonian, an exhibition of artists like Romare Beardon, Jacob Lawrence, Bill Traylor, and William H. Johnson, that they offered their art as an exhibition at the Martin Luther King Library. It remained on display for several months.

Even more miraculous testimonies abound. At one performance workshop, Living Stage performers led the children on an improvised visit to the circus. One child claimed that he was going to walk on a tightrope. The child at that particular time had crutches and braces, but at that moment he put the crutches down and started walking, one foot in front of the other, with his arms balanced out. At another, a fourteen-year old girl joined a Living Stage actor on an improvised taxi ride during which they careened wildly around the room. She suddenly shouted, "Stop the cab! There on the sidewalk is a set of keys. Pick them up!" After a moment of silence with the imaginary keys in her hand, she confided to her new friend that they were the keys to her heart. These were the first words she had spoken in seven years.

While these stories of personal transformation are compelling, they are hard to translate into models of empowerment. The work that Living Stage does to empower disempowered groups actually runs much deeper as it uses participation in the theatrical event to give them the tools to reclaim knowledge from the dominant structure and to produce new knowledge.The performative event in which spectator becomes artist parallels the concept of "conscientization" introduced by Paulo Freire who developed a literacy program that not only taught reading and writing, but also critical thinking about one's world. Freire claims that the hallmark of oppression is a passivity and an unthinking acceptance of one's reality and that to be fully human, one must be active and reflective. Conscientization is the process in which oppressed people develop a critical awareness of their social reality and their ability to transform it through their own actions, rather than through help from the outside. In *Pedagogy of the Oppressed,* he examines how conscientization occurs through dialogue as people begin to understand institutional injustices and contradictions and learn how to utilize their power, however limited, to challenge the powerful and change their reality. Participants in a dialogic relationship are able to "perceive critically *the way they exist* in the world *with which* and *in which* they find themselves; they come to see the world not as a static reality, but as a reality in process, in transformation."[22] Thus empowerment is the process by which people assume control over their lives by wresting their destinies from those who make their decisions for them.

At Living Stage, Freirean dialogue takes the form of participation in the creation of the theatrical event as the audiences wrestle with the consequences of their choices and actions. In the audience-generated endings and in the environments, unlike in real life, spectators can experiment with a range of solutions to daily problems. In addition, sometimes these performative events give the spectators real information about their neglected, erased, or simply unlearned histories. Through that knowledge, they begin to find their voices. Sociologist Anthony D. Smith emphasizes the importance of understanding the past because it helps a group "to discover a cognitive framework, a map and a location for its unfocused aspirations."[23] Through the past, an individual learns not only the triumphs and defeats of previous generations, but also the impact of individual action on the course of history.

Participation becomes empowerment moreover as the audiences begin to understand how the power structure actually works and to recognize how they unconsciously cooperate in their own oppression. One provocative piece, entitled *Root of Rage,* challenged audiences to action by exposing the "root of rage" caused by racism and injustice. The piece opens with a striking stage picture: a bloodied African-American man hangs upside-down surrounded by other hanging objects, like basketball sneakers and a machine gun—all for sale. This powerful image incorporates the signs of African-American objectification and devaluation in this country and echoes events of our racist past—the sale of human beings, the lynchings of black men. The image is held for a long time, but when the man finally releases himself, he does not destroy the objects exhibited with him; instead, he "consumes" them, literally eating the price tags. The scene challenges the audience both to understand institutional racism and to recognize one's own inadvertent collusion in the system.

With that knowledge of how individuals often participate in their own oppression comes the determination to demand a say in one's individual future, to stand up for one's rights. At Living Stage, that process begins with the improvisations that produce a "social imaginary"[24] that lays the foundation for social change in the creative imagination. Creativity, says Alexander, teaches individuals "to communicate, to daydream, to imagine possibilities, and to stick up for themselves and their hopes."[25] In a workshop with troubled teens, the actors created a scene in which a white store owner accuses an African-American teen of shoplifting and demands to search her. She responds by cursing him. An African-American policeman arrives and yells at her for making a bad name for black people, an action that hurts and confuses her. Several other incidents occur that humiliate her and highlight her apparent powerlessness until she finally runs into a friend who hands her a gun so she can rob and perhaps even kill the store owner. At this moment the scene was frozen. The teens then developed endings as they adopted roles in the scene and experienced the consequences of their choices. After the improvised performance they discussed real-life incidents of such accusations, what they did, and what they would do differently now.[26]

Closely tied to the reappropriation of knowledge and the development of new knowledge is the acquisition of real life skills, notably creative problem solving, collaborating, engaging in dialogue, taking a task to completion, and, of course, literacy. Many of the Living Stage activities work to develop these skills, but one striking example from the teen mother program is the making of a video entitled "That's My Mommy!" The teens wrote the script from improvised scenes, which dealt with childhood fears and dreams. They designed the set and costumes, performed the play, and filmed it. Once the video was completed, all received a copy to show their children. In addition to the thrill and pride the teens felt as their children squealed with delight to see their mothers on television, the imagination and discipline needed to create the video carried over into other areas of their lives. Teachers at the schools attended by the teens remarked on the significant improvement in the girls' attention spans, organizational skills, and creative problem-solving in the classroom after this project.

At every workshop, participants read aloud and write poetry, stories, and song lyrics. And, in fact, several volumes of the creative writings of the audience participants have been "published" in-house. But, at Living Stage, literacy is not just about reading and writing. Social activist John Gaventa examines how "literacy from the top" rarely succeeds even in the small goal of teaching a person to read, and he claims that type of program may even "be a way to expand to the illiterate the skills needed by the dominant society." Instead, he argues, "the process of becoming literate [must be] tied to a process of struggle, of gaining knowledge for action."[27] This principle determines many of the scenes and environments at Living Stage as writing becomes an integral part of solving the problem. In fact, for Alexander, "poetry is the bullet that stops the tyrant. . . . poetry is the kiss that heals the heart that has been mangled by evil."[28]

In one workshop with teen mothers, the Living Stage actors began a piece at the lunch table as they and the teens were finishing the meal. It dramatized an argument between a teenaged boy and his girlfriend who had a baby. The fight exploded into the hall and down the stairs into the theatre with the teen mothers running to keep up. The girl accused the boy of flirting with other girls, and she was desperate with jealousy (a situation easily recognizable for the teen mothers). At the moment of crisis when the scene could easily turn violent, it was frozen and discussed. The young women then divided into three groups to write different endings, all of which explored resolutions without violence or abandonment of mother or child. The endings were developed into a list of "commandments" for respect in a relationship.[29] Hundreds of other examples exist in the Living Stage archives. In an "environment" where the participants became outcasts exiled to some lonely place, they explored tolerance, acceptance, and individual worth. Or in another, where they became objects abandoned in a house deserted by a family on vacation–a dirty sock, the dustball in the corner, the leftovers in the refrigerator, the evening gown, they examined feelings of desertion and loneliness. In one workshop, the audience participants experimented with governance, breaking into groups and "creating" a country. They determined the physical attributes of the landscape and the people, the climate, and the history, and they explored how these aspects formed the basis of their culture. They also established the governmental structure, the economic system, and the social policies. Once the national identities and "laws" of each country were established and a "constitution" was written, the different groups met to discuss issues of mutual concern. Treaties, alliances, and animosities developed among the various groups over the issues.

Underlying this work is the belief that, regardless of small successes or failures, a "self-conscious people, those who are currently poor and oppressed, will progressively transform their environment by their own praxis."[30] At Living Stage, self-worth, self-reliance, and self-determination grow out of the learned ability to take risks, both artistic and personal. And once the participants are willing to take these risks beyond the doors of the theatre, the potential for efficacy is born.

EFFICACY OF THE THEATRE WORK AT LIVING STAGE

The possible efficacy of performance is very difficult to measure, yet it is clear both from the mission statements and the work itself that the goals of Living Stage are just such social transformation. But how is it possible to establish the causal connection between the theatre work and any societal changes no matter how small? Baz Kershaw argues that even that question is not helpful—"what if [instead] we pay more attention to the *conditions* of performance that are *most likely* to produce an efficacious result?" he asks. In order to evaluate efficacy more convincingly, we must "consider the *potential* of performance (both in its specific sense as 'individual show' and in its general sense as 'a collection of practices') to achieve efficacy in a particular historical context."[31] Looked at from this perspective, it is possible to document the increased politicization of the Living Stage participants.

As participation at Living Stage shifts the role of the audience from passive watching to active doing, it undermines the elitism of "Art" by demystifying the process of art production. Creating art encourages the participants to observe their world more carefully which, in turn, makes them *see* it differently. They begin to understand that what is seen and how it is seen is determined more by expectations than by observations, and they begin to recognize that rather than reflecting an objective reality, "art *creates* realities and worlds." Because it is not limited by actualities, art is "the medium through which new mediums emerge."[32] Art supplies a variety of models from which to construct reality. At Living Stage where performances are not gifts to the spectators from the actors, but a joint effort (what Boal calls "rehearsal theatre"), the theatrical event provides a "'model' for oppositional action against hegemony."[33] Active involvement rather than spectatorship forms the core of the event, and this participation signals cultural politicization paralleling one of the principles of community-based theatre, which states that this theatrical activity "is linked to the struggles for cultural, social, economic, and political equity for all people. It is fundamentally a theater of hope and often of joy. It recognizes that to advocate for equity is to meet resistance and to meet with no resistance indicates a failure to enter the fight."[34] The practices of this "theatre of social engagement," must be "considered as a form of *cultural intervention*," and it must be clear that these performances are "committed to bringing about actual change in specific communities."[35] For Freire, this type of "cultural action is always a systematic and deliberate form of action which operates upon the social structure, either with the objective of preserving that structure or of transforming it. . . . Cultural action either serves domination (consciously or unconsciously) or it serves liberation."[36]

Participatory research, the grassroots action that grows out of these ideas, offers specific groups with little power and few resources a strategy by which they can work together toward social justice. It helps them understand what they need to better their lives and how to attain it, and it teaches ways to take effective action towards improving their conditions.[37] "Participatory research attempts to break down the distinction between the researchers and the researched, the subjects and objects of knowledge production by the participation of the people-for-themselves in the process of gaining and creating knowledge. In the process, research is seen not only as a process of creating knowledge, but simultaneously, as education and development of consciousness, and of mobilization for action."[38] So, participatory research is about the right to speak, and "true speaking," warns bell hooks, "is not solely an expression of creative power; it is an act of resistance, a political gesture that challenges politics of domination that would render us nameless and voiceless. As such, it is a courageous act—as such, it represents a threat."[39] Usually with the help of an outside researcher or leader, the people learn to ask: "Who has the right to define knowledge? How does the control of knowledge affect power relations? What is the relation of 'popular' knowledge to 'official' knowledge? How do relatively powerless groups empower themselves through research and information?"[40] Paulo Freire admits that "Participatory research is no enchanted magic wand that can be waved over the culture of silence, suddenly restoring the desperately needed voice that has been forbidden to rise and be heard. . . . the silence is not a genetically or ontologically determined condition of these women and men but the expression of perverted social, economic, and political structures, which can be transformed." But it is through participatory research that they learn to be "the masters of inquiry into the underlying causes of the events in their world"[41] and that knowledge is inextricably linked to social action.

The theatre work at Living Stage uses the principles of participatory research in the performance workshops to awaken the imagination and consciousness of the spectator/actors so that they become aware of the social situation that circumscribes their lives and more critical and creative in their approach to what needs to be done to improve their conditions. Rather than being on the receiving end of knowledge about their problems, which Gaventa argues "is more often than not produced by the powerful in the interest of maintaining the status quo,"[42] they participate in the articulation of the problems, in the research about institutions and issues impacting the problems, and in the determination of appropriate solutions. Transforming spectators into artists at Living Stage becomes a key mobilization strategy in cultural politicization. For Alexander, "the act of creation is to make something where before there was nothing,"[43] and it is not a huge leap from imaginative new worlds to a willingness to test those practiced solutions on real life problems. Creativity, repeats Alexander over and over, will not only "affect the lives of individual participants, but also will radically impact the ways in which they interact with others."[44]

In one case, an inmate at Lorton Prison was so inspired by his work with Living Stage that he began Lorton Voices, a theatre company within the prison. He later received a pardon from President Gerald Ford because of his theatre work, and Lorton Voices remained a strong program at Lorton Prison until the facility was closed. After working with the Living Stage, many prison inmates have insisted that had they participated in such workshops when they were young, they would not now be in jail,[45] and proof of that assertion is evident in the other example, which documents the transformation of a student at Frank W. Ballou High School, an inner city school in the District of Columbia, from juvenile delinquent to graduating senior to a social worker working with troubled D.C. youth. Mac, an arrogant and belligerent student, was awaiting trial for a shooting in which he was involved when he participated in a year of Living Stage workshops. His teacher wrote to Living Stage: "Mac was 'transformed' last year in a really rare, startling and miraculous way. His experiences with the Living Stage . . . gave him the opportunity to take a good look at who he really was and what he was feeling and enabled him to see the great reservoirs of talent inside himself."

In addition to these individual cases, Living Stage has inspired other community-based theatres and programs across the country. Olympia Dukakis' remarks spoken at the benefit reception for Living Stage on April 17, 1989, proclaim that not only is the work "replicable," but necessary to heal the "epidemics raging all over this country . . . Living Stage has discovered a powerful medicine that injects *life force* into severely threatened minds, hearts, and bodies and the possibilities of their young lives. Someday, a visionary scientist will prove, in a form the general public can understand, that creative work that is physically, mentally, and emotionally *whole* and *active* transforms the biological structure of the brain and the nervous system."[46] Dukakis has experienced the power of the work in education programs based on the Living Stage model at Whole Theatre that she founded with Remi Bousseau in New Jersey. Several other theatres, including Red Ladder Theatre Company, the community outreach branch of San Jose Repertory Theatre; Sally Gordon's Teatro de la Realidad in Los Angeles; and Ralph Remington's Pillsbury House Theatre in the Twin Cities, acknowledge their indebtedness to Living Stage. (Remington began as director of Living Stage in July 2001.) In addition, Living Stage has led innumerable workshops for teachers nationwide who then incorporate the ideas and strategies into their classrooms. The parameters of the ever widening circles of influence are impossible to calculate.

Participation is the key strategy for politicization in the work of Living Stage, and for Chantal Mouffe, active involvement is a key factor in democratic politics as well. Democracy, as a concept, guarantees liberty, equality, and justice to all people, but, she argues, these democratic principles are not realized even in societies that claim to be democracies. Rather than a revolution to spawn a new political form of society, Mouffe proposes to radicalize democracy: to renew the idea of citizenship where people work for the "common good" of a society without losing the gains made for individual rights. "A radical, democratic citizen must be an active citizen, somebody who *acts* as a citizen, who conceives of herself as a participant in a collective undertaking."[47] Living Stage strives to create a paradigm of a radical democracy by establishing a microcosm of a society that lives by true democratic principles as audiences transform from compliant observers of events created by others into initiators of action and decision-makers. Through this participation in the democratic process, the theatre work becomes the staging ground for activities that counter the effects of depoliticization, which have rendered racial minorities, the poor, and the disadvantaged politically and socially passive by taking away their initiative to speak and act. "For those without power in the society, theatre offers a means of empowerment and, as a result, has repeatedly been used as a social weapon."[48] Living Stage strives to stimulate the individual to action no matter how small for one action leads to another and another resulting in a cumulative effect: changed attitudes and behavior affect the individual certainly, but also those around him or her. It is here in the "*potential* of performance . . . to achieve efficacy"[49] that we must look to discover the impact of this theatre work on society.

NOTES

1. Baz Kershaw, *The Politics of Performance: Radical Theatre as Cultural Intervention* (London: Routledge, 1992), 1.

2. M. A. Zimmerman, "Empowerment Theory: Psychological, Organizational, and Community Levels of Analysis," in Julian Rappaport and Edward Seidman, eds., *Handbook of Community Psychology* (New York: Kluwer Academic/Plenum, 2000), 46.

3. See Antonio Gramsci, *Selections from the Prison Notebooks of Antonio Gramsci,* Ed. and trans. Quintin Hoare and Goeffrey Nowell Smith (New York: International Publishers, 1971).

4. Robert Alexander, interview by author, tape recording, Washington, D.C., October 13, 1995.

5. Robert Alexander, interview by author, tape recording, Washington, D.C., October 2, 1995.

6. Augusto Boal, *Theatre of the Oppressed,* trans. Charles A. and Maria-Odilia Leal McBride (New York: Theatre Communications Group, 1985), 122.

7. Augusto Boal, *The Rainbow of Desire: The Boal Method of Theatre and Therapy,* trans. Adrian Jackson (New York: Routledge, 1995), 40.

8. Robert Alexander, interview by author, tape recording, Washington, D.C., October 8, 1995.

9. Boal, *Theatre of the Oppressed,* 122.

10. Jan Cohen-Cruz, "Theatricalizing Politics: An Interview with Augusto Boal," in Mady Schutzman and Jan Cohen-Cruz, eds., *Playing Boal: Theatre, Therapy, and Activism* (London: Routledge, 1994), 234.

11. Fredric Jameson, *The Prison-House of Language* (Princeton, N.J.: Princeton University Press, 1972), 58.

12. Oran Sandel, interview by author, tape recording, Washington, D.C., June 28, 1996.

13. Harry J. Elam, Jr., *Taking It to the Streets: The Social Protest Theatre of Luis Valdez and Amiri Baraka* (Ann Arbor: University of Michigan Press, 1997), 131.

14. Mohammad Anisur Rahman, "Participatory Development: Toward Liberation or Co-optation?" in Gary Craig and Marjorie Mayo, eds., *Community Empowerment: A Reader in Participation and Development,* (London: Zed Books, 1995), 30.

15. See Craig and Mayo, especially the article by S.M. Miller, Martin Rein, and Peggy Levitt, "Community Action in the United States," 112–26 and B. Hopson and M. Scally, *Lifeskills Teaching,* (Maidenhead, England: McGraw-Hill Company, 1981).

16. Zimmerman, 44.

17. Mohammad Anisur Rahman, "The Case of the Third World: People's Self Development," *Community Development Journal* 25.4 (1990): 311.

18. Jennifer Nelson, Segment on Living Stage Theatre Company, "All Things Considered," National Public Radio, Washington, D.C., May 28, 1986.

19. Margaret Beyer, "Evaluations of Teen Mothers of Today, 1991–94," Living Stage Archives.

20. Jennifer Nelson, "Living Stage: The Improvisational Process and the Myth of the Black Underclass," Living Stage Archives, August 1988.

21. Robert Alexander, interview by author, tape recording, Washington, D.C., October 5, 1995.

22. Paulo Freire, *Pedagogy of the Oppressed,* trans. Myra Bergman Ramos (New York: Continuum, 1989), 71.

23. Anthony Smith, *National Identity* (Reno: University of Nevada Press, 1991), 140.

24. Janelle Reinelt, "Notes for a Radical Democratic Theatre: Productive Crises and the Challenge of Indeterminacy," in Jeanne Colleran and Jenny Spencer, eds., *Staging Resistance: Essays on Political Theatre* (Ann Arbor: University of Michigan Press, 1998), 289.

25. Robert Alexander, interview by author, tape recording, Washington, D.C., February 18, 1996.

26. Living Stage Production Reports, December 23, 1991, Living Stage Archives.

27. John Gaventa, "Toward a Knowledge Democracy: Viewpoints on Participatory Research in North America," in Orlando Fals-Borda and Mohammad Anisur Rahman, eds., *Action and Knowledge: Breaking the Monopoly with Participatory Action Research* (London: Intermediate Technology Publications, 1991), 125.

28. Robert Alexander, Letter to an Actress, Living Stage Archives.

29. Living Stage Production Reports, Spring 1994.

30. Orlando Fals-Borda, *The Challenge of Social Change* (London: SAGE Publications, Ltd., 1985), 118.

31. Kershaw, 3.

32. Murray Edelman, *From Art to Politics: How Artistic Creations Shape Political Conceptions* (Chicago: University of Chicago Press, 1995), 7.

33. Kershaw, 39.

34. Dudley Cocke, Harry Newman, and Janet Salmons-Rue, eds., *From the Ground Up: Grassroots Theatre in Historical and Contemporary Perspective* (Ithaca, N.Y.: Community Based Arts Project, Cornell University, 1993), 81.

35. Kershaw, 5–6.

36. Freire, *Pedagogy,* 180.

37. See Peter Park, "What is Participatory Research? A Theoretical and Methodo-

logical Perspective," in Peter Park, Mary Brydon-Miller, Budd Hall, and Ted Jackson, eds., *Voices of Change: Participatory Research in the United States and Canada* (Westport, Conn.: Bergin and Garvey, 1993), 1–19.

38. John Gaventa, "Participatory Research in North America," *Convergence* 24.2–3 (1988): 19.

39. bell hooks, *Talking Back: Thinking Feminist, Thinking Black* (Boston: South End Press, 1989), 8.

40. John Gaventa, "The Powerful, the Powerless, and the Experts: Knowledge Struggles in an Information Age," in Park, Brydon-Miller, Hall, and Jackson, 22.

41. Paulo Freire, "Foreward," in Park, Brydon-Miller, Hall, and Jackson, ix–x.

42. Gaventa, "The Powerful," 26.

43. Robert Alexander, "Life, Death, and Creativity," *Simulation and Games* 8 (1977): 112.

44. Robert Alexander, interview by author, tape recording, Washington, D.C., October 13, 1995.

45. Rhea Edmonds, "Fighting Street Crime from the Living Stage," *The Community News,* April 4, 1991, n.p.

46. Olympia Dukakis, "Remarks at the Benefit Reception for Living Stage," Washington, D.C., April 17, 1989, Living Stage Archives.

47. Chantal Mouffe, ed. *Dimensions of Radical Democracy* (London: Verso, 1992), 4.

48. Elam, 139.

49. Kershaw, 3.

7

MANIPULATION OF THE MIND: FICTION IN THE PERFORMANCES OF PENN AND TELLER

Susan Kattwinkel

The experimental theatre of the 1960s developed styles that its practitioners hoped would help communicate a message of skepticism and protest regarding systems of power in contemporary society. Richard Schechner has discussed at some length the reflexive nature of such theatre, and notes that it was often used to "educate the public to the theatricalized deceptions daily practiced on them by political leaders and media bosses."[1] He acknowledges that while the style of theatre with such aims has changed in the intervening years, many of the techniques, including audience participation, have remained. One of today's styles of theatre to use audience participation for much the same purpose is new vaudeville, or contemporary variety theatre.[2] When Ron Jenkins wrote about artists in the form in 1988, he said that they "are linked by the ingenuity with which they subversively attack the oppressive elements of everyday life in modern America."[3]

One of the performing groups at the head of this movement is the magic duo of Penn and Teller. Known as "the Bad Boys of Magic," they resist being classified with other magicians because of their insistence that, unlike other magicians, they acknowledge the skill and practice required to perform the tricks they do, and emphasize the trickery involved. Although most other magicians insist on maintaining the fiction of "magic," and of possessing special skills (what Penn Jillette calls "arcane knowledge"),[4] Penn and Teller present themselves as just a "couple of very eccentric guys who have learned how to do real cool things."[5] What they are especially adept at is manipulating the levels of fiction perceived by their spectators and using that manipulation to draw parallels with contemporary systems of power, with the hope that they will add to the community of skeptics to which they belong. They believe that "You can use trickery to talk about the truth."[6]

At several points in their performances they show their audience how they do those real cool things, and continually remind us that sleight of hand or mouth is not only possible on stage. They make constant analogies to contemporary political and "new-age" con artists. They are not, however, magicians who simply do tricks and then reveal their methods, comparing the tricks to real life scams. The fictionality level in a Penn and Teller performance is layered; new fictions emerge even as the magicians expose truths. Apparent revelations turn out to contain further mysteries, and one is always left wondering at what point the two men have told the truth. Further strengthening the analogy to the everyday lives of their spectators is the constant audience participation, which takes a variety of forms (from the individual participation of spectators to direct address) and involves the audience in the questioning of reality.

This manipulation of truth and fiction unbalances the spectator, engaging them mentally by putting them in a position of continuous interrogation. Daphna Ben Chaim has connected the fiction level of a performance with its success in decreasing distance between performers and spectators. She states that "the most intense personal relationship with a minimum awareness of fictionality is 'low' distance and the combination that the realist film and realistic play aspire to."[7] The difficulty with this "aspiration" is that realistic theatre is shackled to a certain, quite high, level of fictionality, because of its insistence on its presence in a world separate from that of its audience. The spectators will not forget, no matter how brilliant the fiction on stage, that they are sitting in a theatre and that the action on stage is assumed to be happening regardless of their attention to it. A minimum awareness of fictionality is created when there is less fiction in the theatre, not by creating a fiction that is hermetically sealed. The combination of a lack of a fictional plot with a constant acknowledgment of the physical surroundings, as in contemporary variety theatre, provides spectators with a lesser "awareness of fictionality" than the most convincingly presented realistic play. Although Ben Chaim may be correct that "when an element is perceived as only real, it is therefore no longer perceived metaphorically,"[8] the constant unsettling of reality in a Penn and Teller performance heightens the sense of metaphor, because the spectator is not sure at any given moment whether they are being included in the fiction or not. Because they must question their own participation in the performance it is a small step toward questioning their own participation in other performances they encounter in their lives.

Penn and Teller are convinced that their audiences can make the leap from magic skeptic to life skeptic. The difference between themselves and the magic tradition, says Jillette, is that "we start with the assumption that the audience is at least as smart as we are."[9] The attitude is not lost on their fans, many of who share the sentiment of one fan that wrote, "they treat their fans as if they have some brains in their heads."[10] The two reject the assumption that "the people in the audience are ignorant savages who will fall at our feet and worship us for performing supernatural miracles."[11] Instead, they remind the audience throughout the show that these are only tricks, accomplished through practice. In a performance in New York described by Calvin Trillin, "Penn's version of 'Abracadabra!' was a muttered 'Now I give the cards another false cut.' He referred to magic effects not as wonders but as cons or swindles."[12] When Penn and Teller perform the traditional cup and ball trick with clear cups, describing their palming technique throughout, and the scam is still not visible, it makes clear the simplicity of sleight of hand and verbal distraction with a little practice. Ron Jenkins sums up the effect by saying, "While the audience members may not be transformed from suckers to skeptics overnight, they might be a little more prone to laugh the next time a politician or salesman tells them there's nothing up his sleeve."[13]

The direct participation employed by Penn and Teller only increases the spectator's awareness of life as layers of fiction that are open to interrogation. Spectators are brought on stage to look for the deception (which Penn and Teller never deny is there) and are expected to genuinely report their findings. Unlike volunteers for other magicians, who are often expected to conceal their inside knowledge of tricks they observe, they seem to take seriously Penn's instructions to watch closely and reveal any sleight of hand they observe. Occasionally these volunteers are on stage simply to check for cover-ups and to confirm that the sleight of hand involved is not the most obvious method possibly being considered by audience members. More often, however, volunteers are on stage to assist with the trick. In some cases one or both of the men go into the audience, often to the very back, to pick a volunteer, and other times spectators become true volunteers, when they raise their hand to be chosen. In an average show, about half of their sketches will involve audience members, usually more than one at a time.

A fascinating example of full audience participation happens in a Bible trick (where a chapter and verse are chosen by a spectator and then "discovered" through supposedly random means). The chapter to be read is chosen by the audience as a whole through the use of two giant dice that are thrown into the audience from the back of the house and then rolled by the spectators down onto the stage. In this case, hundreds of people are given the chance to test for the "force"—in other words, to try to determine if the dice are loaded.[14] Choosing the "Quote of the Day" from a Bible with darts (thrown by audience members) and crap shooting may offend some audience members, but others will notice the echoes of evangelist meetings, where questions are answered or Bible passages chosen through apparently random, or divine, influences. Although we're not quite sure how the chosen passage was "forced," we know that it was, and if Penn and Teller can do it, why can't the evangelists?

Because much of the humor in the show comes from Penn's patter with the audience,[15] there are times when a spectator's only role is to provide visual contrast to Penn and Teller and to distract the rest of the spectators from the ongoing deception. Certainly this applies to a number that opened several performances in 2000. "We open by entering in giant, inflatable suits that look like us," Teller said, "just like the kind mascots wear at ball games . . . We do an entire card trick with an audience member on stage with us while we're wearing the suits."[16] Another such example is of a card trick performed with giant metal cards and a forklift, in which the participant serves mostly as a size comparison.

Usually, individual audience members are on stage to serve as the eyes of the whole audience—to look for the deception that Penn and Teller constantly remind them is there. But sometimes the audience member is crucial to the process of the trick itself. They may be participating in a knife-throwing bit, picking a card, tying a rope in knots, or timing a drowning Teller. And in many performances, spectators are invited on stage at the beginning of the show to inspect the gadgets being used in the tricks. Mostly they serve as a point of address for Penn, so that he can get the message across clearly. Although his talk sounds improvised, most of it is carefully scripted to point out "the lie that tells the greater truth."[17] Numbers are often prefaced by Penn with a statement such as "Since Penn and Teller are kind of into that debunking thing. . . ."[18] He regularly notes that all it takes is practice, and that most of their tricks can be duplicated by anyone with enough time and money.

Yet even while the duo are insisting that it's all trickery that anyone can learn they are layering other levels of fiction on top of their honesty. Penn and Teller never stop reminding the audience that everything they are seeing on stage is a sham, even while pulling tricks within tricks to confuse them further. One good example is their "Mofo, the psychic gorilla" trick, a traditional favorite with their audiences, where the gorilla is presented as a clear fake—Teller is obviously providing the gorilla's voice—but still manages to provide answers to audience questions that he should have no information about. Teller speaks for the gorilla by walking backstage every time the gorilla has to talk or by holding his hand up to his mouth and speaking behind it, mocking their own performance convention of his silence. Teller also speaks, unintelligibly, in a piece involving a chipper-shredder and a live rabbit. Teller is apparently describing the whole trick to the audience, but cannot be heard because of the noise of the machine. After the rabbit and then Teller's arm are "accidentally" dropped into the shredder, Penn suggests that people might be worried about what the animal rights activists will say and so offers to show the rabbit on so that the audience can see that it had not been harmed. Of course when Teller walks on stage, he carries a rabbit clearly different than the one apparently thrown in the shredder.

This mockery of those who might believe that they would actually harm an animal for their show reflects their feelings on simulated violence in general. Both men believe that the appearance of danger is essential to a good performance. Teller says, "We like the nerve-racking element. It isn't art without danger."[19] And Jillette has described many of their most successful routines as a simple trick with "death in the background."[20] Like most everything in their shows, this concept works on at least two levels. On one level the danger is never real; neither man is ever in any real danger and the audience is told all along that it's all just a trick. In that sense they have no desire for the audience to truly believe in the danger. Jillette says, "If one of us were to be injured in any way that was very unpleasant . . . that would get out in the press, and you would all know that. And when you came to see our show, and we were doing something dangerous, that is, the depiction of something dangerous, that is a story about something dangerous, and we expect you to laugh, all of a sudden that laughter goes away . . . It becomes very, very sick and very, very unpleasant."[21]

It is very important that they illustrate the fictionality of the danger even while they feign its reality in order to produce the moments of fear in the audience that the performance of high-level magic demands. Their ability to make the audience feel moments of danger, even while they know that the danger is not real, is what makes Penn and Teller so exciting. As one reviewer pointed out, "All the time they have us laughing at our own gullibility by showing what's really real, they somehow manage to float a terror above nearly everything they do."[22] They see the simulated violence as a celebration of life and have been very public with their feelings about movements to suppress violence in entertainment because of the belief that it leads to violence in those who view it. In a 1994 interview in *Reason Magazine,* Penn expressed his disgust with then-Attorney General Janet Reno's attempts to decrease the amount of violence on screen: "Lately she's talked about how violence on television has an effect on violence in the real world. This is damn near a textbook definition of voodoo . . . What Janet Reno has talked about is literally voodoo: If you change the representation of something, you will change its territory in the real world . . . When you're watching *Psycho,* there's that moment when you have a visceral reaction to watching someone being stabbed. And then you have the intellectual revelation that you're not, and that's where the celebration comes in."[23] This viewpoint claims that politicians don't give audiences enough credit for intelligence and don't recognize that the perception of simulated violence as real is a choice made in the moment that does not affect their approach to real life.

A relatively new trick in the performance, "Honor System," takes complete advantage of the spectator's willingness to be tricked. Interviewer Elizabeth Fitzsimons described this new favorite of Teller's: "It's an elaborate magician's escape from a plexiglass box inside a wooden crate. But instead of shielding the box with a screen until the magician emerges triumphant, Penn & Teller offer the audience a test of will. If you want to be amazed, close your eyes while Teller makes his escape. If you choose to see how the magic is done, you're welcome to watch, but you must promise never to tell the people around you with their eyes closed. 'You could bribe our crew, you could rush up on the stage and grab the props out of our hands if you really really wanted to find out how things are done,' Teller says. 'In this, we've made it very explicit that you have the option of making it not a mystery if you wanted. I love that bit.'"[24] Leaving the choice up to the audience gives them power, and translates into a real-life message as well: if you want to be fooled in life, so be it. But you can always open your eyes and see the deception. At some performances spectators are invited backstage during intermission to see how a particular trick is achieved. As in "Honor System," spectators are given the choice of having the trick demystified or remaining in the dark. The fact that the deception is made available to them is enough to emphasize the message of skepticism.

Those who insist there is no deception often find themselves on the receiving end of Penn's derision. He talks in performance about the concept of "force," used by magicians, although of course never overtly, to ensure that the correct card is picked by the audience member, who assumes that they are asserting their free will. This idea is connected to advertising, where consumers are "forced" to believe that their own free choice of a product will lead to a better life. Ron Jenkins articulated one of the best examples of the further connection of this idea to politics. Discussing Penn's description of "force," he points out how Penn "connect[s] misdirection on the stage to misdirection in other spheres of life. When a man insists that he has made a free choice, Penn mocks his innocence. 'You must have loved the last election,' he barks."[25] Penn not only assumes the spectators' intelligence, but also insists on it. In moments of audience contact Penn relishes making fun of people who appear to have any pretensions to importance. In a performance in Washington, D.C., he laughed uproariously at a college night watchman that stood up when "peace officers" were requested for a participation number. Some reviewers have termed this belittling attitude toward affectation of Penn's "badgering" and harassment,[26] but acknowledge that the audience clearly loves it and that the harassment is equal opportunity and so much a part of Penn's personality that it entertains rather than embarrasses the rest of the spectators. Rather than coddling spectators who dare to participate, Penn treats them as if he knows them, and just like school students, they seem to love living up to high expectations.

Regular spectators pride themselves on their skepticism, and take up the challenge to question everything. Quite a few Penn and Teller fan pages exist online, and at least two fans have posted pictures of the bullet casings from the famous "Bullet Catch," in which Penn and Teller appear to shoot at each other and catch the bullets in their mouths. "Peace officers" are asked to come on stage to verify that the guns and bullets are genuine. This is one trick not invented by Penn and Teller, and there has been amateur speculation for decades about how the trick is managed. Penn notes in every performance that several magicians have died performing the stunt. Information about the trick can be found on fan sites, where theories are traded and debated.[27]

By the end of the show, Penn and Teller's skepticism has struck a chord with audience members, who are perhaps less likely than before to believe everything they hear. In one popular final act, two audience members, a man and a woman, are brought on stage where Penn and Teller will supposedly make items appear from thin air. They begin by asking the two audience members if they appear to have anything up their sleeves. Whereas at the beginning of the show the two spectators might have been willing to quickly say "no" and go on with the trick, by this point they are more dubious, and inevitably respond with a doubtful "well, I guess not." In response to their doubt, the two men begin stripping off their clothing, down to shorts. Again they ask if they appear to be hiding anything. True to their recent education, the two spectators reply not "no," but something closer to "not that I can see." At this point they are invited behind the screen, where Penn and Teller remove all remaining clothing to reveal that, in fact, there is nothing at all hidden on them, and then proceed to put on t-shirts (checked by the volunteers), step out from behind the screen, and make items appear from apparently nowhere. I have read accounts online of participants in this trick who swore that they did not know what to expect, and other accounts indicate that invariably Penn and Teller receive the skeptical responses to their questions. Indeed, indications are that by this point in the show Penn and Teller have sufficiently educated their audience in the matter of skepticism that the two almost never have to disrobe unasked. An online report from an audience participant is worth quoting at length here:

On stage Penn & Teller removed their shirts, Penn removed his microphone transmitter, and both magicians presented themselves for inspection to me and my audience partner. Penn then asked me if I was satisfied that he had nothing hidden on him. In true skeptical fashion, I certified to the rest of the audience that I was sure there was nothing hidden "any place that I could see" . . . At this point my memory is not clear, but the next thing I knew, Penn & Teller were standing on that stage stripped down to their boxers and asking me if I was satisfied yet! Now I must admit a shameful thing: as Penn & Teller removed their trousers, my deeply ingrained male locker room reflexes overrode my skeptical nature and I was ready to stop right there! I hurriedly asserted that I was completely satisfied that there was nothing hidden on either of the magicians. Were it not for my female audience partner, I fear that that would have been the end of it (yeah, sure). When she was again asked if she were satisfied, my partner echoed my earlier sentiment that there was nothing hidden any place that was visible. Penn immediately thundered "We're Penn & Teller . . . don't call our bluff!" A large, opaque sheet of plastic was brought on the stage and held at waist height between the audience and the four of us on stage. My fellow audience member let out a gasp and my eyes rolled as Penn & Teller proceeded to strip naked and ask once again if we were finally satisfied that there was nothing hidden on the two magicians.

It took all the maturity and will power that I could muster to defeat those inhibitions that have been with me since high school gym class, but I can state, with more certainty than I have about most other things, that there was nothing hidden on either Penn or Teller, anywhere, at all, period.[28]

Clearly recognizing the power of live performance (especially for magic, in which television special effects can render a number like the one described above meaningless), Penn and Teller have been forced to confront the differences between live and recorded performance because of their many television and video appearances. They recognize that it is the live element of the show that makes it special. In their home video *Penn and Teller's Cruel Tricks for Dear Friends*, they present a series of gags for their viewers to play on their "sucker" friends using portions of the videotape as punch lines. In one segment they set up a fake interview with Alan Hunter of MTV. In the interview Hunter says that he's been to many of their shows and, "live you're great, it's terrific, but on TV, well, it sort of blows for me . . . I think the thing is that live, like, you guys are able to interact with the audience, you know, you get the feedback . . . but on TV, it's sort of like a spectator sport." Penn's response is: "I'm really glad we told you to say that, because we have a trick right here that is completely interactive with the people at home."[29] He then sets up a trick saying that Teller will be able to guess a card pick by the people at home from their own personal deck. Of course, it's a set-up and, of course, Teller gets it correct and there's no true interaction with the TV audience. But the two clearly recognize the impact that a live audience has on the show and vice versa. Jillette acknowledges that "There is a slightly different aesthetic between live and TV"[30] and says that in the short performance time they have on TV (on shows such as David Letterman) they have to do something really spectacular and gross to have an effect. "But for the live show," Jillette says, "we have two hours to take the audience on a roller-coaster ride, so we can pace it better."[31] Calvin Trillin distinguishes the crucial difference between the two forms when he says, "on television Penn and Teller can't lure the audience into a constant but ever-changing role in the swindle."[32]

Direct audience participation is clearly the most effective way to induct spectators into their community of skeptics, but Penn and Teller can only reach a very small proportion of their audience at each performance with it. In order to include everyone, they must address them directly and make it clear that they are trying to talk to each individual spectator. The fact that the two do not play characters on stage, but appear as their own selves, without the fancy, distancing glitz of traditional magicians, helps put them on the spectators' level of perception. But even this is problemetized by Teller's silence in performance. Their attention to the structures of lying also has the potential to distance audience members. While they achieve a certain level of what Michael Kirby has called "nonmatrixed performance"—in which the performers are not constrained by a framework of fictional existence[33]—their imposition of their own levels of fiction prevent them from truly connecting with their spectators. Because their message of skepticism, if received, will automatically distance them, they must find other ways of creating what they admit will be a "community" of skeptics rather than a disconnected mass of individual skeptics.[34]

Their acknowledgment of specific performance conditions is one way of being more personal, but even that may be fraught with deception. Jillette's negotiation of the lines between fictions is precarious, as he lies even while admitting he is lying, inducing suspicion of all that he says. In the patter that accompanies a display of Jillette's fire and broken bottle juggling he explains why juggling fire is so easy (the wands are weighted correctly) and why juggling broken bottles is so hard (they are weighted variously and poorly for juggling). At each performance he pays special attention to one bottle, saying that it really is hard to juggle, and that he says that every night, but that at this performance he really means it, but of course he says that at every show, too, so it is nearly impossible to make the audience believe him, but that this particular bottle is really hard to juggle. He even pretends to show someone offstage how difficult it is. Accounts online of spectators indicates Penn's talent at this patter, for very often spectators believe him, feeling that normally this patter is just a hoax, but that in the particular performance they saw he was telling the truth. Certainly this is not the response Penn and Teller would desire.

Another bit before which Jillette addresses the audience directly is when he eats fire, which is the final sketch in the show when performed. The address to the audience is calm and quiet, and Jillette seems more personal. Before this point Jillette has been yelling and running around the audience, living up to his brash reputation. And even in this apparently straightforward bit there is a moment of debunking, when Jillette explains that the danger in fire-eating is not really from the burn risk, but from swallowing small bits of lighter fluid year after year, revealing that even this is not what it seems. Knowing how an audience can be more affected by reality than by a trick, Jillette says, "Now I take the time to explain all of this to you in such detail because I think it's more fascinating to think of someone poisoning themselves to death slowly on stage than merely burning themselves, and after all, we're here to entertain you."[35] This admission, that seems to step outside the world of magic for a moment and into a more personal space, appears in a much longer speech that addresses Jillette's need for personal contact. It is worth quoting at length for its appreciation of the power of live theatre as well as for the acknowledgment of a desire to produce a form of community in their performances. The section quoted here is close to the end of the speech, which begins with Jillette's observations on mystery and skepticism and continues with a detailed explanation of fire-eating.

I realize you've been sitting in these seats a long time, but if you can just bear with us another moment, we'd like to look out at you guys. 'Cause there's an obvious but still unique quality of live theater, and that is that while we're doing the show, you're right here in the room with us. And that means that light will fall on some of your faces. And if light happens to fall on one of your faces while we're doing the show we'll do a small part of the show for you, I mean, just for you, just staring right in your face. And when we do that, and we've picked you, and you know it, and you can feel it . . . we're not paying any attention to you at all. We're trying to get the tricks to work, get the laughs. We can't worry about you individually. So what I'm saying—convolutedly—is that right now is the place in the show we can look at you in the same light we're in, and we can kinda pay attention. And it's really important. And I used to feel that importance should be made explicit, so I would do these little speeches about community and these speeches were superficial and they were contrived, and I really believed them, so they were embarrassing. So now I'm trying to learn to shut up and look at you. Teller's got it down.[36]

There is the potential for great power involved in talking directly to an audience, a power that flows both ways. Direct address pulls an audience into the performance more, making them more susceptible to ideas, and it also allows the audience to express their opinions directly to the performers. But direct address is not by definition only vocal, as evidenced by the entirely nonspeaking performances of contemporary variety performers Bob Berky and Michael Moschen. The silent expressions that Teller shares with the audience are just as powerfully communicative as Jillette's nonstop direct speech. Jillette has become more aware of that power over the years, as indicated by the previous speech.

Willingness to contact spectators outside the performance boundaries also helps to create the community Penn and Teller desire. The two often loiter in the lobby of the theatre, talking to spectators before the show and during intermission, and always remain after for pictures and autographs, until the last audience member is gone. When they perform the "naked trick" at the end of the show they will appear in the t-shirts to sign autographs, and Penn has even been known to put a program under his shirt to give an audience member a "bloody" print of his private parts.[37]

They also connect with their fans regularly outside the performance arena—going out for food after the show with them, hosting "Movie Nights," and recently appearing in *The Rocky Horror Picture Show* in New York. They extend the message of their performances—"using your head in a world full of flim-flam"[38]—to their lives off the stage. Penn and Teller are avid attackers of any movement that calls for faith on the part of its followers. Unflinching atheists, they have devoted a considerable amount of time to unmasking supposed psychics, mentalists, and séance operators. The two men patronize skeptics' societies and strongly dislike any belief that tends toward spiritualism, be it psychics, New Age mysticism, séances, or religion of any type. In the mid-1980s they performed a series of séances for wealthy New Yorkers in which they announced their trickery up front, and then proceeded to amaze the participants with the usual séance surprises.

Both on and off the stage, Penn and Teller have taken popular entertainment and made it an analogy for American society. While they present themselves as "regular guys," they traverse the rocky ground of American politics and consumerism, exposing the fraud through the metaphor of magic. The aspects of their performance discussed here—demystification of certain magic tricks, the orchestration of the appearance of danger, and most of all the various types of audience participation—are all part of Penn and Teller's manipulation of fictionality in order to make a point about skepticism in everyday life. Many of the levels of fiction juggled by Penn and Teller are not so explicitly revealed as the trickery of their magic is. Questions remain that spectators must consider on their own, that keep the sense of wonder that is necessary for a successful performance. If the performance has truly been successful, spectators will learn to participate in the demystification of the deceptions they encounter in the larger world of mass media, culture, religion, politics, and human relations.

NOTES

1. Richard Schechner, *Performance Theory* (New York: Routledge, 1988), 121–122.

2. Ron Jenkins was the first to write a book-length study using the term "new vaudeville," and I chose "contemporary variety theatre" for my dissertation. See Ron Jenkins, *Acrobats of the Soul* (New York: Theatre Communications Group, 1988), and Susan Kattwinkel, "Contemporary Variety Theatre: Using Techniques of Performance to Decrease Performer/Spectator Distance" (Ann Arbor: UMI Research Press, 1993).

3. Jenkins, xii. Penn and Teller are one of the groups discussed by Jenkins in this study.

4. Lloyd Dykk "Penn and Teller," *Vancouver Sun*, 22 July 1993: 2C1.

5. Linda Winer, "Penn and Teller: Up to Their Old Tricks," *Newsday*, April 4, 1991: 66.

6. Penn Jillette, "Penn and Teller," Bravo Profiles, Bravo channel, air date 12/28/01.

7. Daphna Ben Chaim, *Distance in the Theatre: The Aesthetics of Audience Response* (Ann Arbor: UMI Research Press, 1984), 67.

8. Ben Chaim, 77.

9. Dykk 2C1.

10. Miriam Callisto, "Re:New P&T Fan," October 1, 1995, online posting, newsgroup alt.fan.penn-n-teller, Usenet, October 1, 1995.

11. Calvin Trillin, "A Couple of Eccentric Guys," *The New Yorker*, May 15, 1989: 75.

12. Trillin, 62.

13. Jenkins, 176.

14. I observed this trick July 12, 1995, at a performance at the Wolf Trap in Wash-

ington, D.C., but the trick is a popular one and has appeared in many of their performances since that time.

15. Penn is the ringmaster, who talks constantly and loudly and often abuses audience members. Teller is silent throughout the performance.

16. Carol Pucci, "Teller speaks(!) about duo's sort-of-magic act," *Seattle Times,* December 13, 2000: D4.

17. Quoted in Pete Bell, "The Icon Profile," *Icon Magazine,* June 1998, 88–95, 110.

18. Penn Jillette, performance, "Penn and Teller," Bally's, Las Vegas, January 4, 1997.

19. Richard Nilsen, "Sleightly Warped: Penn and Teller Merge Onstage," *The Arizona Republic,* October 6, 1993: E1.

20. Harrison, 280.

21. Jillette, address, Smithsonian Institution. Transcription found at http://www.pennandteller.com/sincity.

22. Kevin Kelly. "On the Funny Side of the Fridge," 70. *Boston Globe,* February 17, 1991.

23. Steve Kurtz, "Voodoo and Violence," *Reason Magazine,* April 1994, 35–39.

24. Elizabeth Fitzsimons, "Two for the Road; The Penn & Teller Show Is a Magical Mystery Tour if Ever There Was One," *The San Diego Union-Tribune,* November 15, 2001: Night & Day, p. 47.

25. Jenkins, 171.

26. David Richards, "The Lord of the Rings Meets Penn and Teller in Malice Afore-thought," *New York Times,* April 7, 1991: H5. Richards does recognize that the audience "seems to adore" the harassment.

27. For pictures of the bullets and descriptions and theories by participants, see particularly http://www.well.com/user/lord/penn-and-teller/ and http://www.donath.org/Rants/PennTellerBulletTrick/.

28. Gregory Aicklen, "NTS Examines Penn and Teller," *The Skeptic: The Newsletter of The North Texas Skeptics,* Vol. 9, No. 12, August 1995.

29. *Penn and Teller's Cruel Tricks for Dear Friends,* dir. Art Wolff, perf. Penn Jillette, Alan Hunter Teller, 1987.

30. Nilsen, E1.

31. Nilsen, E1.

32. Trillin, 85.

33. Michael Kirby, "On Acting and Not-Acting," *The Art of Performance: A Critical Anthology,* Gregory Battcock and Robert Nickas, eds. (New York: E.P. Dutton, Inc.,1984), 97–117.

34. Penn Jillette, "Eating Fire," online, SinCity, URL http://www.sincity.com/penn-n-teller/ (The Penn and Teller Web site has been updated since I found this speech and it no longer appears there.)

35. Jillette, "Eating Fire."

36. Ibid.

37. The trick ends with the appearance that the two have been injured and are drenched in blood.

38. Teller, in Trillin 80.

8

---•◦•◦•---

LOOKING AT LOOKING
[AT LOOKING]:
EXPERIMENTS IN THE
INTERROGATION OF SPECTATING

Joanne Klein

We watched from above. We thought we were safe.
—Tilly, quoted in Nagy, *Weldon Rising*

My principal focus as a stage director has been on disrupting spectator/spectacle relations in order to inflect and interrogate practices of looking. Situated as we are in a culture of gazing, the power of spectacle and of our engagement with its material-semiotic attractions strike me as primary in my approach to making theatre. As TV/VCR remote controls, digital imaging, cybermedia peripatetics, and other viewing technologies spawned by economies of electronic mediation, tourism, shopping malls, and the like blur boundaries between spectator/spectacle, subject/object, consumer/producer, and other convenient dichotomies,[1] I find myself drawn to the vortex of those confluences. This vortex also supplies a circulation of histories and practices, and I have often appropriated strategies from antecedents; even in Western theatre conventions, which divide the audience definitively from the performance, attempts at transgressing and troubling audience/performer borders have occurred in notable historical and current work. Attracted by these histories and practices, by the problematic technologies of mediation and observation, by traditions of participant-observer instrumentality in otherized cultures, and by my desire to decenter the naturalized gaze of the straight, white, middle-class, male spectator, I have attempted various experiments in the inflection of spectating as a performed component of stage productions I have directed.

This chapter will describe my attempts to disrupt the material-semiotic coding of "reality" that is produced by historically specific habits, conditions, and apparatuses of looking. Meanings are made in the moment of reception.

By making production choices that intervene in or foreground those (never-stable) processes, I have attempted throughout my career to shift moments of impact onto questions of epistemology. Particular strategies and goals have recurred in various productions I have mounted for college and university audiences over the past twenty years, but I have focused this chapter on a production of Phyllis Nagy's *Weldon Rising* that I staged at St. Mary's College of Maryland in the spring of 2000.[2] Facilitated by this script, which positions the pleasures, perils, dynamics, and technologies of *looking* at the center of its relations, I developed a plan to interrogate spectating practices by pointedly and instructively transferring their encumbrances onto the audience. For example, by setting the action in a world of surface fragments that reflect elsewheres, elsewhens, and closed-circuit TV images of the audience, and by delivering the twice-reenacted murder in styles suggestive of VCR functions and hypertext surfing, I situated the audience in a problematic role of authority in relation to their viewing. Nothing on stage secured designation of a bottom-line (artifactual) realism or truth.[3]

I chose to direct *Weldon Rising* for our 1999–2000 main stage season in the wake of the mayhem at Columbine High School.[4] My readings of Columbine and *Weldon Rising* converged in their shared incrimination of cultural practices mapped on late capitalist economies of looking. In *Weldon Rising,* Nagy interrogates a fictive incident of hate crime by focusing attention on the acedia produced by proliferating technologies of *watching* and *being watched.* The characters embody a series of subject positions—inscribed by various gazes and credited with apocalypse—that are constitutive of hate and passivity. Nagy's attribution of hate crime to numbness effected by the otherizing technologies of sales-driven spectator positioning and "enterprised-up"[5] looking practices tallied with my sense of what had happened at Columbine. For me, the challenge of staging *Weldon Rising* resided in troubling these technologies not only as they are situated in diegetic (or story-bound) relations but also as they pertain to the (complicit) strategies of audience relations with live performance.

The components of *Weldon Rising* are fixtures of two places and the non-space of reverie. Most of the action takes place on Little West 12th Street in New York City's meat-packing district, where we learn that Natty Weldon's lover, Jimmy, has been casually butchered by a homicidal homophobe. The other characters—Tilly and Jaye, a lesbian couple who watch from their apartment window, and Marcel, a transvestite prostitute who cowers in the street below—are witnesses. At the moment of the murder, which recurs twice in slightly different (recollected) reenactments during the play, Natty flees the scene in terror. In an aftermath marked by soaring temperatures and the meltdown of false dichotomies and urban infrastructure, the characters struggle to escape their guilt-induced (socially produced) torpor.

For the limited purposes of this chapter, I shall identify four sites we chose for troubling and shifting practices of looking and then describe the first three of those—the exterior street, the interior lookout, and the virtual space of screen media—in more detail. Nagy's inflection of bodies—those of the characters and those of the performers—as a fourth site of specific discursive and corporeal practices is elaborately contrived. Despite their primacy as markers in both the script and the production, I am limiting address of bodies for the sake of brevity and will consider them merely according to their inscriptions by emplacement within the remaining three loci.[6]

THE STREET

Nagy describes Little West 12th Street as a shadowy cobbled back street of possibly deserted factory buildings and prescribes that "One surface must be covered entirely by a[n] [enormous, overwhelming] detailed map of the meat-packing district."[7] The significations produced by this doubled representation of place and its map are reinscribed by diegetic circumstances and practices. On the street, we see Natty, dressed in boxer shorts and a wool beret, sitting at an art deco vanity covered by cologne bottles before a mirror pasted over with postcards, and Marcel, dressed in "something ridiculous, like a plastic dress and platform shoes,"[8] rinsing out pantyhose. At the opening of the play and throughout most of its duration, Natty's discourses and practices take "place" in the nonspace (elsewheres and elsewhens) of reverie, and Marcel is positioned by self-commodifying rituals of work. Between them, they gloss the ambivalences of Benjamin's *flâneur*, whose transgression marks a reversal of (paradigmatically segregated) public and private practices.[9] Together with the backdrop of the meat-packing district, they also mark the street as a discursive site of abjection and display.

The script concludes in paired transcendances that are conspicuously transgressive, gendered, and troublesome, from several perspectives. As bridges collapse and Jones Beach falls into the Atlantic Ocean, Natty and (apparitional) Jimmy cut their way through the map as a gesture of "tear[ing] up the world," while Tilly and Jaye make love naked in the street to the unlocalized music of Donna Summer and then disappear in a "glorious flash of white light."[10] My big worry about this moment was the design and function of the map. Given the specific subject formations of the male figures (principally Natty and Marcel, because Jimmy and the murderer, Boy, are second-order apparitional manifestations), I could read their passages-beyond only as consummations of their (dissimilarly constituted) desires for effacement and disembodiment. Marcel, who refers to his mostly prosthetic, enterprised-up "self" in the third person and *as* the third person, opts for dematerialization earlier, in a business transaction that secures him the ultimate customer. The plainly symbolic gesture of slashing through the map—modeled on a regime of adversarial violence, performed by an abjected character (Natty) with his apparitional lover (Jimmy), and qualified by a concurrent orgy (doubled by performer nudity and agency!) of lesbian sensuality—persisted in its troubled resonances for me.

The standing of cartography in contemporary Eurocentric culture—given current hegemonies of gene-mapping, border-patrolling, mind/body splits, race/gender categories, subject/object divides, performance/audience boundaries and so on—positions it as a key figuration of our times. As Donna Haraway has argued, tropes of mapping (along with banking) secure the discourses and practices of both technoscience and the New World Order.[11] Nagy's featuring of the map of Little West 12th Street evokes these material-semiotic territorializations (Helen Watson-Verran's "advanced case of hardening of the categories"[12]), signaling transgression and blurring as predicted routes for progress, or better, egress. My particular strategy was to spread this sensation not only throughout the diegetic space of the performance but also across the border between performance and audience.

Our realized design was an accommodation of three overriding solutions to questions of how to portray the (climactically implicated) map, where to put Tilly and Jaye's lookout, and how to manage the legion of technical and aesthetic challenges posed by my desire for multi-media effects. Because theatrical constitution of the map-slashing moment would prove so redolent and because representation of the street relied on our reading/portrayal of the discursive operations of the map, we gave that decision primacy in our design of space and place. My readings of the script had already assigned the moment to reinscriptive fantasy, so I was tempted by the prospects of mediatization as an address of it. Thusly liberated from the need to slash and violate the map, we chose to paint it on the floor. We chose also to inflect the (doubled) performative practices of the street/script by depicting it as a raked deck, which had an irregular (island-like) shape and was skirted in black velour. The deck was flanked on either side by a curved drop on which was painted a planetary diagram, including the editorial contribution by my student designer, William A. Jamieson, of an apocalyptic supernova.[13]

Tilted, prominent, and crudely drawn, the map charted not only fragments of the meat-packing district and certain cartographic references from the script but also eras, local idioms, cuts of meat, and virtual spaces, in order to locate (and territorialize) these within the discourses of mapping and to echo Haraway's astute insight that, " . . . maps are fetishes in so far as they enable a specific kind of mistake that turns process into nontropic, real, literal things inside containers."[14] Our map also included, down left center, the crime-scene outline of Jimmy's body.

Because the deck fixture was raised to an inaccessible height and all access was hidden from view (actors slipped on and off stage—through slits in the drops or by going underneath the deck—via ramps and stairs at the rear), the "street" seemed to float in space like a metonymic exhibition of constructedness. The image/view was decidedly of a world carved up—bordered, classified, inscribed, fetishized, privatized, and re-presented. For me, at least, its visual impression evoked ruminations on hermeneutic circles and Christo's islands. Except for the evocation of carving and the map label designations, however, we regrettably lost the imprint of meat-packing on the place.

THE LOOKOUT

If the street is initially (and ambivalently) gendered male by virtue of its occupants, the space from which Tilly and Jaye watch the street is (also ambivalently) gendered female. Nagy intervenes in facile readings of these genderings by confounding the sexual practices of all four dwellers and by specifying feminized activities for the men (Natty sits at his vanity dousing himself with cologne; Marcel wears a dress and rinses pantyhose) and masculinized activities for the women (Tilly and Jaye sprawl in squalor and guzzle beer). Nagy describes Tilly and Jaye's "apartment" only as littered by spent beer bottles and separated from (preferably above) the street, advising that it "should not be represented naturalistically."[15] The architectural limitations of our performance space (which is a flexible black box), together with our plans for media technologies and desire to inflect *watching* as a key discursive operation, freighted the siting of this outpost. Furthermore, I was engaged by the need to place these mimetically intimate scenes in close proximity to audience seating as well as by prospects for defusing potentially controversial sexual depictions by making them vivid and down stage rather than "artistically" remote.

Our solution came from the ingenuity of Bill Jamieson, my student scenic designer, who proposed siting the "apartment," which I had already reduced to the exclusive territory of a couch, down stage of the street, nearly in the midst of audience seating, so that it produced the effect of serving as "privileged seating" for the scripted onlookers. Through this placement of the couch, we also achieved a doubling formation in the technologies of looking/ seeing, because Tilly and Jaye "watched" the street action through an undepicted window over its back, turning them toward audience seating, but away from the locale of events they "see." This configuration positions Tilly and Jaye with their backs turned alternately (and contradictorily) on spectators and on the street, and it places "looking/spectating" squarely in quotes by queering the apparent spatial relations between the lookout and the street. The effect produced by Tilly and Jaye's reactions to and descriptions of events that occurred "behind" them proved productively disorienting. As one audience member stated, "In a way, it felt that if we, the audience, were to look over our shoulders, we might see what Tilly and Jaye did."[16]

My thinking with respect to the lookout and its potential to enact inquiries into looking practices was strongly informed by Foucault's work on constructions of power and privilege by the optics and spatializations of surveillance.[17] The script situates Tilly and Jaye as a kind of surrogate audience, whose role is marked by vested witnessing as well as by privileged positioning. In terms

of my desire to inflect this shared condition, I wanted to identify their subjectivity with that of the audience so that Tilly and Jaye's subsequent migra-
tion onto the scene of the street might be read as a challenge to blur and
transgress given (naturalized) boundaries, thereby reorganizing the power
dynamics performed by those spatializations. Furthermore, I intended the
"misdirection" of Tilly and Jaye's gaze upon the street as well as the preva-
lence of falsely registering specular surfaces on the scene of the street to
disrupt habitual looking practices in order to pronounce their role in the
shaping of ideology and understanding. These optics share Haraway's alluring
preference for diffraction as an epistemological trope: "Diffraction patterns
record the history of interaction, interference, reinforcement, difference. . . .
Unlike reflections, diffractions do not displace the same elsewhere, in more
or less distorted form, thereby giving rise to industries of metaphysics. Rather,
diffraction is a metaphor for another kind of critical consciousness at the end
of this rather painful Christian millennium, one committed to making a difference and not to repeating the Sacred Image of the Same."[18] My effort to
interpellate the audience within the material-semiotic discourses of the play
relied partly on the optics of diffraction, which, as Haraway elsewhere notes,
"is not a reflection; it's a *record of passage*."[19]

A follow-up survey of audience members elicited some canny reactions to
the effects of our siting of the lookout. In response to the question, "Did
the positioning of Tilly and Jaye's couch cause you to form any particular
thoughts about the performance?" a student wrote: "Not until after establishing that they were witnesses to the crime. After that, their position in
physical space created a bridge between audience & stage action. My first
thought was one of following them into the rest of the stage action. . . . The
rest of my thoughts on that all had to do with pondering in what ways they
were (not) linked to the rest of the stage action (& consequently—how I
was)." Other responses, these two admittedly from faculty members, were
likewise attuned to the effect I had hoped to produce: "For me a couch always
creates—that is, produces—a living space and marks the inside/outside
boundary. . . . In a sense this means that I was looking "in" on something,
but the effect [of gazing at the couch's back] for me was much more that I
was excluded from the space the characters share—and this is heightened by
the fact that they are always looking "out" and seeing things that are sometimes not revealed to me. So the sum effect was probably to multiply perspective and disrupt any simple lines of the gaze: the couch prevented any
simple viewer/subject dichotomy." And:

Tilly and Jaye's positioning on the sofa immediately evoked a spatial and spectatorial
dynamic reinforced by the action that took place "behind" them. . . . Tilly and Jaye's
watching disrupted my expectations: I expected them to function as conduits, or as
liaisons, to the background action (since we're supposed to see through their eyes as
they watch and report on what they're seeing on the street below their apartment).

Instead, as Tilly and Jaye confronted us with their observations—as if they were eaves-dropping on us in some kind of voyeuristic game—I was continually forced to tally their perceptions and positioning against what I was seeing behind them, which they're supposed to be seeing from "behind" the action, looking down from their apartment window. I also felt strangely implicated in the action that took place behind them: Natty, Marcel, Jimmy. It created a kind of vertigo. This vertigo was borne out by the action on the stage proper and the impact of the projection screen, which ran a con-tinual feed of images, related and unrelated to the action of the play, including those of actors performing and in rehearsals.

THE SCREEN

Paramount to my analysis of visual culture and looking behaviors as culprits in the mayhem of Columbine and *Weldon Rising* are the conditions of our postmodern society of spectacle and simulacra.[20] Images and practices of gaz-ing are omnipresent in this historical moment, which is marked by prolifer-ation of simulation and the virtual. Nagy's foregrounding of looking and re-visioning as activities in the script signals a strategic interrogation of sub-jectivization as the effect of these processes. In other words, the subject-positions enacted by the characters are produced by specific techniques and practices of looking. These ways of looking are situated in larger cultural technologies associated with consumption and leisure.[21] As Margaret Morse describes these dynamics in her study, *Virtualities: Television, Media Art, and Cyberculture:* "Cultural forms from television graphics and shopping malls to the apparatus of virtual reality, as well as practices from driving to conducting war to making art employ various forms of engagement to construct a *virtual relationship* between subjects in a here-and-now. . . . Cyberculture is built upon such a proliferation of *nows* in diverse modalities and inflections and *heres* that are not single, material, and contiguous but multiple, discontinu-ous, and virtual. . . . Furthermore, the very notion of "liveness" is more and more compromised by algorithmic image processing that erases the difference between *having been there* and *being there now.*"[22]

Engaged by the notion that techniques and technologies of "self" (subject-positioning) are problematically constituted in relation to screen media, I planned from the beginning of our production process to perform the script against a projected backdrop montage of sampled electronic imagery. I hoped to achieve at least two overarching effects by this choice: the assignment of postmodern subjectivity[23] to ubiquitous simulacra and the confrontation of audience members with an instructive viewing dilemma. With respect to the latter goal, I wanted to situate the audience in a problematic (authorial) re-lation to spectator/reception practices and to pose Susan Bennett's questions in her recent preface to *Theatre Journal:* "What happens, then, when our eyes turn more often to the "jumbotron" screen than to the live performers whose images are brightly illuminated above us, dwarfing the "real" presence doing the "real" work on stage? Have we more readily embraced the televisual screen in an anxious denial of the presence of the body?"[24] Theorizing that electronic media attract our gaze not only because of their promise of de-materialization (or pixilated Deliverance?) of flesh but also because of their provision of an internalized managerial surveillance that performs us as Foucault's "docile bodies"[25]—and that these processes were articulated in the discursive formations of this script—I wanted to use screen media to incriminate both dimensions of that attraction/distraction. If we are ever to modulate the postlinear hegemonies of "Fast-Forward, Rewind, Eject, Delete, Insert, Quit,"[26] we must first make their operations and formations plain.

The locus for our display of virtual distraction was a $10' \times 10'$ black projection screen, suspended directly up stage of the street deck and flanked by the two astronomical map drops. Projection on the screen was in progress when the house opened and was continuous throughout the performance. The momentum for the eventual montage potpourri was supplied by a team of three digitally inspired students who were experienced in both theatrical performance and electronic media.[27] They dodged my ambitious and possibly misguided suggestions for fine-tuning the fit between live and virtual media in favor of cobbling together several specifically keyed cassettes of clips and videography, which they dubbed the Main Vomit Feed or MVF. The MVF cassettes were pastiches that included almost-subliminal excerpts from films, television, video games, Web sites, biotelemetry, and rehearsals. In order to convey the notion that the subject-positions interpellated by mediated "reality" and simulacra are always-already constituted,[28] we projected occasional footage of the performers watching videotape of their own performances in rehearsals. By timing the MVF cassette that included one such diffractive whirligig to coincide with Boy's direct hate-speech address of the audience, we particularly designated hate as an embodiment and interpellation proposed by the discourses and technologies of media.[29]

In addition to continuous screening of the MVF, we schemed to put "looking" in quotes by interjecting live, closed-circuit images of audience members watching (notably during the second re-enactment of Jimmy's murder, which "pans out" on stage to include the witnesses) as well as doubled images and close-ups of the simultaneous stage action. One audience member summarized the impact of this choice as follows:

Then, of course, there's the projection screen and the play of images: particularly those moments when a live feed was introduced to show audience members watching the play. I was caught in one of those feeds. I watched myself on screen watching the play, acutely aware of being watched (as an image and by other audience members in the auditorium). A very, very uncomfortable moment. And those live feeds seemed to be introduced at moments when the action referred us to the murder of Jimmy and to Natty's inaction (his fleeing the scene). As if we're implicated in the watching, accused (as Natty is) of "not doing," of not taking action. We're passive: watching, and feeling uncomfortable about it.

The culminating operation of this phantasmagoric screen aperture, however, was its accommodation and inscription of the male character evacuations at the end of the play. We accomplished Marcel's god-like dematerialization in headlight beams of "the biggest motherfucking car I've ever seen"[30] by lifting his image—as he approached the down stage lip of the deck and then stepped off its edge unlit—onto the screen, where he was swept away along a z-axis in a premediated zoom. Similarly, we represented the triumphant, map-slashing flight of Natty and Jimmy as a deliverance, avenging knife and all, onto the surface of the screen, where the Hollywood version of their (disembodied) reunion broke up into visual static as Tilly and Jaye celebrated carnal pleasures on the deck below.

The gendered bifurcation of virtuality and sensuality (text/flesh) that was constituted by this moment allowed both realms of pleasure full amplitude, but secured them within the larger diegetic trajectory of apocalypse. All of these ambivalences were plotted on what I read as Nagy's conclusion of the play and inflected by my groping with Columbine. By delivering the idealized transcendence of the male figures onto the screen, I hoped both to reify and unravel masculine coding of this culturally privileged desire for the ethereal. The gendering of this conclusion corresponded with Haraway's claims that, "One stream of American feminism deemphasizes—really anathematizes— eyes and visual process and foregrounds the oral and the tactile. The specular is always under suspicion. 'Spectacle,' 'specular,' 'spectacular,' 'speculating' are coded white, coded masculine, coded powerful, coded extraterrestrial, full of domination. . . . "[31]

In terms of this gendered schema and in terms that reach beyond it, looking is likewise positioned as male and privileged by race and class.[32] Haraway's interrogation of the historically produced and endorsed scientific gaze (the modest witness) serves to trouble the looking practices that Nagy's script and my efforts aimed to disrupt. "The kind of visibility—the body—that women retained glides into being perceived as "subjective," that is, reporting only on the self, biased, opaque, not objective. Gentlemen's epistemological agency involved a special kind of transparency. Colored, sexed, and laboring persons still have to do a lot of work to become similarly transparent to count as objective, modest witnesses to the world rather than to their "bias" or "special interest." To be the object of vision, rather than the "modest," self-invisible source of vision, is to be evacuated of agency."[33] By blurring boundaries between the lookers and the looked-at, between subjects and objects, between self and other, I tried to destabilize these positions as a gesture toward redistributing agency and deconstructing cultural sources of hate.

Nothing is more obvious than Nagy's call in this script for de-mapping, for violating the borders of paradigmatic territorializations. To the extent that such boundaries are fixed in place by practices and technologies of looking, Nagy makes these visible by disrupting the uses and rituals of related (discreet) sites. The characters mediate across boundaries of gender, sex, and sexuality; Natty and Marcel negotiate the borders between the ethereal and the material; the performers (and characters) blur lines between mimesis and authenticity. Instances of shifting, negotiation, and mediation are numerous in the script, and we tried to amplify them in our staging (for example, in our siting of Tilly and Jaye to negotiate between audience and performance spaces, and in our transfiguration of Natty and Marcel onto the screen) in order to constitute third-term positions as viable in re-mapping of subjectivity and space.

SOME IMPACTS

Because the project of determining whether we achieved these intended effects is freighted with difficulties and dubiousness, I don't want to argue that audience members "got it" or didn't "get it." As Sturken and Cartwright put it in their book, *Practices of Looking*, " . . . meanings are created in part when, where, and by whom images are consumed, and not only when, where, and by whom they are produced."[34] My horizon of artistic tyranny, in other words, ends at the moment of a viewer's reading. Nonetheless, audience reactions during our post-performance discussion and in response to my survey included indications that our intentions were to some degree accessible. As examples, I quote two responses to my question: "Did anything material to the production cause you to question or be aware of your own looking practices or position as spectator?" "Yes, yes, yes is the only easy answer I have here. My experience of the play was not to have my position of looking questioned in any SPECIFIC way (e.g. you are objectifying objects of desire or something like that) but simply to throw into relief the very FACT of my position as spectator—not to allow it to remain invisible, to refuse to let it drift into the background. So I continued to watch and continued to be aware of my own watching. . . . " And: "I was always aware of my own looking practices and position as spectator throughout the play. First, there's the placement of Tilly and Jaye . . . then, the moment when all actors are situated on the "stage"—as though on an island, disconnected from surrounding space—and there's a sense of containment: of me being able to "take it all in in one glance." A safety space, if you will, that isn't a safety space for the characters (or is it?)." Another audience member ruminated on the questions posed by the nonstop display of virtuality on the projection screen.

What attracts me as spectator? The mediatized body or image, or the image of the "live" performer? Am I attracted to the live body, in all its immediacy and rawness, or by the contrived body, projected on screen? But isn't the "live" body, in its fictional context (the play), contrived as well? The projection screen created another space, another place that questioned how we look at things, how we read things (the body, our culture, sex, gender, pleasure, etc.), and to what we are immediately drawn. The images on the projection screen created a dialogue with the action situated below it. I was forced to tally my perceptions and readings of the images with my reading of the live action. It kept me extremely busy and engaged!

The technologies of numbness that enable discursive practices of hate and apathy are constituted by a disconnect between mind and body that is anchored by baggage of the Cartesian split, but newly facilitated by proliferation of virtuality and simulacra. In her description of cyborgs, Margaret Morse sums up this scopic regime:

For couch potatoes, video game addicts, and surrogate travelers of cyberspace alike, an organic body just gets in the way. The culinary discourses of a culture undergoing transformation to an information society will have to confront not only the problems of a much-depleted earth, but a growing desire to disengage from the human condition. Travelers on the virtual highways of an information society have, in fact, at least one body too many—the one now largely sedentary carbon-based body resting at the control console that suffers hunger, corpulence, illness, old age, and ultimately death. The other body, a silicon-based surrogate jacked into immaterial realms of data, has superpowers, albeit virtually, and is immortal; or rather, the chosen body, an electronic avatar "decoupled" from the physical body, is a program capable of enduring endless deaths.[35]

When sites (categories) harden, as they do for Morse's dichotomous cyborg, they become constitutive of otherizing discourses that form the social practices of hate crime. Nagy's project in *Weldon Rising* is a de-mapping of these boundaries, agitated by thermal apocalypse. Citing the multiplex cinema as a virtualization of the speculative activities of shopping combined with the mobilities of tourism (and I note that both shopping and tourism are prominently featured in this script), Anne Friedberg states that, "as the mobilized gaze becomes more and more virtual, the physical body becomes a more and more fluid site; in this 'virtual mobility' the actual body—gender-bound, race-bound, ethnicity-bound—becomes a veritable depot for departure and return."[36] Friedberg's model of site/body-as-depot might form the basis for more fluid practices that could constitute the subject positions and dramaturgy of the future. We keyed our work on *Weldon Rising* to a privileging of such fluidity, seeking with Nagy a reevaluation of theoretical accounts of looking, the body, and temporality. Hate thrives on boundaries—those produced by the taxonomies of alterity, dualistic thinking, binary organization, mapping, re-mapping, classifying, prosceniums, and so on. A world that shifts and blurs—in which subjectivities are unstable and performed in many contexts—slips the roots of hate.

NOTES

1. For a range of extended descriptions and analysis of looking practices associated with these cultural developments and technologies, see Donna Haraway, *Modest_Witness@Second_Millennium.FemaleMan©_Meets_OncoMouse™: Feminism and Technoscience* (New York: Routledge, 1997) and *How Like a Leaf: An Interview with Thyrza Nichols Goodeve* (New York: Routledge, 2000); Margaret Morse, *Virtualities: Television, Media Art, and Cyberculture* (Bloomington: Indiana University Press, 1998); Walter Benjamin, "The Work of Art in the Age of Mechanical Reproduction," in *Illuminations*, trans. Howard Eiland and Kevin McLaughlin (New York: Harcourt Brace Jovanovich, 1968) and *The Arcades Project,* trans. Howard Eiland and Kevin McLaughlin (Cambridge, Mass.: Harvard University Press, 1999); and Anne Friedberg, *Window Shopping: Cinema and the Postmodern* (Berkeley: University of California Press, 1994).

2. The student cast and crew were as follows: Joshua Gembicki (Natty Weldon), Rob Hendricks (Marcel), Alana Smith (Jaye), Marianne Koch (Tilly), Michael Boynton (Jimmy), and Timothy Riordan (Boy). Erin Schuenzel was the stage manager, assisted by Scott O'Neil and Benjamin Siggers. The costume designer, Heather C. Jackson, and scenic designer, William A. Jamieson, also were students.

3. Unlike past productions I have directed—such as those of Fornes's *Fefu and her Friends* and Brecht's *The Threepenny Opera,* both of which called on their audiences to participate vocally and physically—I attempted in *Weldon Rising* to make the politics and practices of looking visible to audiences by reifying their naturalized, passive role and causing them to *perform themselves as audiences.*

4. As I complete revisions of this chapter in November 2001, I want to acknowledge that the events of 9/11 have superseded Columbine as a marker of cultural shock in the United States. At the time of the terrorist attack, I was rehearsing *The Laramie Project,* which is a similarly effective (and timely) address of hate crime as the product of villainous paradigms rather than of villains, and is similarly staked on disruption of conventionalized audience habits. From its baseline mingling of the "real" and the "fake"—these are authentic speeches, faked by performers—*The Laramie Project* likewise interrogates formations of hate by blurring borders that hold territories and categories, such as those that sustain suspension of disbelief, in place.

5. For a discussion of how narrative devices and commercial interests conflate nature and culture with respect to looking practices, see Haraway, *Modest_Witness,* 85.

6. See, for example, Denise Varney, "Focus on the Body: Towards a Feminist Reading of Brecht in Performance," *Communications* 29 (2000): 29–38, for an excellent discussion of this topic.

7. Phyllis Nagy, *Weldon Rising & Disappeared* (London: Methuen Drama, 1996), 4.

8. Ibid., 5.

9. For a discussion of *flaneurism,* see Benjamin, *The Arcades Project.*

10. Nagy, 44.

11. Haraway, *Modest_Witness,* 131–72.

12. Helen Watson-Verran, "Renegotiating What's Natural." (Paper read at Meetings for the Society of Social Studies of Science, New Orleans, La., October 12–15, 1994). Quoted in Haraway, *Modest_Witness,* 131.

13. The effect of these drops, while accurately evocative of mapping and cataclysm, was somewhat more turgid than what I had envisioned.

14. Haraway, *Modest_Witness*, 136.

15. Nagy, 4.

16. Audience responses in this chapter come from two sources. For more general characterizations of audience responses, I have relied on a videotape of our traditional TalkBack Night session with audience members who took part in a moderated discussion of the performance. Quotations of audience members, however, are excerpted from an audience questionnaire that posed the following three questions: Did the positioning of Tilly and Jaye's couch cause you to form any particular thoughts about the performance? Did the presence and uses of the projection screen cause you to form any particular thoughts about the performance? Did anything material to the production cause you to question or be aware of your own looking practices or position as spectator?

17. See Michel Foucault, *Discipline and Punish: The Birth of the Prison,* trans. Alan Sheridan (New York: Vintage, 1979).

18. Haraway, *Modest_Witness*, 273.

19. Donna Haraway, *How Like a Leaf,* 103, italics added.

20. For discussions of looking and the spectacle of simulacra, see Guy Debord, *The Society of the Spectacle,* trans. Donald Nicholson-Smith (New York: Zone Books, 1994) and Jean Baudrillard, *Simulacra and Simulation,* trans. Sheila Glaser (Ann Arbor: University of Michigan Press, 1995).

21. For further discussion of looking based on cultural technologies associated with consumption and leisure, see Benjamin, *The Arcade Project;* Marita Sturken and Lisa Cartwright, *Practices of Looking: An Introduction to Visual Culture* (New York: Oxford University Press, 2001; *Visual Culture: The Reader,* ed. Jessica Evans and Stuart Hall (London: Sage, 1999); *Representation: Cultural Representations and Signifying Practices,* ed. Stuart Hall (London: Sage, 1997); and Theodor Adorno and Max Horkheimer, "The Culture Industry: Enlightenment as Mass Deception," in *Dialectic of Enlightenment,* trans. John Cumming (New York: Seabury Press, 1972).

22. Morse, 4 and 15.

23. Anne Friedberg describes the postmodern subject position as a "subjectivity that posits 'presence' in a virtual elsewhere and elsewhen" in *Window Shopping,* 8.

24. Susan Bennett, "Comment," *Theatre Journal* 51.4 (1999): 358.

25. Foucault, 25.

26. Susan Kozel, introduction to "Post-Linearity and Gendered Performance Practice" in *The Routledge Reader in Politics and Performance,* ed. Lizbeth Goodman with Jane de Gay (London: Routledge, 2000), 262.

27. The video and sound designer, Peter Welsch, was assisted by John McDonald and Sarah Mercure.

28. For a discussion of interpellation, see Louis Althusser, "Ideology and Ideological State Apparatuses," from *Lenin and Philosophy and Other Essays,* trans. Ben Brewster (New York and London: Monthly Review Press, 1971).

29. We also, in a more joking vein, "videated" the performers' bows.

30. Nagy, 39.

31. Haraway, *How Like a Leaf,* 102.

32. Among the many excellent studies of looking in terms of its privileging by gender, race, and class, I recommend Haraway, *Modest_Witness,* as well as Laura Mulvey's seminal essay "Visual Pleasure and Narrative Cinema," in *Visual and Other Pleasures* (Bloomington: Indiana University Press, 1989); bell hooks, "The Oppositional

Gaze," in *Black Looks: Race and Representation* (Boston: South End Press, 1993); and Jill Dolan, *The Feminist Spectator as Critic* (Ann Arbor: University of Michigan Research Press, 1988).

33. Haraway, *Modest_Witness,* 32.

34. Sturken and Cartwright, 46.

35. Morse, 125.

36. Friedberg, 110.

9

THE AUDIENCE IN CYBERSPACE: AUDIENCE-PERFORMER INTERACTIVITY IN ONLINE PERFORMANCES

Nina LeNoir

Cyberspace performance has as a distinguishing element an implied interactivity through the mediation of the computer interface. Interface, Brenda Laurel notes in *Computers as Theatre*, is a "trendy word," and to those not versed in computers, smacks of computer jargon, but, in simple terms, an "interface" according to Laurel can be viewed as "a shared context for action in which both [the person and the computer] are agents."[1] Even more simplistically, the dictionary defines "interface" as the "common boundary between two parts of matter or space." In traditional stage performance, the interface is the set of shared conventions that establish the relationship between performer and audience in the imaginative space between them. In technologically mediated forms of production, such as film and television, the interface becomes tangible, embedded in the equipment that transfers the performance to the viewer. On either side of the performance interface are the agents of the action—the spectator on one side and the performers and technicians on the other. In pre-technologically-mediated days, the agents on the other side of the audience were the physically present, live performers, but with the advent of technology that expands the means of performance, the performers may now be prerecorded in film and television, broadcast from another space in television or radio, or mediated by software programs and computers in cyberspace.

This notion of "mediation" is a key element in understanding Internet performance. Theatre is a relatively unmediated performance form, governed by shared conventions rather than technological interfaces. The audience and the performers are in the same space at the same time, able to interact. All performance on the Internet is mediated by the hardware and software that allow participants to convene virtually. Similarly, radio, film, and television are mediated by technology that enables the performance to reach the audience; however, as opposed to computer-mediated forms of communication, these earlier forms of mediated-communication used to transmit performance are one-way. Computer-mediated communication has the potential to be not only bi-directional but multi-directional, allowing interaction between and among performers and audience, very like the live interaction between audience and performers that occurs in theatre performance.

In order to begin to understand how computer-mediated performance compares to traditional, "live" performance, it is necessary to explore the artistic conventions that govern the interactions of performers and spectators through the conventions defined at the computer interface. Within the digital information stream that makes up the Internet, a myriad of conventions are used to communicate, dictated by the rules imposed by the hardware and software that construct the space of interaction. In cyberspace, these conventions determine the behavior of the individual even more tenaciously than agreed-on artistic conventions govern an individual's behavior in the theatre, for certain actions become impossible in cyberspace, depending on the software and hardware design. Despite the limitations on behavior within the realm of cyberspace, or perhaps because of these limitations, performances are occurring that take advantage of the opportunities for human connection beyond the physical limits of space and the human body. What are these performances? How is the spectator-performer relationship altered in virtual performances as compared to "live" events? The following is an examination of two online performances and a new form of online performative experience that will be used as a basis to begin answering these questions.

INTERACTIVITY IN MUD THEATRE

Multi-User Domains, often known as MUDs, are participative online environments that have been in existence since the early beginnings of networked environments.[2] A MUD is a virtual space in which communication and interaction occur among the participants (known as "players") through characters created in the online world. MUDs are similar to online chat rooms in that communication occurs primarily through text, but differ by creating an environment, and objects within the environment, with which the characters can interact. Many MUDs are specifically designed for role-playing interaction—rather like interactive story-making. In these environments there is no passive audience, as all involved are creating characters, storylines, actions, and dialogue as the role-playing game proceeds. However, within these MUDs, players often will design public events that are planned, prepared, and designed for audiences. Many role-playing MUD communities hold weddings, coronations, court hearings, even wars, and occasionally performances labeled as plays, that are designed to engage an audience. Although it is possible to "watch" such a performance on the screen as it is generated by other players without interacting, the lure of these virtual environments is in the interactive opportunities available to participants.

One early online MUD theatrical performance in which I was an audience member took place at ATHEMOO, a text-based MUD[3] designed for theatre educators and professionals.[4] On March 24, 1996, The Virtual Drama Society performed *Playground*, a scripted science fiction piece by Cat Hébert,[5] a theatre director, playwright, and computer programmer, as part of Crosswaves, a five-day festival of technology and the arts at the Annenberg Center, University of Pennsylvania. Physically present at the Annenberg site were about seventy-five audience members who followed the action in the ATHEMOO site by listening to live actors read the performance text as it scrolled on the computer screen and was projected on a large video screen. Online in ATHEMOO, about fifteen audience members gathered virtually, in addition to the performers. The performance, as it took place online, was in a virtual room that was designed to resemble a theatre.[6] There was a stage space, an audience space, and even an usher (a robot character who operated without a human agent), who would shush people who spoke in the auditorium. As an alternative choice, the Rowdies Balcony could be used for viewing, a space in which participants could read what happened on the stage and on the main floor below, but could communicate openly with each other without an usher's interference. The characters "onstage" did not see the conversation in the balcony or on the main floor. They could only read text from other characters onstage. This created an interesting situation, because the actors received no audience feedback.[7] One actor, Robert Garland, commented in the postshow discussion that took place in ATHEMOO, "one of the primary forces for any actor, what gets one on the stage, is the response from the audience. This is the first time in my life that I 'got on the stage' and didn't feel that. At all."[8] Such feedback reinforces the significance of the active audience role in performance, made all too obvious by its absence.

The text of the play had been previously typed and recorded, and the actors could "play back" the prerecorded text using special commands. Characters included the Narrator, Citizen1, Citizen2, Citizen3, GB1, GB2, and GB3 (the 'GB' stands for 'Global Being'). Set descriptions also had been prerecorded and were to scroll past on the viewer's screen at the appropriate moments under the control of one of the players; however, because of a technical problem, set descriptions appeared as "type mismatch." To give a flavor of the text and experience, below is an excerpt as it appeared on my computer screen from the performance's opening:

[on stage] Narrator A long time ago, before there was stuff in the universe, or a universe to put stuff into . . . two GALAXY-SIZED beings herded along a pretty unruly group of beings about a quarter or *[sic]* their size. Got the picture?
[on stage] GB3 says, "ready in puddletown"

[on stage] Type mismatch
[on stage] GB2 They're driving me NUTS! They can't just "be". They always have to be "doing" something, as they like to call it.
[on stage] Type mismatch
[on stage] GB3 says, "Where'd they come from, anyway?"
[on stage] GB2 Uh. . . . they just sort of. . . . . uh. . . . . popped up.
[on stage] Type mismatch
[on stage] GB3 says, "And you didn't have anything to do with that?"
[on stage] GB2 ME?! No way. They just. . . .
[on stage] GB2 [CALLS OFF] Fourteen! Stop that!

This remnant of text provides several pieces of information. The bracketed text, "[on stage]," was a programmed function of the room used throughout to clarify for the online audience, reading as the text scrolled by, the location of the action. During the performance, a viewer's screen could show the performance, a private message from another person viewing, the action of the robotic usher, and so on; thus, preprogrammed functions were designed to help audience members orient themselves to the source of the text and differentiate the "performance" from other activity. Below is an excerpt from later in the performance that demonstrates some of the actions taken by audience members (Cordelia, Shakespeare's_Guest, SusanW, and RickS were names given to the audience members) at the event:

[on stage] GB2 No. . . . We make a whole BUNCH of "real" something or other and. . . . :. . . . and we put them in charge of taking care of it. . . .
   [on stage] GB2 I don't know about that . . . I. . . .
   Cordelia takes a bow and the curtain falls: poof, she's gone.
   [on stage] Type mismatch
   Shakespeare's_Guest claps
   <Clap Clap>
   SusanW starts to wonder if the performers are talking about us..!
   RickS nods
   [on stage] GB2 I don't know if I want them in CHARGE of it. I mean. . . . .look at 'em. Do you want "Fourteen" in charge of ANYTHING?
   SusanW claps her toes together but they don't make much sound..
   [on stage] GB3 says, " . . . and they can "do" and "do" and "do" and "doooo" all they want! "Oh, they'll "do" just fine. . . . . All WE need to do is to make something "real" and . . . "
   RickS says, "off"
   [on stage] Type mismatch
   The Usher walks over to RickS, "Please, not so loud . . . "

Because the rooms that comprised the ATHEMOO theatre space were designed/programmed to mimic a real theatre space, there was a clear delineation between actors and audience during the performance. The script had been created to be "played" to a passive audience rather than an interactive one. Despite this, as the above excerpt shows, interaction by and among audience members occurred. The technical glitch that created the reoccurring statement "[onstage] type mismatch" was a source of much discussion and even humor among audience members,[9] until the technical malfunction was explained. Discussions among audience members were interspersed on the screens of all those attending throughout the performance, becoming as much a part of the performance experience as the play created by the actors. Although the audience members did not interfere with the actors on the stage during the performance, once it was over several audience/characters leaped onto the stage and interacted with the actors' characters. The performance itself was not designed to be interactive, but MUD space is inherently so, prompting spectator/players to engage their characters in virtual actions throughout, actions that were reflected on other players' screens. Audience members clapped, whispered to others, talked aloud, nodded their heads, and paged each other in private communications.

Networked communications control how the spectator interacts within performances through the design of the software and the interface. In the previous example, an early experiment in ATHEMOO, the performance and room design prescribed a fairly traditional audience role, although much interaction occurred among audience members. Other performances in ATHEMOO have experimented with the role of the audience in performance, such as having audience members become performers, as in Rick Sack's "MetaMOOphosis," or providing audience members with options to choose their level of interaction, as in Stephen Schrum's "NetSeduction."[10]

In all Multi-User Domain performances, it is important to realize that MUD space is highly interactive space. Even when watching a performance presumably passively, without interacting with the performers, there is a great deal of chatter among players, reminiscent of what is known of pre-Wagnerian Western theatre, in which, during performances, audiences came and went, visited each other, held conversations among themselves, indulged in refreshments, and openly interacted with performers on stage. The goal of attending a theatre performance, particularly in the seventeenth and eighteenth centuries, was not necessarily only to see a performance, but to see and be seen by others. Changing theatre architecture in the nineteenth century that divided the audience firmly from the stage was instrumental in altering audience behavior, allowing audience conventions of polite and silent viewing to be developed.[11] The addition of controllable lighting that focused attention on the stage area and darkened the audience area was introduced in the mid-nineteenth century, further reinforcing the audience/performer division and relegating the audience to a more passive role than they previously had in performance situations. Interestingly, Ken Schweller, programmer/designer of the ATHEMOO theatre, included a function entitled the "Cone of Silence," which could be lowered over the main floor and prevent audience comments from being seen on other audience members' screens. It was not lowered for the *Playground* performance. Other controls that can be implemented in this virtual theatre space are controls on the Usher's behavior, enabling or disabling applause or booing, dimming the houselights, raising the curtain, and putting a net over the Rowdies Balcony so that players there cannot shout or throw objects.[12] Audience conventions can be, indeed need to be, programmed into the space to allow for or prevent certain types of interactivity. Although Cat Hébert had designed a performance for passive spectating, without the proper controls in place, the interactive audience did not cooperate. Monica Wunderer, who studies and creates Internet performances, suggests in her essay "Presence in Front of the Fourth Wall of Cyberspace" that "Some basic rules for an audience participating via the lines of the Internet have to be clarified," and that Internet audiences need training in both the conventions for specific performances, and "Netiquette," the term used for a code of etiquette that guides written net communication.[13]

Lacking audience conventions that are either prescribed by tradition or by programming, interaction among audience members in MUD space is inevitable. Because each audience member's action or comment scrolls across the screens of other audience members, a MUD performance becomes as much about audience behavior as about the preplanned, prerehearsed actions of the performers. The presence of an audience creates a sense of immediacy provided by participation with other audience members in the virtual space.

INTERACTIVITY IN MULTI-MEDIA PERFORMANCE

In an attempt to capture this immediacy—the quality of "live event"—other networked performances use the Internet to transmit an experience in the moment of its occurrence. Webcasting is a means of allowing viewers to see a live performance on their computer screen. Performance artists have played with Webcasting as a means to create a moment-to-moment, synchronous, "live" art form by incorporating a degree of audience interactivity into the mix. A performance event in June 1998, *Kidnap,* by the United Kingdom multi-media arts group, Blast Theory, provides an example of audience interactivity in online performance through the use of the Web and Webcasting.[14] In this performance piece, rather than buying tickets, potential audience members applied (and paid £10 for the privilege) to be kidnapped by the group. From all of the applicants, nine were chosen at random as semifinalists. Members of the company stalked each of these nine individuals for a day on foot and by vehicle. Records of these stakeouts were posted to a Web site accessible to anyone interested in the performance.[15] Finally, two people were chosen as "kidnappees," brought to an unknown location, and kept captive for two days. Those who paid the £10 fee could also visit the Kidnap Centers set up in London and Manchester, where they could use dedicated Web terminals there to e-mail the kidnappers and control the direction of the video cameras that were recording the room in which the hostages were kept. Each entrant also received a copy of the final videotape made of the event. Throughout the *Kidnap* event, viewers from anywhere in the world could access the Web site and watch the captives through live Webcasts, read a log of what had happened, or converse via an online bulletin board with those in control. Observers could even post suggestions for interrogation.

After their two-day captivity, the two "victims" of the kidnap were released to a press conference to discuss their experience, and ultimately, a videotape of the entire encounter was made and distributed. *Kidnap* was featured on several British television stations and was nominated for a Creative Freedom Award in Britain. The stated purpose of the performance encounter, according to a posting on the Liveart discussion list, "Re: Kidnap," was that by "invoking issues of voyeurism and power, *Kidnap* sought to bring the world of Hollywood and the news media into the lives of ordinary people."[16]

This performance event was a combination of live and Internet performance. A scenario for the event was constructed, set in motion, and overseen by the creators, but the audience was both the focus and the means of performance. For the two chosen audience members who became the kidnappees, a transformation occurred from audience to star. Those watching could engage with the event by visiting the Kidnap Centers in person or connecting through the World Wide Web. These audience members could affect the event by making suggestions to those in control or by altering the angle of the camera that observed the kidnappees. Another audience was created by those who had not paid the fee to participate but who, having heard of the event through e-mail or other means, connected to the Web site only (although this audience could also communicate via the bulletin board with the artists in control). The hostage performance continued in real time throughout two days, but audience members controlled how and when they viewed it, and whether or not they became involved directly through Web bulletin board communication or visits to the captors and kidnappees at the Kidnap Centers.

ANALYZING INTERACTIVITY IN THEATRICAL TERMS

The *Kidnap* performance was interactive, but in a different way than the ATHEMOO performance described earlier. The German theatre scholar Wilfried Passow, in "Analysis of Theatrical Performance," suggests that there are five levels of interaction occurring in a traditional stage performance: (A) The interaction of fictional characters and objects in the world of the play, (B) the interaction of the audience and stage action within the fictional world, (C) the interaction of the performers to each other within the real world, (D) the interaction of the audience and the performers in the real world, and (E) the interaction of audience members with each other in the real world.[17] Applying this model of interactivity to Internet performances is a means to compare and differentiate the type of interactivity possible in networked performance forms with theatrical interactivity.

In the two examples give previously, the fictional interaction (A) is present, clearly occurring in the MUD theatre example and in *Kidnap*. There was a fictional structure within which actions and reactions took place. In ATHEMOO, it was the fictional world of the play; in *Kidnap*, it was the creation of the mock hostage-taking event. The second level of interaction (B) was also clearly visible in *Kidnap*, for the audience could choose to believe in the fictional kidnap and captivity of the two selected hostages as a means of propelling interest in the event—what would happen next? They also chose not to take an overt action, such as rescuing the hostages or calling the police. It is less clear in the ATHEMOO performance, for the audience was not receiving all of the performance (the stage setting error), and most of the audience spent the performance time questioning what was going on, because they lacked the necessary information to decode the event.

The next level of interaction (C), real interaction among the players, occurred in both performances, although in *Kidnap*, the division between fictional and real was elided within the view of the audience, for all actions of the artist/hostage takers in view of the audience resulted in actions that could have real consequences for the kidnappees—when to feed them, what to feed them, what questions would be asked in the interrogation, and so on—because of the improvisatory nature of the performance. In the ATHEMOO performance, these real actions were occasionally visible to audience members, such as Hébert, the director, asking onscreen (visible to everyone, rather than in a private page to the actors) if the performers were ready to begin the second scene. Other messages among the performers may have taken place in private page messages that were not shown on the audiences' screens. The audience/performer interaction (D) was precluded in the ATHEMOO performance by the programming of the space, which did not allow audience reactions to be perceived by the performers because the audience had not been taught how to interact with the limited, preprogrammed options available. In *Kidnap*, the audience/performer interaction was foregrounded by the Web page bulletin board for questions between audience members and the artist/captors and by the improvisatory nature of the performance, which allowed for audience input into the events. The audience interaction amongst themselves (E) was clearly evident in the ATHEMOO performance, but only possible in the *Kidnap* performance in the physical environment of the Kidnap centers if more than one audience member was present at the same time. There was no audience interactivity potential for those watching the Web performance of the capture, although this could have been made possible through the use of an ancillary chat space created specifically for the performance and linked to the Web site.

Passow's model of interactivity in the theatre provides challenges for those designing interactive Internet performance. In examining Internet performances, the type and scale of interaction can be determined so that similarities and differences from "live" performances can be examined. What do Internet performances have in common with live performances? What do Internet audiences have in common with live audiences? What traditions of theatrical "spectating" are drawn on in creating Internet performances? And what new forms of interactive participation are being developed in cyberspace? In the above examples, I have attempted to demonstrate this type of analysis, but it is still necessary to define more clearly the term "interactive."

Interactivity in theatrical performance is a cornerstone of theatre's definition. As Passow's model demonstrates, theatre performance is a multi-layered matrix of encounters that involve performers, audience, a constructed fictional world, and the external frame of reality in simultaneous engagements that affect and define the experiences for those involved. Interactivity in theatre suggests a continuing feedback loop of responses—performers respond to the fictional world by creating fictional behaviors, audiences respond to the fictional world and performers by creating real behaviors, real audience behavior affects the performer's behavior, possibly strengthening or weakening the attachment to the fictional world. Performers respond to the real and fictional behaviors of other performers with new behaviors, structured to fit within the framework of the fictional world, or perhaps even shatter the fictional world in response to a received behavior (as examples, a fellow performer is hurt on stage, or an audience member disturbs the performance). Audience members interact with each other through their behavior created in reaction to the performance, enhancing or disturbing the experience for fellow audience members. Interactivity is predicated on behavior—on external signs of actions of the performer and the audience that can be perceived by those involved.

Critics who dismiss digital performance as theatre will argue that there is a spiritual dimension to the interaction among performers and audience members that cannot exist without physical presence. Many performers, including myself, speak of a feedback loop of energy that is constructed in the physical space of a theatre. Such a bond, whether spiritual or through a feedback energy loop, manifests itself in real actions. A nod of the head, a physical leaning toward the stage, more rapid breathing or a holding of breath, gripping a playbill more tightly, all are behaviors that appear as an audience engages itself fully with a performance on the stage. For a performer, small changes such as increased effort in a move across stage, a change in breathing, an increase or decrease in vocal levels, or a change in pitch or tempo in delivering the lines are overt, although possibly minute, behavioral changes that happen in response to audience feedback. An energy loop may indeed be present in the physical space of traditional theatre, but this energy interaction manifests itself through numerous subtle behavioral changes in everyone involved in the performance. The challenge for interactivity in digital performance is that the behavior must be made overt in order to manifest the energy to be transmitted between and among performers and the audience. Methods of interaction must be planned, programmed, taught, and learned by performers and by audience members in order to create fully interactive performances. Interfaces must be created to allow as much information in the form of defined behaviors as possible to flow between and among those involved.

Interactivity is a key element in digital media, and yet the term presents problems for those who attempt to define it within the realm of cyberspace. Janet H. Murray, author of *Hamlet on the Holodeck,* suggests that the terms *procedural* and *participatory* "make up most of what we mean by the vaguely useful world *interactive.*"[18] Brenda Laurel, in *Computers as Theatre,* suggests that interactivity be looked at "on a continuum of three variables: frequency (how often you could interact), range (how many choices were available), and significance (how much the choices really affected matters)," but she also backs away from this reliance on so technical a specification by saying that this is only part of the definition: "There is another, more rudimentary measure of interactivity. You either feel yourself to be participating in the ongoing action of the representation or you don't."[19] Steve Holtzman, in *Digital Mosaics,* suggests that interactive experiences "respond to you, pull you in, demand your participation."[20] Again, interactivity in cyberspace is predicated on behavior, on taking action, on engaging in a participatory fashion with the experience. This can be as simple as clicking a button on a Web page, or writing a textual description or comment in MUD space, or sending e-mail to the creators of an event or other audience members. Without participation, without some outward sign of behavior, there is no interaction.

Of course, all communication is interactive or communication does not take place. In the simplest and earliest forms of communication, gesture and speech, interaction is simultaneous—sender and receiver are in the same space and time. With the development of writing and printing, the sender and receiver no longer need to share the same physical space at the same time for communication to occur. Electronic communication technology both expands and contracts the limits of space and time, providing options depending on the medium. Telephones, for instance, create simultaneous transmission over distances, but limit the type of shared behavior created and transmitted to the spoken word and other aural communication. Film, by contrast, widens both the time interval from creation to reception and the distance between those involved, much as writing does. With the introduction of recording, radio and television can either operate as film, or they can be "live" and simultaneous, although the distance between creator and receiver delays a direct response.

What networked digital communications offer that is new (at least for electronic communication) is the ability to create the simultaneous multi-media interaction of a sender and receiver over distance. In many ways, what this returns to is the framework of oral traditions—simultaneous (albeit virtual) presence in time and space and mutual reception of (limited forms of) behavior.[21] The difference is that the interaction of audience and performer behavior is no longer limited by geographical distance, although it is limited by the interface, which allows only a small range of responses to stimuli to be made concrete to others within the networked connection because of limitations in technology. But even within this limited range, I can be virtually and simultaneously there in cyberspace with other creators and receivers, creating and receiving behaviors that can be perceived as a performance (although Gertrude Stein, via cyberbard William Gibson, reminds me, "There's no there there"). I can laugh and cry, and although I may be alone at my computer, I can create behavior at the interface that signals my reactions to others involved. I can also, if allowed by the design of the networked space, affect the performance by clicking on buttons or sending messages that may be suggestions, ideas, or responses to performer behavior. My online behavior as an audience member can create a chain of reactions that affect the overall experience of an online performance for the performers and others. I can react with the fictional world, with the performers, with other audience members, as Passow suggests are the interactive options in theatre for audience members. Or if a performer, I can react to the fictional world, the other performers, or the audience. The virtual stage of cyberspace becomes the town courtyard, and cyberperformances become gatherings of the global village at holiday.

With world-wide networked digital communication, the world returns, as Paul Levinson points out in his book on communication history, *The Soft Edge,* to a potential means of communication that is ubiquitous, that places the same means of communication in the hands of producers and consumers, unlike prior technological innovations of print, radio, film, and television, which separated production from consumption.[22] The question becomes, when we all have the tools to be artists, will we be? And here lies both the promise and the problem with technologically mediated performance over the Internet.

The promise of vast audiences connected worldwide by the Internet to experience performances is tantalizing to artists. But the problem is that the audience demands involvement in the performance, because the digital connection goes both ways. The rise of interest in role-playing games on the Internet is evidence of a growing interest in escaping to fictional worlds, not just passively as traditional forms of entertainment allow, but through immersion and participation in the fictional event. Technology allows us to act, to react, to play in fictional worlds; to construct characters that we can become; and to engage in fictional conflict. We can act out our stories in cyberspace, rather than watch others act them out for us. Role-playing games make everyone into an actor and an audience member at the same time. Creating the mask of character becomes a matter of writing a character description or, in some games, even simpler, choosing from a menu of options.

And at the same time that players are participating, they are enjoying the inventiveness and artistry of other players as they encounter new fictional situations together.

NEW INTERACTIVE WORLDS

When it was first released in March 1999, *EverQuest,* a multi-player role-playing game on the Internet, was a near instantaneous success.[23] In three months time, the game, created by Sony's 989 Studios, acquired over one hundred thousand players who paid for the software needed to play and continue to pay a monthly connection fee, and players online averaged thirty thousand nightly.[24] While its origins rest in the text-based Multi-User Domains described earlier and other computer games such as the action-driven *Doom* and the puzzle-solving *Myst,* advances in software and hardware allow *EverQuest* to develop much more complexity than previous games. As the game manual states, "In the world of EverQuest you assume the Persona of [a] mythical figure traveling across a magical world in search of fame and riches."[25] An elaborate fictional world consisting of several continents and numerous towns, castles, forests, deserts, and other locations is rendered visually in three-dimensional graphics, allowing players' characters to move to different places and interact with other players and objects at the point and click of a mouse or through a few keystrokes. Conversations still occur in a text-based mode through a chat window, but characters are visually rendered and can take actions such as fighting, putting on costumes, picking up objects, or even waving hello. Players design their characters from a menu of options including race, gender,[26] occupation, special abilities, equipment, religion, and appearance. Nonplayer characters (NPCs) also exist, much like the robotic usher in the ATHEMOO theatre, but these *EverQuest* robots are much more sophisticated, incorporating advances in artificial intelligence programming. These automated characters consist of beasts that attack, guards at city gates, or other characters who have repetitive functions. Similar to other computer games, a player's character moves through the fictional world and encounters new experiences, gaining points and improving its abilities. But unlike other multi-player online games, *EverQuest*'s design strongly encourages interactive role-playing. An incentive is built into the game for players to band together in teams of up to six characters to accomplish certain difficult objectives. The pleasure of the experience comes from accomplishing tasks, interacting with others, and gaining rewards.

That there is pleasure is clear from the game's overwhelming popularity. Edward Umheiser, a computer games reviewer for an online gaming magazine, wrote: "To me, EverQuest has become more than a game . . . it's another life! Every emotion comes out as you play the game . . . anger, fear, hatred, joy, and even love. Yes, it's true. Just recently a couple were married, with a large reception held in the ButcherBlock Mountains. Just about anything and everything can happen in this game."[27] The game taps into emotions of players in much the same way that theatre emotionally engages an audience. The difference is that the *EverQuest* audience member is also the player watching his or her own actions translated through technology into the actions of the character on the screen. The player decides what the character is going to do, rather than watching an actor on stage make the choices. The play is improvisatory rather than pre-scripted, but scenarios can be planned with other characters for quests, or weddings, or duels. Preplanned festivals held in an *EverQuest* town include concerts and even plays.

EverQuest is an interactive performance form that fulfills all of Passow's definitions for theatrical interactivity. First, there is (A) interaction in the fictional world among characters. Clearly, the characters interact with each other, with the nonplayer characters such as beasts or guards, and with the fictional objects in the world. Characters can eat, drink, put on clothing and armor, engage in battles and events such as plays or concerts, or just talk. There is (B) interaction between the audience (the players) and the fictional world of the characters, because the players are directly controlling the characters. There is also interaction among actors in the real world (C) through a communications function similar to the page or whisper function in a MUD. Thus, direct player-to-player contact can take place. Interaction between audience and actors in the real world (D) is also present, again through the same function. A player can send communication to another player after a battle with a "nicely done" message, or congratulations for having gained a new level for the character. And (E) audience/players can affect each other by stepping out of the role-play mode.

As happens in MUDs, *EverQuest* is a performative space that engages its players in an audience/actor duality. Indeed, the game encourages player and character interaction in its design. When a new character is created, it begins its existence in a populous town, sure to encounter other characters. Membership in guilds is encouraged, and guilds often hold meetings or other gatherings. Planned events such as weddings, tournaments, and festivals encourage large groups of characters to congregate in the same space to participate in a public way as characters. Events such as concerts or plays held in the space become performances within performances, just as Shakespeare's play-within-a-play in *A Midsummer Night's Dream*.

EverQuest is a simulation of life, just as theatre is a simulation of life. Both are based on action, both engage participants in encounters within a matrix of the real and the fictional, both occur through simultaneous transmission of behavior. Whereas theatre creates and transmits behavioral encounters through physical presence, *EverQuest* encounters occur in the virtual space of the Internet, mediated by hardware and software. But both theatre and role-playing games such as *EverQuest,* together with other Internet performances, share a common characteristic of playing, of acting out, of experimenting with life by creating fictions and fantasies.

Interactive audience experiences hearken back to earlier cultures in which theatre-making was not the exclusive preserve of highly trained specialists but an integral part of a culture. Ancient and Medieval festivals and pageants serve as the model for many of these interactive role-playing performance forms, rather than what is perceived as the traditional theatre-making of the post-Gutenberg civilization. Interactive audiences are also a guaranteed part of our future. As Stewart Brand, the former editor of *The Whole Earth Catalog* and a prescient observer and developer of innovative digital technology, points out, advances in communications, such as the VCR, the satellite dish, and the personal computer have "made audiences into something else—less 'a group of spectators, listeners, or readers' and more a society of selectors, changers, makers."[28] This opinion is echoed by Derrick de Kerckhove, Director of the McLuhan Program in Culture and Technology in Toronto, when he states in his book *Connected Intelligence,* "We are moving from an era of 'replay' to 'remake.' We are developing computer-assisted cognitive habits and computer-assisted forms of collaboration—new forms, in fact, of connectedness."[29] And this connectedness demands interaction. Online, audiences shapeshift into the selectors, changers, and makers of new stories, of new fiction, of new dramatic encounters. Cyberspace has the power to unleash an individual's creative potential. Umheiser, the game critic cited earlier, confesses in his review of *EverQuest,* "I actually find myself dreaming about my character and some of the adventures I've been on!"[30] A 1998 advertisement for the Sony computers aptly paraphrased Shakespeare: "To sleep perchance to dream perchance to mess with reality—do you dream in Sony?"[31] Apparently, Umheiser does, along with the rapidly growing number of *EverQuest* players.

This dream of immersive dramatic experience was suggested by theatre designer and theorist Adolphe Appia at the turn of this century: "We shall arrive, eventually, at what simply will be called the *House:* a sort of cathedral of the future, which in a vast, open and changeable space will welcome the most varied expressions of our social and artistic life, and will be the ideal place for dramatic art to flourish, *with or without spectators.*"[32] What Appia possibly recognized was that the audience would merge *into* players. But he also dreamed that dramatic art would take place in a vast, open, changeable space—the space now made possible by the glimmerings of the virtual. Today's programmers and designers are beginning to create the cathedrals of the future on the Internet. A stage for dramatic interaction can be created through the malleable bits of digital information to frame and shape the varied expressions of social and artistic life, as expressed by the actions, interactions, and stories that emerge in these new worlds on the Internet. Just as theatre artists shape the production on a stage, the programmers and designers of virtual worlds are designing the possibilities for new dramatic forms in cyberspace.

NOTES

1. Brenda Laurel, *Computers as Theatre* (Reading, Mass.: Addison Wesley Publishing Co., 1993), 4. Brenda Laurel was one of the first writers to suggest that much could be learned by computer program designers from theatre. In *Computers as Theatre,* she applies Aristotle's dramatic elements, as outlined in *Poetics,* to create satisfying, interactive, interface design.

2. For detailed information on the operation of Multi-User Domains and their similarity to theatrical environments, see Nina LeNoir, "Acting in Cyberspace: The Player in the World of Digital Technology," in *Theatre in Cyberspace: Issues of Teaching, Acting, and Directing,* ed. Stephen A. Schrum (New York: Peter Lang, 1999), 175–200.

3. MUDs are either text-based, in which all description and actions are rendered in text that scrolls across the computer screen; or graphical, in which images are rendered visually and may be supplemented by sound, although conversation may still be rendered through text.

4. ATHEMOO, [MOO site], telnet://moo.hawaii.edu:9999/.

5. Information on the playwright and his experiments with online performance can be found at Cat Hébert, "Virtual Drama Society," [online] 1996 (27 June 2001), available from the World Wide Web at http://www.virtualdrama.com/.

6. The theatre space in ATHEMOO is called the Schweller Auditorium, named after its creator/programmer, Ken Schweller. It includes rooms that serve as lobby, main floor, balcony, control room, stage, and backstage. The "properties" of the space include raising and lowering the curtain, the ability to display various prebuilt "sets" (text descriptions), and the ability to raise or lower a "cone of silence" over the main floor, which keeps audience comments from being displayed, among other features. Although some of these features are discussed herein, a full description of the virtual space and how a play can be performed within it is provided in Ken Schweller, "Staging a Play in the MOO Theater," in *Theatre in Cyberspace: Issues of Teaching, Acting, and Directing,* ed. Stephen A. Schrum (New York: Peter Lang, 1999), 147–57.

7. Interestingly, the actor/players could have received feedback through certain programming codes available within the space that would have allowed specific responses to be shown on the screens of those manipulating characters on stage; however, the audience was not taught how to use them and did not use them. Consequently, no feedback was provided to the actor/players until either an audience/player moved his/her character onto the stage, or the actor/player's character left the stage, as the stage was considered a separate room than the main floor. See Schweller's article for a full description of audience options.

8. The performance of *Playground* and the postshow discussion are contained in my personal computer files, which captured the text generated during and after the performance on March 24, 1995.

9. At one point, everyone was literally typing "mismatch":

RickS says, "Type mismatch? Type mismatch?"
[on stage] Type mismatch
RickS descends the spiral staircase down to the Lobby . . .
FabioP says, "What'st thoiss *[sic]* mismatch?"
[on floor below] Neuber's_Guest types mismatch :)

[on stage] Type mismatch
[on floor below] Shakespeare's_Guest types mismatch:)
FabioP types mismatch but cut it out
[on floor below] SusanW types mismatch to be like everyone else . . . :-)

10. Information about MetaMOOphosis can be found in Rick Sacks, "Meta-MOOphosis: A Visit to the Kafka House," in *Theatre in Cyberspace: Issues of Teaching, Acting, and Directing*, ed. Stephen A. Schrum (New York: Peter Lang, 1999), 159–74. Information about "NetSeduction" is archived online at Stephen A. Schrum, "Netseduction," [online] June 27, 2001, available from the World Wide Web at http://socs.ntu.uc.ak/archive/netseduction.html.

11. Susan Bennett, *Theatre Audiences: A Theory of Production and Reception* (London and New York: Routledge, 1997), 3.

12. Schweller, 153–55.

13. Monica Wunderer, "Presence in Front of the Fourth Wall of Cyberspace," in *Theatre in Cyberspace: Issues of Teaching, Acting, and Directing*, ed. Stephen A. Schrum (New York: Peter Lang, 1999), 204–20. Also, although many Web pages exist defining Netiquette, one of the most complete is the award-winning site of Arlene Rinaldi, "Netiquette Home Page," [online], 1998 (June 27, 2001), available from the World Wide Web at http://www.fau.edu/netiquette/netiquette.

14. Blast Theory, "Kidnap," New Media Center, Manchester, England, May–June 1998, archived information available from the World Wide Web at http://www.blasttheory.easynet.co.uk/work_kidnap_body.html.

15. The records of the stakeouts are available at Blast Theory, "Kidnap Surveillance," [online] November 9, 2001, available from the World Wide Web at http://www.blasttheory.co.uk/kidnap/surveillancedetect/surdet.htm.

16. [ds98@mttp.net.uk], "Re: Kidnap," [online posting to LIVEART], September 21, 1998 (October 1, 1999), available from the World Wide Web at http://www.mailbase.ac.uk/lists/liveart/1998-09/0016.html.

17. Wilfried Passow, "The Analysis of Theatrical Performance: The State of Art Today," trans. R. Strauss, *Poetics Today* 2:3 (1981): 240.

18. Janet H. Murray, *Hamlet on the Holodeck: The Future of Narrative in Cyberspace* (New York: Free Press, 1997), 71.

19. Laurel, 20–21.

20. Steven Holtzman, *Digital Mosaics: The Aesthetics of Cyberspace* (New York: Simon and Schuster, 1997), 127.

21. Marshall McLuhan first made this observation of the reversion to older forms of culture: "Not only does the visual, specialist, and fragmented Westerner have now to live in closest daily association with all the ancient oral cultures of the earth, but his own electric technology now begins to translate the visual or eye man back into the tribal and oral pattern with its seamless web of kinship and interdependence." Marshall McLuhan, *Understanding Media: The Extensions of Man* (Cambridge: Cambridge University Press, 1964), 50.

22. Paul Levinson, *The Soft Edge: A Natural History and Future of the Information Revolution* (London and New York: Routledge, 1997), 117.

23. The *EverQuest* Home Page, together with reviews of the game, related sites created by players, and demonstrations on television shows that focus on computer games, originally provided me with information on the world of *EverQuest*, because

my personal computer was not compatible with the software. I have since had the opportunity to play in the world of *Everquest*, which has verified what is described herein. Sony Corporation, "Everquest," [online] (June 27, 2001), available on the World Wide Web at http://www.station.sony.com/everquest/.

24. Michael Krantz, "Grab Your Breastplate: Everquest Reinvents the Web Role-playing Game," *Time*, June 21, 1999, 63.

25. Sony Corporation.

26. According to the online game manual, *EverQuest* is an equal opportunity world, in that gender does not affect skills or performance. It only affects how the character appears on the screen.

27. Edward Umheiser, "Everquest Review," in *3Dgaming* [online magazine] July 14, 1999 (July 14, 1999) no longer available from the World Wide Web.

28. Stewart Brand, *The Media Lab: Inventing the Future at M.I.T.* (New York: Penguin Books, 1988), 252.

29. Derrick de Kerckhove, *Connected Intelligence: The Arrival of the Web Society* (Toronto: Somerville House Publishing, 1997), xxxix.

30. Umheiser.

31. Sony Computers advertisement, in *Wired*, July 1998: 20–21.

32. Adolphe Appia, "Actor, Space, Light, Painting," in *The Twentieth Century Performance Reader*, ed. Michael Hurley and Noel Witts (London: Routledge, 1997), 23.

10

ONCE UPON A TIME: THE STORY OF THE PANTOMIME AUDIENCE

Dawn Lewcock

The English Christmas Pantomime is the quintessential entertainment involving the audience and encouraging their active participation in the happenings on stage. It has been presented for the past two and a half centuries and has, of course, changed in both form and content over that time, yet still attracts and holds its particular audience. This chapter explores why and how the audience has influenced and participated in the show across the years, causing changes in both presentation and casting while continuing to expect traditional elements. Paradoxically, there is little evidence for the ways in which audiences join in a pantomime performance, yet there is a tradition of particular kinds of behavior and modern presenters know they need to include certain characters and dialogue that appear to be rooted in particular actions or ways of presentation in the past. In order to examine audience responses today, it is necessary to give some description of the origins of the genre to understand the traditions that the present-day audiences expect to find honored. This chapter, therefore, examines the historical background and follows through those links from the past to see both why they have endured and what the expected response is to each manifestation. This can only be relative and conjectural, as no direct academic study has been made in this field.

The Pantomime is a uniquely British occasion first presented for adults in the eighteenth century but since the nineteenth century, it has gradually been aimed more and more toward children. However, it often makes concessions in the form of double entendres and satirical references to topical personalities or political or other issues in order to attract the adults who accompany the children. Pantomime's success depends to a large extent on meeting the audience's expectations for novelty, topicality, extravagant spectacle, and titillating wickedness. The attractiveness of wickedness and the need to resist it is always one of the hidden lessons. It always has a strong moral story with both virtuous and wicked characters and the audience is encouraged to participate in working toward the final triumph of the forces for good. The genre has evolved by adapting to contemporary tastes and attitudes toward good and evil while keeping the same basic parameters as well as by changes dictated by commercial and financial considerations in enticing audiences to attend.

The traditions and characters derive from many varied sources, some of which can be traced back to the comedies of Menander and Plautus. An afterpiece called *The Loves of Mars and Venus, an entertainment of dancing in imitation of the ancient Greeks and Romans,* presented at Drury Lane by Weaver in 1717, is usually thought of as the first English pantomime. But later pantomimes owed more to the characters of Commedia dell'arte and the harlequinade, which developed from it. The eighteenth-century pantomime afterpiece opened with characters from a children's story. There was usually a pair of lovers, with her father and a servant who were changed by supernatural magic into Harlequin, Columbine, Pantaloon, and the Clown. The adventures of Harlequin and Columbine formed the basis for comic chase scenes, acrobatic evasions and magical rescues that became translated into the trials the hero and heroine in modern pantomimes have to go through before evil is overcome and they can live happily ever after. The ideas of the Harlequinade were adapted by John Rich into a repertoire of pantomimes. Under the stage name of Lun, he used his own talent for mime and acrobatic dance as a mute Harlequin who contrived to overcome adversity by magic. Although Garrick introduced a speaking Harlequin in 1759 Harlequin still continued mute in many productions until, as the audiences' tastes inclined toward burlesque and Gothic melodrama, his role diminished.

At first Harlequin was masked as in the commedia dell'arte, but Rich soon allowed his Harlequin to take any disguise. One report speaks of him playing a dog and another of hatching from an egg in which "every limb had its tongue and every motion its voice."[1] From this came the tradition of animal characters played by humans in later productions; the cat in *Puss in Boots* or in *Dick Whittington* will often be played by an actress. The cow in *Jack and the Beanstalk* will be usually played by two actors (or actresses) inside a painted skin who probably do a comic dance on the way to market, where it/they are exchanged for the magic beans. The audiences expected and expect this as part of the topsy-turvy world where nothing is quite what it seems to be and/or unexpectedly changes into something else. The in-built ambiguities confirmed and confirm the audience in the certainties of their own existence while allowing a delicious thrill of fantasy.

Rich used all the possibilities of the eighteenth-century stage—the sliding shutters, flying trapezes, stage traps, explosions, and smoke to enable sudden appearances and quick scene changes, and many of the sequences seen earlier in Ravenscroft's *Scaramouche a Philosopher, Harlequin a Schoolboy, Bravo,*

Merchant and Musician (1677), and Behn's full-length *The Emperor of the Moon* (1687), became traditional in the pantomime. Harlequin might enter as a gentleman in his coach but become a farmer in his cart by dropping the sides or would have a sedan chair that suddenly turned into an apothecary's shop by a similar sleight of hand. Characters would jump out of the walls, pop up through traps in the floor, or descend to the stage in elaborate chariots. Pope in Book III of *The Dunciad* summarizes very clearly the total impression given:

> And look'd, and saw a sable Sorc'rer rise,
> Swift to whose hand a winged volume flies:
> All sudden, Gorgons hiss, and Dragons glare,
> And ten horn'd fiends and Giants rush to war,
> Hell rises, Heav'n descends, and dance on Earth:
> Gods, imps, and monsters, music, rage and mirth,
> A fire, a jigg, a battle and a ball,
> Till one wide conflagration swallows all[2]

Then and now the astonished audience would wait enthralled for the next extraordinary event.

There was opposition to the early pantomimes by the managers of the rival theatres and much written by the intelligentsia deriding the absurdity of the eighteenth century pantomime and its attraction to the ill-educated. Hogarth satirized it in caricature, castigating the managements for preferring Harlequin to Shakespeare for commercial concerns.[3] The managements were only following popular esteem. Pantomime was so successful with the audiences that the managements of both patent theatres found they had to present them in order to make a profit. Colley Cibber, who had objected to "the barbarous entertainments so expensively set off to corrupt" the public taste when he was managing Drury Lane in the 1700s, confesses that he "had not virtue enough to starve by opposing a multitude, that would have been too hard for me."[4] His son Theophilus, writing in 1753, said, "So great was the run to many of the Pantomimes that the advanced Prices by their frequent Use, became rather the common Prices."[5] That is, the higher admission prices charged for a pantomime became the general prices for all shows. But the audience insisted on what they saw as their right to enter the theatre at half price just to see the pantomime presented after the mainpiece drama. Garrick attempted to stop this custom on January 25, 1763, by not allowing any reduction for those who wanted to see the pantomime afterpiece after *The Two Gentlemen of Verona*. A riot ensued and when another riot was threatened for the next night Garrick gave in.[6] The same thing happened at Covent Garden in February. That management also had to give in and eventually the pantomime became the mainpiece. The financial records of Covent Garden for the eleven years from 1810 to 1821 show the theatre had been maintained by the success of its pantomimes.[7]

Eventually the transformation of the characters into the harlequinade became less important than the transformation of the scenery. The techniques of the Victorian extravaganza, painted gauzes and special lighting, were added to Rich's original spectacular opening scene to manage the transformation scenes and once electricity and hydraulics were available these became even more astounding. A program for *The Sleeping Beauty in The Wood* at Covent Garden in 1840 lists twelve scene changes including a Banquet Hall, a Magic Forest, and the Illuminated Palace and Gardens of the Fairy Antidota.[8] It was the transformation scene and the spectacle that drew the audience all through the nineteenth century. The *Echo* of December 27, 1900 wrote of *The Sleeping Beauty and the Beast* that it "has got to fill the stage of Drury Lane in the eye of the pit and topmost gallery, is forced to satisfy a taste that insists on great and accumulated masses of color, winding processions, and blinding electric illuminations."[9] The effect on the children is seen in Arthur Quiller-Couch's account of his first visit to the "new and unimagined world, stretching deeper and deeper as the scenes were lifted; a world in which solid walls crumbled and forests melted, and loveliness broke through the ruins, unfolding like a rose."[10]

Commercial considerations continued to affect productions all through the nineteenth century and the profits from the annual pantomime are still important to some extent for a modern theatre. With modern computer-controlled technology, "magical" effects are easier to arrange but, with more technical knowledge and experience, audiences' expectations are higher and the expense of the special effects account for much of the modern outlay. Other expenses include the many changes of gorgeously outrageous costumes, the obligatory chorus of singers and dancers, and the accompanying musicians. In the smaller professional or amateur shows, these may be less elaborate with the local dance academy or schoolchildren acting as the chorus accompanied by a single piano. Even so, the audience will expect to be affrighted by the wicked characters, charmed by the good, startled and surprised by the magical effects, be invited to shout and sing themselves, and see traditional "magical" special effects and a transformation scene in any and every production. In *Sleeping Beauty* the cobweb strewn palace, covered in ivy, in which the princess and her court have slept for one hundred years, is transformed by clever lighting and fast scene changing into a brand new one at the instant the prince wakes her with his kiss. In *Cinderella,* the pumpkin and the mice are turned into a full-size coach drawn by actual ponies at the wave of a wand.

Whatever the casting and the special effects, the presenters know from experience that the audience will not tolerate departures from tradition and that much of the success of the actual presentation will depend to a great extent on the ways in which the audience is invited to participate during the performance. Scripts allow for participation, sometimes by cueing a character to "ad lib," sometimes deliberately including dialogue with and to the audience. The basis comes from much earlier in theatrical history.

The comic characters often behave in ways similar to those found in plays by Plautus. The Prologue in *The Prisoners* deliberately singles out one member of the audience as the butt of a joke, pretends that he is complaining he cannot hear him and tells him to "go take a walk outside . . . Do you want to make a poor actor loose his job / 'I'm not going to rupture myself to suit you, don't think it." Most of Plautus's characters tell the audience their thoughts and feelings or comment on the other characters' actions as the play continues.[11] This is what Bernard Beckerman calls direct presentation, in which the performer acknowledges the presence of the audience and the show makes that acknowledgment explicit and this is exactly the kind of playing that is traditional in pantomime.[12] It has a very long history and was used in Medieval plays but more particularly in the sixteenth century. In John Heywood's play *Johan Johan the husbande, Tyb his wyfe and Syr Johan the preest*, published in 1533, Johan Johan tells the audience he is going to beat his wife when she returns home but they discover that he is actually henpecked. He asks one of the spectators to look after his gown but insults him by suggesting he is "so nere the dore he myght ron away" and then orders the one he gives it to to "skrape of the dyrt."[13] He tells the audience in asides exactly what he is thinking about his wife's behavior and his suspicions about her and the priest. However, Tyb and the priest do not confide in the audience so their inner thoughts are not known and their illicit relationship is not confirmed until Johan Johan has had to perform many chores that deprive him of his share of a pie. This makes for a complicated relationship between Johan Johan and the audience. They see he is a henpecked coward whom they should despise yet they are drawn to sympathize with him because they see how badly he is treated and because he relates to them by talking to them about his fears. This is very much the kind of ambivalent relationship that can be established between certain pantomime characters such as Baron Hardup in *Cinderella* and the audience. They see him as a weak person and feel sympathy while at the same time slightly despising his behavior in not standing up for Cinderella against the Ugly Sisters.

In *Gammer Gurton's Needle* (c. 1553/54), Diccon is an obvious mischief maker. The Prologue explains that Gammer Gurton has lost her needle and Diccon lies to her that Dame Chat has found it, which causes Gammer Gurton to attack Dame Chat and then several others whom Diccon wrongly accuses. The audience is aware that Diccon is lying and enjoy the mayhem caused by his trickery until the needle is found when Hodge "drew it out of his buttock, where he felt it sticking."[14] Elements of this Medieval vice figure, the mischief maker, are found in Harlequin who became subsumed into the acrobatic clowns of the English farceurs to become the nineteenth-century clown buffoon of the pantomime, who instigates exactly this kind of crude and rough humor in the tricks he plays on everyone. He "teases, titillates and seduces"[15] the audience.

Some of the clown's traditional business drew on roots in the earliest representations of Harlequin and Scaramouche. In *The Emperor of the Moon*, Harlequin and Scaramouche are rivals for the hand of Mopsophil. When Harlequin thinks he has lost her he tries to tickle himself to death in a kind of acrobatic frenzy, an act still occasionally used by some comedians. One can also find echoes of several of their other actions. The mock fight that turns into a dance, the mimed encounter in the dark, and the acrobatic fooling with a ladder appear in the turns performed by today's clowns. These were incorporated with tumbling in and out of scene doors and windows and comic business such as a chasing with a red-hot poker, wearing a coal scuttle, fighting with strings of sausages or becoming stuck in wallpaper paste. These acrobatic transformations were not without danger but this seems to have added to the audience's enjoyment. A psychotherapist writing about the attraction of Houdini's daredevil escapades suggests the explanation lies in the anticipation of the audience that something horrific may occur. That this time he will not free himself from the chains, the trunk, or whatever before the water reaches him.[16] It seems likely that this is also the response to the possible danger the audience perceives in some of the pantomime scenes. Although the fights and the chases are known to be just pretend, there is the ambivalent feeling that maybe this time it is real, that the red poker is really hot.

In the mid-eighteenth century, it was reported that "a tumbler . . . [fell and] beat the breath out of his body, which raised such vociferous applause that lasted longer than the venturesome man's life, for he never breathed more. Indeed his wife had this comfort: when the truth was known, pity succeeded to the roar of applause."[17] At the Britannia Theatre on January 2, 1865, a "Ballet girl burnt tonight . . . ascending a pillar for the transformation scene, alone, in the absence of the man to assist her up, her under-dress caught fire from the Gas wing lights . . . she was badly burnt."[18] Accidents with star traps, when characters being propelled on to the stage were caught in them and badly hurt, were very common.

The Victorian taste for melodrama added the moral philosophy of good overcoming evil villainy, which made for a proliferation of wicked wizards and fairy godmothers drawn from folklore who took over the control of magic from Harlequin. Indeed, in 1871, *Entr'sacte* called the pantomime at the Britannia Theatre "a melodrama played in large masks."[19] The rather gentle world of the earlier Harlequins, in which the lovers were simply chased by an angry father through various adventurous exploits, had changed to a more frightening one in which the storyline began to involve something wicked that had to be overcome. Audiences now expected to be scared by the villains, amused and shocked by the antics of the clown, and see the hero and heroine undergo death-defying ordeals before virtue triumphed.

The first true clown was Joseph Grimaldi. He had appeared as a small child in a monkey costume with his father but began his career in 1806 in *Harlequin and Mother Goose or The Golden Egg*. He was an acrobatic dancer like Rich but, where Rich had been a romantic Harlequin always searching for his Columbine, Grimaldi was an anarchic, deliberately mischievous clown akin to Autolycus. "Joey" became the nickname for this kind of clown after him. This Harlequin delighted in playing nasty tricks on his friends and picking their pockets and this side of the original Harlequin's character became subsumed into the servant-clown rather than the hero. Here was the attractive side of mischievousness, trickery at which one could laugh but should not emulate. Grimaldi himself became crippled by his tumbling acrobatic exertions and on his last appearance in 1828 had to perform sitting on a chair.

Nowadays the clown may take on the role of Pantaloon as a mean Baron Hardup or Stoneybroke, or two comedians may play the bumbling Broker's men who want to foreclose on Jack and his mother (in *Jack and the Beanstalk*) or the men who fail to smother the *Babes in the Wood*. The roles still provide scope for similar comic slapstick routines when played by a well-known comedian, but occasionally a retired sports personality, a boxer, or a footballer is seen as a draw and then the comedy is usually found in outrageous puns and comic routines.

The commercial draw of the casting necessarily reflected the changing tastes in the audience. The nineteenth-century audience male's inclination toward sexual titillation meant that a vivacious and good looking girl began to be cast as the hero in a breeches part, drawing on the dress and actions of the soubrettes from eighteenth-century burlesque. Aladdin or Prince Charming in *Cinderella* would be played by what became known as Principal Boys. By the beginning of the twentieth century, the girls had become the buxom corseted Principal Boys preferred by the Edwardian fathers. However, in the more open modern society, the Principal Boy is seen less often and today the hero may be played by a male pop star or a good-looking young actor from a popular TV soap whom both parents like to see in the flesh.

The other character who cross-dresses is the Dame, always played by a man. Ever since the time of the ancient Greeks, actors have specialized in playing the silly older woman; this broadened under the influence of comedians like Dan Leno in the late nineteenth century into the modern Dame, a transvestite character unique to this form of theatre. Part of her appeal is that she is often dressed in an extravagant parody of current fashion. The Dame was and is more scripted than the clown whose actions were often improvised foolery, but she is also the one who now often instigates the slapstick and with her advent the prominence of the clown declined. She is a virtuous character, often the foolish but lovable mother of the hero, who builds a relationship with the audience by confiding her troubles to them. Depending on the story, this could be the laziness of Jack and her lack of money in *Jack and the Beanstalk* or the effect on her hands of all the washing she has to do as Widow Twankey in *Aladdin*. It was said of Dan Leno, one of the most popular Dames at the end of the nineteenth century, that "Part of Leno's amazing success was his gift of taking you into his confidence. The soul of sympathy himself, he made you sympathetic too. He told you his farcical troubles as earnestly as an unquiet soul tells its spiritual ones. You had to share them. His perplexities became yours."[20] This expresses the whole relationship between a Dame and her audience. She asks them to help her by telling her when the villain appears or some other occurrence happens. The audience is sympathetic to her and willing to help her by shouting out "He's behind you" or "Look out" when someone like the Rent-collector comes on stage. There are links with the traditions of the Music Hall from which Dan Leno had come, when both male and female comics would sometimes cross-dress and always play out to the audience.

Depending on the storyline virtually any of the characters may address the audience and include them complicitly in their plans. In a modern *Sleeping Beauty* the Good Fairy, when invited to the christening, says:

Goodness ! I haven't a thing to wear for the Palace. Now that I'm a Fairy
Godmother at last, I should have a beautiful shawl. Hm-m.
Spiders, Spiders on the wall,
Weave for me a dainty shawl,
Spin your threads with special care.
Oh yes—and make it wash and wear[21]

Spells are usually still cast in rhyming couplets but often the rest of the text is in prose. Here the Fairy is involving the audience in both her feelings of pleasure and in her spell-making. They will empathize with her common problem of "not having a thing to wear." The adults will laugh at the prosaic last line and the children will believe in the magic she wields as they see the dainty shawl drop from the flies. Magic is an important ingredient of the pantomime and has deep roots in Harlequin's magic bat. Slapstick is named for the slap of the bat or wand with which he seemed to cause the scenery to change, or rather gave the signal to the stagehands to effect the next change. In 1771, there was a complaint that Harlequin "does nothing but run away with his Mistress and give signals with his magical wooden Sword to direct the Men to shift the Scenes."[22]

But children believed the bat was magic. A theatre critic wrote how as a boy he had had one of the very bats used by the Harlequin at Covent Garden in the late 1820s and how he retained his belief in their magical properties despite "the persistent obstinacy of any article of household furniture to become something else after administering to each the proper word and a blow."[23] Peter Pan uses the same social interaction when asking those who believe in fairies to clap their hands so that Tinkerbell may live in *Peter Pan*.

However, the wicked witch or the enchanter will set out to subtly antagonize the audience. The Vice figure Merygreeke in *Roister Doister* (c. 1553) builds up this kind of relationship by implicitly inviting approval of his mischief making. He tells the audience that he lives on other men and that his latest and "chief banker/Both for meat and money" is Ralph Roister Doister.[24] He makes asides to the audience that allow it to understand the trickery that he is instigating to fool Ralph. A wicked pantomime character behaves in the same way by telling the audience of the plans he/she is making to overthrow the good characters and achieve his/her ends. But they also use a particular approach. It is the same approach found in the Prologues and Epilogues of the seventeenth century after the Restoration of Charles II when the audience was often deliberately insulted—"flighted," as it was called. The effect was to make the audience complicit with the speaker. Each member of the audience would feel the insult did not apply to them and thus feel superior to those to whom they thought it did apply. This kind of insult is the style that the wicked characters, the witches and wizards, use in pantomime, setting the audience against them, and implicitly inviting them to respond with hisses and boos. The audience is therefore deliberately made partisan and subtly inclined toward supporting the good characters. This is a very specialized way of acting which not everyone can manage and keep control but it is a predominate feature of pantomime. On Abanazer's first entrance in *Aladdin* in 1861, he immediately addresses the audience:

> Well, after travelling for many years,
> I find myself in Pekin, it appears.
> At once, perhaps, I'd make admission,
> That I am Abanazer the Magician;
> Not a mere conjuror, I'll have you know,
> I keep no caravan, and make no show:
> No Houdini, Anderson, Frikel, you see—
> There's no deception my good friends, in me.
> I am the real thing—a HORRID spirit,
> A downright British brandy as to merit.[25]

This would be said with the utmost venom in order to antagonize the audience and a similar technique of alienation is employed today. The audience hisses and boos (led by the musicians if it does not happen spontaneously) and will continue to hiss and boo whenever the villain appears. The wicked witch in a modern *Sleeping Beauty* is even more objectionable:

> To a Witch of Evil—a Witch of Night,
> Right is wrong and wrong is right
> I'll think of some terrible thing
> To do to the Princess and do to the King!
> For I LIKE to be evil—I LIKE to be mean,
> I like to mix the nasty spells that turn my fingers GREEN.[26]

The witch or the wicked fairy or the enchanter like the evil Abanazer will make the audience privy to their plans and they will therefore become concerned for the innocent, naive Aladdin and his silly washerwoman Dame mother, or worry about the Princess. The audience becomes involved in the action because its sympathies have been invoked. It means that those playing unpleasant characters must not mind being disliked, which can sometimes be a problem for pop star or TV personality whose popularity is sustained by being loved and admired by their usual audiences.

Unscripted repartee with the audience is often allowed for as in *Sleeping Beauty and the Beast* in 1900.[27] Beauty's Tutor holds an arithmetic class to demonstrate the prowess of his pupil but the King and Queen, played by the comedians, take over. The "King" says he is a lightning calculator and asks the audience to shout out numbers that he will total in his head while the "Queen" writes them on a blackboard. He gives any number as the total and the Queen rapidly cleans off the blackboard before anyone can see that it does not add up. This would be a cue for the characters to ad lib. One character will challenge the King saying he has not reached the right total and appeal to the audience to agree. The King will in turn appeal to them to say he did and they will orchestrate choruses of "Oh, yes he did" and "Oh, no he didn't." This has no rational meaning; it adds nothing to the plot, but it allows the audience to interact with the comedians. *The Times* in December 2000 wrote, "They are drawn into the drama because they are made to feel they are constantly one step ahead of the daft, camp, accident prone lunatics on stage."[28] They can therefore feel privileged in an ambiguous relationship in which they both recognize the comedians as themselves and as the characters in the story. Before the interchange can become too unruly another character will initiate the next part of the action and the scripted story will move on.

This encouragement of interjections from the audience in response to certain actions or behaviors on stage is deliberate and helps to bring out the conflict between good and evil, or wickedness and innocence, in which the audience is implicitly invited to take sides. This was seen particularly in the behavior in the Penny Gaffs, the rough popular entertainments enjoyed by the poorest audiences in London slums in the nineteenth century. In 1881, a *Sunday Times* correspondent decided to report on the pantomime in one and described how much the young audience encouraged the crude humor, the chases, and the slapstick, shouting at each other as well as the actors and particularly enjoying the clown battering at the actor dressed as a police constable. They were experiencing a kind of catharsis in seeing the characters behave as they might wish to themselves against the forces of law and order, whom they saw as their enemies. This would have been a reversal of the usual partisanship but a sign of their own allegiances.[29] But it was not only in the slums that this occurred. Dickens describes a visit to the Britannia Theatre when the actors were chased by policemen and dropped to the ground "so suddenly as to oblige the policemen to tumble over them, there was much rejoicing among the caps [the men in the gallery]—as though this were a delicate reference to something they had heard of before."[30] The Penny Gaffs no longer exist and nowadays it is less likely that such direct partisanship would occur; nevertheless, audiences still enjoy seeing an authority figure such as a policeman or a teacher come to grief.

Sometimes the audience is asked to behave as extras in the cast. In a modern version of *Sleeping Beauty*,[31] a Captain of the Guard (a descendant of the braggart soldier from the commedia dell'arte) drills the audience in the way to behave when the King and Queen enter. Again there is no logical point to this; it is simply one way of involving the audience and coaxing them, especially the children, into believing for a few minutes that they are at the King's Court. It helps them believe the make-believe.

Mother Primrose [the good fairy] . . . Do they all know how to behave?

Elf. Why, is there some special way?

Mother Primrose. Oh, goodness me. Of course there is. It's known as Court Etiquette.

Captain of the Guard. That's right ma'am. Perhaps we'd better make sure they know the drill. (Addressing the audience) Parade. Listen to me. ER-umph. When the King arrives do you all know how to greet him?

Elf. (in case audience do not respond.) I don't.

Mother Primrose. But perhaps we had better have a rehearsal Captain.

Captain Good idea ma'am. A little extra drill makes for a good soldier. Now when I give the word everybody stand—wait for it, wait for it. STAND UP (Audience to stand encouraged by Mother Pink and the Elf.) Very good. When I mark the time everybody shouts together. One, two three, Long live his Majesty the King. (Repeat two or three times as necessary, improvised according to the response until the fanfare.)

Captain Parade. QUIET. Everybody sit down again.

Mother Primrose. I think they're all very good. The King will be very pleased if you are as loud as that.
(Fanfare of trumpets)

Captain. That's the signal. He'll soon be here. Quick. PARADE, PARADE STAND UP. One, two (A very large Cook played by the Dame, comes up behind him and he stops and turns as she taps him on the shoulder.)

[The scene continues as the Captain is upbraided by the Dame for shouting and making her cakes collapse, which cues a later slapstick cookery scene when everyone becomes covered in dough as they prepare for the Princess's birthday feast. Eventually a second fanfare brings on the King and the audience perform their role.]

In many productions there is an invitation to the children to come on stage
to take part in impromptu action such as simple gestures that they are told
will cause a spell to work or something else to take place. They may receive
a small gift of sweets or a memento. If numbers are too great it will be
restricted to those with a near birthday or under a certain age. Much of this
involvement is unscripted and evidence is circumstantial and implied in reports and comments but it is traditional embellishment.

Most characters will pause for a song, the hero and heroine will perform a
sentimental duet, others will add topical words to a well-known tune. There
has always been a chorus who sing and dance items like "Somewhere Over
the Rainbow" and give "There's no Business like Show Business" for a grand
finale. Every pantomime has an episode of community singing led by the
Dame, who conducts patter songs from song sheets dropped from the flies.
This tradition is believed to have begun with Grimaldi, who sang a song called
"Hot Codlins," in which the audience supplied missing "naughty" words
until the "rude" last verse:

> This little old woman, then up she got,
> All in a fury, hot! hot! hot!
> Says she, 'Such boys sure, never were known;
> They never will let an old woman alone'.
> Now here is a moral, round let it hiss
> If you mean to sell codlins, never get—[piss'd][32]
> Ri tol iddy, iddy, iddy, iddy,
> Ri tol iddy, iddy, ri tol lay.

This was so popular that it continued to be called for after Grimaldi's death.
At Drury Lane in 1870 a visitor said, "Last night from the topmost seats of
a house crowded to suffocation they did their musical duty to perfection."[33]

Ten years later the *Daily Telegraph* was complaining that, despite the encouragement of the conductor who turned his back on the orchestra in invitation to join in the popular songs of the overture, the gallery "was as
artistically solemn as if a Wagner opera were being presented." He recalled
that formerly "the gallery on Boxing Night was the best fun of the evening."[34]

Some thirty years ago, a semi-professional Dame had always sung "There's
a Hole in My Bucket, dear Liza." He would ask one side of the audience to
sing the question and the other side to sing the answer. One year he decided
they must be bored with it and rehearsed something else instead. However,
when he began he was not allowed to continue and was shouted down until
he gave the audience "The Bucket Song," in which they joined with gusto.[35]
Spontaneous community singing seems peculiar to Britain. Football and
rugby (but not cricket) crowds break into sometimes indecent song before,
during, and after the match. The last night of the Promenade Concerts at
the Royal Albert Hall each year finishes with renditions of "Land of Hope

and Glory" and "Auld Lang Syne" sung with feeling by the classical music lovers. While allowing for a release of tension in certain circumstances, it also emphasizes both a sense of community and of continuity.

Part of the fun in performance is the response to topical or satirical references to personalities or affairs, which may arouse as much vociferous behavior as the riots over ticket pricing did. A Frenchman described his visit to *The Prince of Pearls* in 1858 just at the end of the Crimean war. His own patriotic fervor was aroused when Harlequin magicked a tricolor to appear with a three-year-old child representing liberated Turkey. He wrote, "My heart was thumping and I had an overwhelming desire, which fortunately I suppressed, to kiss every pretty English girl in the theatre."[36]

The ambivalence of pantomime presentation and the response to it is summed up in a hostile review of *The Sleeping Beauty and the Beast* in 1900:

The Drury Lane pantomime, that national institution, is a symbol of our Empire. It is the biggest thing of the kind in the world, it is prodigal of money, of invention, of splendor, of men and women; but it is without the sense of beauty or the restraining influence of taste. . . . only an undisciplined nation would have done it. The monstrous, glittering thing of pomp and humor is without order or design; it is a hotch potch of everything that has been on stage; we have the Fairy Prince and the Sleeping Beauty and the quite different legend of Beauty and the Beast, we have President Kruger and the President of the French Republic hinted at in the same figure, . . . we have the motor car, the tuppenny tube and the flying machine, we have a transformation and a harlequinade, we have a coon dance, music-hall songs, ballets, processions, sentimental songs and occasionally even a good joke.[37]

The modern pantomime still draws on these elements of nationalism, fantasy, and spectacle laced with comedy and the audience find their view of themselves as patriots with a sense of ridicule reinforced.

A pantomime is often the first introduction to theatre a child has, whether performed by a professional cast in a large city theatre or in the only theatre in a shabby provincial town or by a cast of amateurs in the local village hall. It has become a traditional presentation for the Christmas season, now ostensibly for children but always containing material to attract their elders, with speciality acts or particular stars from TV. Over the centuries each generation has always said, "It's not like it was in my day," but it continues to evolve and change, adapting itself to the latest taste while still maintaining its original structure. It has even adapted to the World Wide Web on which one can find the nearest performance, read about its history, superstitions, and traditions, view pictures of personalities and performances, or download a script. Maybe this adaptability is its strength, for there are still comedians who specialize in playing the Dame, sometimes girls who play Principal Boys, often an animal that is played by actors. There are usually spectacular transformations and gorgeously outrageous costumes, songs and activities for audience participation, all based on a children's story such as *Cinderella*, or *Aladdin*, in which the good characters overcome the bad to end happily ever after. There is a reciprocity between actors and audience during a pantomime performance that is unlike any other theatrical presentation. What Social Scientists term interactionism, the reciprocal effect that insensibly occurs between groups of people engaging in a communal activity, takes place between those on stage and those in the audience. The familiarity and continuity of these traditions provide a sense of consistent stability in an uncertain world for both adults and children alike.

NOTES

1. Andrew Saint, *A History of the Royal Opera House, Covent Garden, 1732–1982* (London: Royal Opera House, 1982), 42.

2. Alexander Pope, *Poetical Works* (Oxford: Oxford University Press, 1965), 540–41.

3. Hogarth Etching, "A Just View of the British Stage," 1724.

4. Colley Cibber, *An Apology for His Life* (London: J.M. Dent, 1914), 263.

5. Theophilus Cibber, *Lives and Characters of Actors and Actresses 1753,* 68, quoted in Alvin Thaler, *Shakespere to Sheridan* (Cambridge, Mass.: Harvard University Press, 1922), 231.

6. Allardyce Nicoll, *The Garrick Stage: Theatres and Audience in the Eighteenth Century,* ed. Sybil Rosenfeld (Manchester: Manchester University Press, 1981), 134.

7. Michael Booth, *Prefaces to English Nineteenth Century Theatre* (Manchester: Manchester University Press [reprint n.d.]), 149.

8. Allardyce Nicoll, *Development of the Theatre* (London: Harrap, 1927), 190.

9. Michael Booth, *Victorian Spectacular Theatre 1850–1910* (London: Routledge & Kegan Paul, 1981), 89.

10. J.C. Trewin, *The Edwardian Theatre* (Oxford: Blackwell, 1976), 164.

11. Plautus *The Pot of Gold and Other Plays,* trans. E. F. Watling (London: Penguin Books, 1965), 57.

12. Bernard Beckerman, *Theatrical Presentation: Performer, Audience and Act Theatrical,* eds. Gloria Brim Beckerman and William Coco (New York: Routledge, 1990), 111.

13. Edmund Creeth, ed., *Tudor Plays* (Anchor Books, 1966), 82–3.

14. Frederick S. Boas, ed., *Five Pre-Shakespearean Comedies* (Oxford: Oxford University Press, 1970), 209.

15. Beckerman, *Theatrical Presentation,* 117.

16. Adam Phillips, *Houdini's Box on the Arts of Escape* (London: Faber and Faber, 2001), 120.

17. Fitzgerald, *A New History of the English Stage,* 2 vols (London: Tinsley Bros., 1882), vol. 1, 428.

18. Jim Davis, ed., *The Britannia Diaries of Frederick Wilton* (London: Society for Theatre Research, 1992), 89.

19. Ibid., 20.

20. E. V. Lucas, quoted in Gerald Frow, "*Oh Yes It Is!*": *a History of Pantomime* (London: British Broadcasting Corp., 1985), 167.

21. Anon., *The Sleeping Beauty.* Headley Theatre Club, 1972. It is as it was in Shakespeare's day as far as pantomime texts are concerned. There are few published scripts even for professional productions. They guard them and reuse them year after year with additions/alterations/new material. *The Sleeping Beauty* was a production by an amateur theatre group that wrote its own script. There are records of the production on the Web under the name of the Headley Theatre Club.

22. Victor, *History of the London Theatres from the Year 1760* (1771), quoted in V. C. Clinton-Bradley, *All Right on the Night* (London: Putnam, 1954), 212.

23. E. L. Blanchard (1820–89) writer of pantomimes, dramatic critic for the *Daily Telegraph* from 1863 and the *Era* from 1850–1879, quoted in A. E. Wilson, *Pantomime Pageant* (London: Stanley Paul and Co Ltd., 1950), 44.

24. Boas, *Five Pre-Shakespearean Comedies,* 116.

25. Frow, "*Oh Yes It Is!*": *a History of Pantomime,* 101.

26. Anon., *The Sleeping Beauty,* Headley Theatre Club, 1972.

27. Michael Booth, *English Plays of the Nineteenth Century, Vol. 5, Pantomimes, Extravaganzas and Burlesques* (Oxford: Oxford University Press, 1969–76), 400–3.

28. "Love it? Oh Yes We Will; Festive Entertainment," *The Times,* December 1, 2000.

29. Quoted in Sheridan, *Penny Theatres of Victorian London* (London: Society for Theatre Research, 1981), 88.

30. Charles Dickens, *All the Year Round* (1860), quoted in Wilson, *Pantomime Pageant,* 114.

31. Anon., *The Sleeping Beauty,* Headley Theatre Club, 1972.

32. Scott, *The Drama of Yesterday and To-day,* 2 vols. (London: Macmillan and Co. Ltd., 1899), vol. 2, 179.

33. Quoted in A. E. Wilson, *Pantomime Pageant,* 56.

34. Ibid.

35. Personal memory of the author.

36. Francis Wey, *A Frenchman Sees England in the Fifties,* quoted in Wilson, *Pantomime Pageant,* 49.

37. Booth, *Victorian Spectacular Theatre, 1850–1910,* 89.

11

AUDIENCE AT RISK: SPACE AND SPECTATORS AT FEMINIST PERFORMANCE

Judith Sebesta

From 1980 to 1983, a small audience regularly gathered in the living room of the rented home of Patricia Van Kirk in Seattle, Washington. There, the Front Room Theatre Guild (FRTG) produced plays with feminist, lesbian themes for an audience of approximately seventy. Van Kirk describes the room for which the theatre was named as housing "two overstuffed couches, two overstuffed chairs, a dining room table and chairs, and had room to spare. It was just a mammoth square room with a fireplace and bookcases and a trap door that went to the cellar. . . . I think it was built to house a theatre in."[1] Their first production, Sarah Dreher's *This Brooding Sky,* was a choice that, according to Charlotte Canning, was influenced by the "romantic, gothic quality of the room and its furnishings."[2] The FRTG's choice of the space was largely economic—an inexpensive, free location in which to perform productions that they feared would not get a widespread following. But the house was full every night. Their "economic" haven was very likely a spatial haven for audiences. Van Kirk's house may have represented a safe, comfortable space for the audiences as well as the members of the FRTG, drawing on the common image of home as haven.

This theatre and other feminist performers and theatres often have at the heart of their mission the desire to further women's condition in society—to provide a safer world for women, for example. Often they have emphasized communal experience, attempting to provide a "safe" space in which the audience can participate.[3] Ironically, however, some form of risk to the audience, most often emotional, is usually involved in these endeavors, and that risk is often linked to both the location of the performances and the demands on audience members as participants in the event. Audience spaces at various feminist performances often have been chosen to enhance the participation of spectators.[4] As a result, audiences have worked within those spaces, consciously or unconsciously, to shape the performance itself. This chapter will focus on the play of subversion versus fulfillment, of safety versus risk, of efficacy versus inefficacy, among audiences of feminist performances in the United States in the 1970s and 1980s—the peak of feminist performance— and how that play affected the performances, by examining some of the most common spaces in which they occurred: outside in nature and on the street, in the work of Suzanne Lacy and Leslie Labowitz; and inside in the home and at work, as represented by the work of the FRTG, Barbara Smith, the Waitresses, and Lacy. This chapter will further demonstrate how those spaces affected audience participation.

It is necessary, however, to first consider definitions of feminist performance. Because *feminist* is a relative label, there is little point in attempting precise definitions of the term. As Charlotte Canning suggests in *Feminist Theaters in the U.S.A.,* the "project of struggling toward a definition [of feminist theatre], however provisional" is "artificial, exclusionary, and discriminatory." Instead of working toward a definition, Canning focuses on the "uses" of the label "feminist theater groups" by the groups, by those writing about the groups, and by the individuals within the groups,[5] concluding that in its varied manifestations, the analysis of feminist theatre focuses on "performance, in the dramatic texts and the audience/performer interaction; on structure, both in the creative process and the group itself, focusing on the relationship to collectivity and collaboration; and politics, in the extremely varied manifestations of feminisms and the way they shape theatrical expression. All three of these relationships are intertwined in a notion of feminist community."[6] Because Canning's book examines groups that were consciously organized, if only for a brief time, around a commitment to creating theatre, structure or organization plays an important part in her analysis of the groups.

However, structure is less important to this chapter, which examines "theatre" under the more encompassing rubric of "performance," following Peggy Phelan's conception of performance in *Unmarked: The Politics of Performance* as the exchange of gaze across diverse representational mediums.[7] Within this extended conception of performance, events can involve only one performer or might include hundreds, and they might not involve a dramatic text, so "structure" is less important. What is important to this study, and to the women studied, is the performer/spectator dynamic—the various ways that the performers examined configured themselves and any spectators involved (for the presence of spectators separate from the performative action is not a given)—and the politics. Some of the performers examined here call themselves "feminist"; others are indifferent to the term, while some vocally deny it. But no matter what the label or category, all of the performers in this chapter were in some way, and often in addition to other goals, politically invested in women-centered efficacy—that is, investing women with increased power through their performance.

AUDIENCES OUTSIDE IN NATURE AND ON THE STREET

Having found only sporadic opportunity within the architectural confines of traditional theatre spaces, many feminist performers of the past few decades have embraced the various opportunities inherent in using outdoor space. For some women, especially radical feminists, found, undeveloped natural space, relatively untouched by humans, provided an unparalleled background for performances focused on the power of nature itself, and they saw little point in elaborate recreations within architectural theatrical spaces.[8] Natural spaces represented spiritual/communal arenas in which to recoup a collective past and celebrate women.[9] Within these spaces, the line between spectator and performer often blurred, making the performances—like Suzanne Lacy's *Whisper, the Waves, the Wind*—more congruent with modern-day notions of "ritual," focusing on efficacy over entertainment as well as audience participation, than "theatre."[10] Women who performed in the street protested elements on the street that made it unsafe. The street performers examined here, Leslie Labowitz and Suzanne Lacy, used the street as a place for public protest.[11] Whether in nature or on the street, the uninhibited spatial movement possible outdoors mirrored and reinforced the uninhibited, liberating material within the performance, counteracting the tendency in society to teach girls to expect and accept spatial limitation. Also, outdoor locations helped to blur boundaries between art and life, merging artist and audience, fulfilling what performance art historian Lucy Lippard calls a "fundamental notion of feminist art"—exchange,[12] and emphasizing efficacy by working with the audience to get results in order to transform themselves and others.

Transformation—changing the nature or condition of something or someone—is a crucial element in all of these performances, both for performer *and* spectator, and figures in the work of an artist who chose a natural setting for one of her pieces, *Whisper, the Waves, the Wind*. Although Suzanne Lacy rarely works in nature and is not concerned with the spiritual or metaphysical in the same sense as many feminist performers, she deals with the transformation of the "communal psyche" in her work. Through her performances, Lacy has attempted to increase awareness of societal conditions, such as rape or the treatment of the elderly. As Lucy Lippard points out: "Her imagery rarely refers to 'nature' in the environmental sense; she has never made a case for the female identity with and of the earth. Yet her deep and consistent concern for the lives and spirits of women in (and on the peripheries of) this society implicitly involves a respect for the mythical levels of her subjects. And it would be impossible to deal with transformation—which is her primary goal—without acknowledging the psyche."[13] Lacy's subjects are anger and love, violence and empowerment. She plays the shaman, trained in the cultivation of enlightened mental imagery through the use of communal ritual.

Lacy, one of the first and most well-known feminist performance artists, is a veteran of the Woman's Building, where she staged several of her germinal events. Opened in Los Angeles in 1973, the Woman's Building was a continuation of the feminist consciousness-raising performance work begun by artist Judy Chicago in 1970 at the Feminist Art Programs of Fresno State and then the California Institute of the Arts. Through the latter, Chicago, her colleague Miriam Schapiro, and their students designed Womanhouse, an old mansion that they renovated and devoted to feminist art and performance. Dismantled after a brief life, Womanhouse led to the more permanent Woman's Building in 1973 and its principal tenant, The Feminist Studio Workshop, and some of the most cutting-edge performance work in the country. The Workshop nurtured the talents of many groups and individuals in Los Angeles—the Waitresses, Barbara Smith, Rachel Rosenthal, Terry Wolverton and the Oral Herstory of Lesbianism, Leslie Labowitz, the Feminist Art Workers, and Suzanne Lacy. By 1974, Lacy was teaching for the Feminist Studio Workshop, and in 1977, collaborated on two events that represented major steps in the development of feminist performance, bringing it out into the open as public media events.[14] *Three Weeks in May* and *In Mourning and in Rage* focused on feminist, action-oriented issues, such as rape. But starting in 1979, Lacy's artistic concerns shifted from the rather angry, specific agendas of her previous protest/demonstration pieces to more comprehensive issues related to women's histories and communities, and she began building large-scale projects that gently gave voice to communities of women often silenced by society.

Lacy set one such work, *Whisper, the Waves, the Wind,* on a beach at Children's Cove in La Jolla, California, against a backdrop of blue skies, crashing waves, and swooping seagulls. Supported by the Older Women's League and various San Diego arts organizations, Lacy began working on the project early in 1983 with the help and advice of a steering committee of fifteen women over the age of sixty-five. Lacy led a series of meetings and media events educating the non-senior community about issues concerning the older women, and the year's work culminated in the beach performance on May 19, 1984. According to Lacy, it was about "the plight of older women's cultural invisibility, the potential loss of dignity and respect we face as we age, and the resources that this society shuts off in its flight from death. . . . but it will also be above and beyond being a woman. It's about being in a body that's part of a life process, a cycle, like the wash of waves on the beach."[15] Two secluded, adjacent coves provided the performance space, and an audience gathered to observe the event from the cliffs above. On May 19, the beach was deserted (thanks to help from municipal agencies), and Lacy arranged twenty-six card tables with white tablecloths and four white chairs on one beach, thirteen identical seating arrangements on the other. The weather was beautiful, the setting idyllic.

Sounds emitting from speakers placed on the cliffs heralded the start of the performance. Susan Stone's taped score, played during the entire event, opened with a collage of women's voices, their conversations layered with laughter, waves, the cries of gulls, and the blast of foghorns, as the participants, 160 women between the ages of sixty-five and one hundred and of diverse national, ethnic, and socio-economic backgrounds, entered dressed completely in white. Each one was escorted to a seat at a table by male and female monitors—volunteers from the community—also dressed in white. As the tables filled, the women began to speak to one another, too distant from the spectators gathered on the cliffs to be heard. The sound score ebbed and flowed until the tape turned entirely to dialogue: "Young people look at me and see the end of the line. This makes me angry, very angry." "I compare myself to the rest of nature. Everything wilts." "I want to live because it's so much fun to be alive, so this would be a hell of a time to *die!*" Audience members gathered around the speakers, straining to hear the words that they mistakenly took for conversations among the women below them on the beach. They could not hear the actual exchanges of the women, who before the performance had been given such questions about the cycle of life to discuss as: "How do you feel about the physical process of aging? Has age brought freedom, or a different philosophy of life?" After an hour, the white-clad monitors invited the spectators to wander down the cliff steps to the beach, to sit where chairs had been deliberately left open and join in the conversations. Most of those who accepted the invitation were younger than the performers. Toward the end of the performance, the tide began to come in, underscoring "the evolving of human life cycles so evident on the beach."[16] In her description of the event, Lucy Lippard relates the reactions of some spectators: "The audience's tears were an admission of identification, accompanied by many emotions, among them love, guilt, pride, fear, regret, and memory. At the end, a sobbing student helper was offered comfort and he said, "It's okay. It's good for me. I never cry." A young woman rushed off to call her grandmother. The presence of absent women was almost tangible."[17] Two hours after they appeared, the participants and spectators began their exodus from the beach, crying, exuberant, smiling, talking.

Lacy set *Whisper, the Waves, the Wind* in the San Diego area because of its large retirement community.[18] That the performance occurred in Southern California was no doubt largely because the artist is from the area, but the proximity of the location to Hollywood and its myths and images of the ideal American woman (young) might have lent pathos to the plight of the elderly women on the beach. Lacy chose the beach location for a number of reasons. According to Lacy herself, the beach setting was intended to underscore the cyclical themes of *Whisper, The Waves, the Wind*: "It's about being in a body that's part of a life process, a cycle, like the wash of waves on the beach."[19]

Indeed, during the latter part of the performance, the tide started coming in, forcing the monitors to interrupt the performance in order to move the tables further up the beach; the rising tide and the performers' response to it emphasized the theme of inevitable, unceasing cycles.

The oceanside location also supported Lacy's populist vision, in which art is public and accessible in order to disseminate its message widely and enhance performer/spectator interaction and exchange. According to Diane Rothenberg, an anthropologist who has studied Lacy's work extensively, "Lacy believes in the possibility of changing the world through art making . . . in the direct appeal to a mass audience. For Lacy there is a continual push in the direction of making works public and accessible because of the urgency of the message contained. The gesture is populist, as is much of the performance art emanating from a feminist orientation; Lacy has a vision of an expanded audience that includes those not familiar with contemporary art and not accustomed to accepting political stimuli to action through art. . . . Her proposed audience is not the hermetic art world, though they are certainly invited—it is society."[20] At Children's Cove, all of society was given access to *Whisper, the Waves, the Wind;* no tickets were taken, no admission charged, no limit to the number of spectators save their ability to find a space along the cliffs, and approximately one thousand people observed the well-publicized (through a variety of media) event. The beach location enabled Lacy to present her own ideas, through the performers, to a potentially more diverse spectatorship, to an audience that might not attend a performance within the confines of an architectural theatre space. It also provided an environment conducive to performer/spectator exchange. Although the height of the cliffs provided a natural barrier between the audience and the action below, steps leading from those cliffs down to the sand insured that there was no Wagnerian "mystic chasm" that in a "traditional" theatrical environment might prove daunting to anyone encouraged to cross. And according to observer Lucy Lippard, Lacy managed to create a feeling of intimacy during the event despite the grandeur of the location: "The whole piece created an extraordinary intimacy. We saw the faces of the performers up close, one by one, as they proceeded down to the beach . . . Despite the noise and passersby, I was drawn *into* this spectacle as I am in the quiet privacy of a dark theater."[21] Undoubtedly, the pleasant picture that Lacy painted on the beach (the glistening tables and women against a backdrop of white sand and blue skies) coupled with the compelling sensitivity of the piece and the likely conditioning of the audience to view the beach as a pleasant place for play, drew the audience members into it, both physically and emotionally. And as Diane Rothenberg points out, "Particularly when the audience replaced the women on the beach in La Jolla there was a hint at issues of generation sequencing and replacement."[22] This audience participation was obviously crucial to the meaning of the piece. It enlarged and expanded the experience of the performers as well as the spectators; exchange with nature and each other led to the retrieval of a collective past, transformation, harmony, and, ultimately, power.

During the 1970s and 1980s, feminist performers demonstrated that locating women in the space of *culture,* where society has transformed natural space to meet its needs, could lead to equally powerful events through their use of the street as performative space. Although, like the performances that occurred in nature, these events took place outdoors, they took on a whole different set of connotations related to the *man-*made environment. The feminist performances on the streets were often designed to "take back" those streets, to empower women and transform perspectives of them from victims to women in control. They were often performances of protest, using the open, easily accessible spaces to gather large groups together to speak out against some societal condition. The artists were more pragmatists than mystics or spiritualists, choosing to isolate specific feminist issues in their performances and locating them on the streets for maximum visibility and performer/spectator exchange. Much of this work came out of Southern California's art community and included collectives as well as individuals.

Leslie Labowitz, born in 1946, grew up in Southern California and attended the Otis Art Institute in Los Angeles. In 1972, she traveled to Germany to study with Joseph Beuys. For four years, Labowitz developed a body of feminist performances—*Menstruation Wait, To Please a Man, Today is Mother's Day,* and *Paragraph 18*—influenced by the theories and practices of Beuys, Bertolt Brecht, and the Russian Constructivists. She also began developing strategies to control media coverage of her events so that the feminist messages of the work would be "clear." When she returned to Southern California in 1976, she became involved with the increasingly vital community of feminist artists there and began work on a large-scale, public, media-centered events.

On December 13, 1977, Labowitz and Suzanne Lacy, who had met during an earlier collaboration titled *Three Weeks in May,* staged *In Mourning and in Rage.* They designed the large-scale, public performance specifically to address the media, whose sensational coverage of the Hillside Strangler, a Los Angeles serial killer who had taken his tenth victim a few months before, had further terrorized the women of the city by helping to cultivate the image of woman as victim. Their purpose was twofold: to provide a public space for women to come together to share their grief and rage through a ritual, and to provide a framework for the participation of women's organizations and governmental representatives who wanted to share in the collective statement against the violence.[23] Unstated but implicit in their work was the desire to position the media as an audience member in order to implicate the media as a participant in the violence—and to utilize it to spread their message of anti-violence just as they had spread messages of violence through their sensationalistic reporting of the events surrounding the Hillside Strangler.

In Mourning and in Rage began when seventy women dressed in black met at the Woman's Building. Soon ten actresses came out of the building to join them. They all formed a motorcade—the actresses in a black hearse, the others in twenty-two cars with signs that read "Funeral" and "Stop Violence Against Women"—and processed to City Hall, where a large group, including the news media, waited. There, the ten seven-foot-tall veiled mourners, nine dressed in black, the leader in scarlet, emerged from the hearse and approached the steps in the front of city hall. The rest of the women formed a chorus on either side of the steps, unfurling banners that read "In Memory of our Sisters, Women Fight Back." They paused as the media positioned itself all around. Then each mourner in turn approached a microphone and made a statement that connected the Hillside Strangler cases with the greater picture of nationwide violence toward women. The first mourner proclaimed, "I am here for the ten women who have been raped and strangled between October 18 and November 29!" while the last of the nine mourners said, "I am here to mourn the reality of violence against women." To each, the chorus echoed, "In memory of our sisters, we fight back!" while the leader wrapped the mourner in a brilliant red scarf. After each mourner received her red cloak, the unveiled leader in scarlet forcefully declared, "I am here for the *rage* of all women. I am here for women fighting back!" For the remainder of the event, the artists read a brief explanation of the rationale behind the piece, a member of the Los Angeles Commission on Assaults Against Women read a prepared list of three demands for women's self-defense, and the singer Holly Near performed as the audience joined in a spontaneous circle dance.

Like their two previous events, Lacy and Labowitz carefully choreographed this event with the media in mind, in an attempt to control coverage that is rarely "feminist" in its reporting. As the mourners traveled in their motorcade, a woman was at City Hall, preparing press arrivals for the subsequent event. During the performance, this woman and others directed the press to obtain the footage that would best represent the piece's conceptions and convey to the women in the media audience the feminist ideas being presented. The artists used the media's own language of high drama and arresting visuals in creating the event, ever mindful of the camera lens;[24] they designed a banner reading "In Memory of Our Sisters We Fight Back" to fit the proportions of a television.[25] The performance was featured that evening on most major television newscasts and received some national attention, although it is doubtful that Labowitz and Lacy's attempts to direct the press led to its complete "feminization." However, the media as audience member had a profound affect on the event itself, causing the creators to carefully arrange and choreograph the event within the public space to allow for its maximum mediatization. The media also became a catalyst for extending the visibility of the piece and its message, creating a whole new (television) audience for it that otherwise would not have existed.

Labowitz and Lacy's work, which promoted the democratization of art, is similar to other radical street theatre of the late 1960s and 1970s. According to Henry Lesnick in his introduction to *Guerilla Street Theater,* street theatre is a return to the communal drama of earlier societies and eschews "the alienation of the players from the audience which is a manifestation of the social fragmentation caused by the division of labor of class society" that results in the theatre "industry," in which performance becomes a commodity for sale to an anonymous audience.[26] Street theatre "represents not only an attempt to bridge the gulf between players and audience, but also an attempt to provide a new model for the relationship between society and social reality; that is, it suggests that social reality can be influenced and even determined by the members of society through collective action."[27] With their performance events, both Labowitz and Lacy seemed to be attempting to create a communal experience in which the audience is drawn into the collective action of the event and persuaded to transfer the message of the action to society. The street provided an excellent space for such creation. It promoted maximum visibility for the performers, as well as maximum exchange between performers and a twofold audience. Furthermore, performing in the street, where large numbers gathered without paying admission, allowed Labowitz and Lacy to eschew theatre as a commodified product and embrace theatre as a democratized, communal experience—and, ultimately, to make room for the all-important media-as-audience.

AUDIENCES INSIDE AT HOME AND AT WORK

At the same time that feminist artists were challenging the spatial boundaries imposed on them by society, locating performances outside both in nature and on the street, performers also were working within those boundaries to expand notions of what they could contain. For centuries, women's movement and activity have been confined mainly to the home, an image long associated with women. Leslie Kanes Weisman, in *Discrimination by Design: A Feminist Critique of the Man-Made Environment,* points out: "Women's social and biological roles, and the human attributes and emotions associated with them, merge in the strong and cherished image of the dwelling."[28] Long relegated to the home, women made a place for themselves within it; when men began to equate this space with femininity, women had little choice but to accept the association. Conversely, when women were "allowed" out of the home and into the workplace, they were again confined to male-defined roles and "appropriate" tasks and places of employment. Feminist artists of the 1970s and 1980s would challenge such confinement of women, locating their performances both within the home and the workplace for a variety of reasons but all proving that the so-called private and public spheres of home and workplace are not so bifurcated, and that women could choose to "belong" anywhere they wanted. This section examines the work of one performer, Barbara Smith, who chose "domestic" spaces for her performance, as well as the work of the Waitresses and Suzanne Lacy, each of whom chose the workplace as the site of their performances.[29]

Since the nineteenth century, the home has come to be viewed as an idealized, safe haven and the center of women's activities.[30] Such attitudes about the home pervaded the performances of the Front Room Theatre Guild, mentioned at the beginning of this chapter. The audiences, relaxing in the intimate, comfortable living room, no doubt helped to provide a welcoming atmosphere for the Guild's sometimes extreme, often hilarious lesbian viewpoints. They also inform Barbara Smith's piece *Feed Me.* On February 2 and 3, 1973, the Museum of Conceptual Art in San Francisco hosted an all-night series of art and performance titled *All Night Sculptures.* In Smith's installation, she created a "boudoir environment" in a small room at the gallery, filling it with rugs, pillows, a mattress, and other personal items. Incense burned and a heater kept the space warm. From dark until dawn, Smith, nude, received visitors, who were encouraged to choose a medium of interaction, something with which to "feed" the naked, exposed woman: oils and perfumes for rubs, food and wine, tea, books, music, flowers, even marijuana. According to Smith: "It was all a source of food—food meaning sustenance. This could include conversation and affection." The only limit that Smith placed on the visitors was that their interactions be "positive": "I didn't want anyone who wasn't positive, whose emotions weren't positive towards me. I would have felt very defensive about that, and I would prevent any action which I did not consider food."[31] How Smith was able to gauge the positivity of her guests'/audience's emotions is unsure.

Although Smith did not perform *Feed Me* in her own, or anyone else's, house, she transformed the small room in the gallery from a bare, stark space to a home-like environment—personalized with Smith's own possessions. In this room private acts and images of domesticity (nudity, massage, eating, personal possessions) became public. Smith's environment was designed to take advantage of "traditional" connotations surrounding the image of the home: home as a safe, nurturing space. This environment, and ideally the spectator/participants within it, in turn aided Smith in the completion of her performative goals, which Jeannie Forte describes as "unabashed exploration of new possibilities boldly assert[ing] her ownership of her body and her desire, allowing for both vulnerability and strength. . . . Smith's work invited the re-examination of cultural standards as well as participants' own sexuality."[32] However, although she questioned "cultural standards," Smith, in taking advantage of prevailing attitudes about the home as haven, seemed to have no interest in questioning society's perceptions of the home and a woman's place within it. She was even criticized by feminists for promoting the image of woman as courtesan or odalisque.[33] Furthermore, inadvertently, Smith played with notions of public and private, transferring what are traditionally considered private acts to a public (gallery) space. Although the space may have been safe and nurturing for Smith, it might not have seemed so to the visitors, witnessing private acts in what was, no matter how it was disguised from the inside, a public space. Indeed, their very presence transformed the space from private to public. And, as with any solo performance, they were essential to the event-as-performance, as was their willingness to "take risks" by becoming active participants.

If women historically have had little control over domestic spaces, they have had even less within public buildings, where they have been either excluded or relegated to inferior spaces. Such institutions as churches, universities, and theatres, among others, all have a history of gender-based exclusion and segregation. But, since the inception of the industrial revolution, this has been particularly true in the workplace.[34] It was under a cloud of seemingly unending occupational inequality that some feminist performers—such as the Waitresses and Suzanne Lacy—chose to perform in the workplace.

Not surprisingly, the restaurant as a workplace teeming with inequality became the target of feminist artists during the 1970s. The Woman's Building in Los Angeles, birthplace of so many pivotal feminist performers, spawned one such group of artists, the Waitresses, in 1977. Founded by six former waitresses—Jerri Allyn, Leslie Belt, Anne Gauldin, Patti Nicklaus, Jamie Wildman-Webber, and Denise Yarfitz—the group converted their experiences in restaurants into performance art that explored the stereotype of the "waitress." According to Allyn, "waitress" is a metaphor for the position of women universally as a mother/nurturer, a servant/slave, and a sex object: "I think often people don't realize that there are a lot of other expectations tied in with food and being served. Also, within the restaurant business, the waitress is far lower on the social ladder than the waiter."[35] Jeanie Forte points out that the Waitresses "have foregrounded the connections between images of femininity, women's oppression, and the patriarchy. . . . Apart from the obvious content regarding the exploitation of women in underpaid labor, these performances evoke an awareness of Woman as a sign, blatantly portraying the master/slave relationship inherent in her exploitation; Woman is merely the negative in relation to Man; a sign for the opposite of man, in service to his needs and dominance."[36] The Waitresses, in themselves, had found an excellent metaphor for the inequalities between women and men in the workforce—and beyond.

Belying the seriousness of the content of their work, the Waitresses' performances were both campy and satirical. Although they performed in "conventional" settings—art galleries and theatres—much of their work was presented in front of employees and patrons of various Los Angeles restaurants, such as the Brown Derby and Sneaky Pete's, in both "guerilla" and pre-planned events. Wearing white coffee-shop-style uniforms, the women burst into an eatery, presenting various personas to the bewildered customers. One woman posed as a variation of the Bionic Woman, "Wonder Waitress," who "helps the harried and hassled waitresses of the world by confronting impatient customers and nasty employers.[37] Another played the Waitress Goddess Diana wearing a soft sculpture with multiple breasts, a debased modern version of the nurturing goddess. Still another, armed with oversized radar equipment, ran through the restaurant reporting on hazards to waitresses spotted at such stereotyped, hypothetical locations as "The Greasy Spoon," "The Hole in the Wall," "The Grinder," and "Mom's Kitchen," all of which hire waitresses strictly for their looks, then force them to run between tables in three-inch heels. Sometimes the group presented "Millie Awards" in an ironic, Oscar-like ceremony to outstanding area waitresses.[38] The Waitresses blurred lines between art and life, performing/demonstrating in spaces that undoubtedly contained a captive audience either already indoctrinated to the issues against which they demonstrated, or guilty right at that moment of the attitudes against which they protested. By performing in coffee shops and restaurants, the Waitresses were able to make what was already public even more visible, creating a sort of "metapublic."

Unfortunately, no record exists of the audience reaction to the Waitresses' "invisible theatre," beyond that they often looked "bewildered."[39] One can imagine, however, how uncomfortable many spectators might have been as they found themselves implicated in the oppression of waitresses portrayed by the performers. And, as is the danger of invisible theatre, their reaction on discovering the "theatrical" nature of what unfolded before them (and they likely did discover this) might have included anger at being "fooled," feeling at risk in such an out-of-control position. This would be somewhat counterintuitive to the goals of the performance, which would have been to incite anger against the patriarchal hegemony that contributed to the plight of the waitress in the first place—not anger directed at the Waitresses themselves. But regardless of what it was, audience reaction to the Waitresses would have certainly been a part of the performance itself.

Suzanne Lacy helped to alleviate the image of the office tower as a cold, anonymous environment in which to work, if only for a day, when in 1987 she staged a new version of her 1984 beach piece, *Whisper, the Waves, the Wind*, in the lobby of a Minneapolis skyscraper. She was invited by the Minneapolis College of Art and Design for a six-month residency beginning in September of 1984. Lacy accepted, hoping to use the residency as a springboard to a longer project in Minneapolis: a large-scale performance thematically relevant to the city that continued Lacy's previous work on aging. With the California *Whisper* experience behind her, Lacy knew the importance of community support to such a work, and for a year she sought the interest and support of the Minnesota Council on Aging, the Humphrey Institute of the University of Minnesota, Minneapolis feminist theatre At The Foot of the Mountain, community leaders, and others; her collaborators became Susan Stone, Lacy's sound engineer and composer for *Whisper;* Miriam Schapiro, who with Judy Chicago developed Womanhouse; Phyllis Jane Rose, director of At the Foot of the Mountain; and local quilter Jeannie Spears.

Slowly *The Crystal Quilt* began to take shape. The project received a "boost" when B.C.E.D. Properties, Inc. donated office space in the high-profile Investors Diversified Services Building (better known as the "I.D.S. Building") downtown, a mirrored glass skyscraper designed by the prolific architect Phillip Johnson, as well as the use of the building's lobby, known as the Crystal Court because it is constructed of tiers of glass, for the performance and its preparation. In all, a pool of fifteen hundred volunteers, half over the age of sixty-five, worked to realize the performance that took place three years after *Whisper, the Waves, the Wind* on Mother's Day, May 10, 1987.

On that day, several thousand viewers gathered on balconies above the floor of the large Crystal Court, and a living quilt of black, yellow, and red unfolded before them. At the start of the performance, four hundred older women from throughout the state of Minnesota, each wearing black, entered, proceeding ceremoniously to one hundred tables covered in black cloths. When the women had seated themselves, four to a table, they unfolded the black tablecloths to reveal red and yellow patterns beneath. As the women talked among themselves, they slowly moved their arms and hands in unison, a sort of "laying on of hands," altering the patterns viewed from above through their choreographed movements. This dance of the arms was accompanied by Susan Stone's taped sounds indigenous to Minnesota: local women speaking of growing old, their fears and memories; Native American songs; thunder claps; loon cries; and church bells. The tape ended with outspoken octogenarian Meridel LeSeur, famous for her writings and radical activism, exclaiming, "I say I'm not aging, I'm ripening." At the conclusion of the piece, some audience members went down to the floor, taking hand-painted scarves to the performers and engaging them in conversation. The work slowly dissolved. This action by the audience members was crucial to the piece; as Diane Rothenberg points out, the performance " . . . progressed from art into life as the stunning image was broken by the audience, which was invited to intrude, and as the performers were reabsorbed from their liminal condition of isolation and elevation into real life, embodied by the audience."[40] This "elevation into real life" could not have occurred without the presence and eventual participation of the audience members, and their need to participate, to engage with the performers and images presented below them, was likely heightened by the rather cold architecture of the building juxtaposed with the warmth of the living quilt.

The Crystal Quilt embraced culture in the form of a highly architecturalized environment, the Crystal Court of the I.D.S. Building, and the advantages that came with it, such as office space for preparations. Rothenberg claims that the performers "were protected from the world of nature by the world of culture and social structure inherent in the architecture of a commercial center."[41] However, viewing the project as a clash between nature and culture seems inaccurate because nothing in the taped dialogue led the audience to believe that Lacy saw nature as the root of the problems associated with aging.

Lucy Lippard seems more accurate in her assessment of the locating of the project in a skyscraper when she writes that "in Minneapolis, potluck became patchwork as the black-clad women brought 'home' to an impersonal corporate environment."[42] Lacy personalized the skyscraper, adding a human element to the glass and steel structure with her living quilt. The quilt, with its history in this country as a unique artistic outlet for American pioneer women, hungry to express themselves, as a source of relief from isolation for the women who gathered for "quilting bees" and, more humbly, as a source of warmth, became an ironic image against the backdrop of cold steel and glass. On that Mother's Day in 1987, women seemed to belong in the skyscraper, transforming it from a "Cathedral of Commerce," to a more inviting chapel of community.

CONCLUSION

The artists examined here, the places in which they performed, and the audiences who viewed and participated in their performances, are not meant to be a comprehensive overview of audience participation in feminist performance during the past thirty years. But they are a representative sampling of the kind of work that was being done, of the places in which it was done, and of the audiences who attended and affected the events. Feminists also have performed in churches, in universities, at conferences, in traditional theatre spaces, even in cyberspace. But the "marginalized" spaces examined here often helped to prepare the audiences for a certain emotional risk that was conducive to the missions of the performances, while avoiding physical risk— or facing it head on, if necessary. They enhanced the building of a community of women and men committed to promoting the equality of, or celebrating the uniqueness of, women, while often questioning the patriarchal status quo by eschewing traditional spaces and conventional spectator/audience configurations. They demanded an active, engaged audience willing to risk their own emotional and intellectual safety in order to, in Brechtian fashion, leave the spaces empowered and, ideally, prepared to empower others.

NOTES

1. Charlotte Canning, *Feminist Theaters in the U.S.A.: Staging Women's Experience* (London: Routledge, 1996), 106.
2. Ibid.
3. In her *Feminist Theaters in the U.S.A.*, Charlotte Canning includes a chapter titled "The Community as Audience," in which she examines both ways that some feminist theatres (none of which are examined here) "initiated contact with their audiences other than in the actual moment of performance" (182) and the performer/spectator relationship in general.
4. Gay McCauley, in *Space in Performance: Making Meaning in the Theatre* (Ann Arbor: University of Michigan Press, 1999), examines related issues: "Emerging from

many recent discussions of theatre space is the vital and somewhat mysterious question of the way the arrangement of auditorium and presentational space facilitate (or impede) the flows of energy between the two" (58).

5. Canning, *Feminist Theatres*, 29.

6. Ibid., 32.

7. Peggy Phelan, *Unmarked: The Politics of Performance* (London: Routledge, 1993), 4.

8. Jill Dolan, in *The Feminist Spectator as Critic* (Ann Arbor: University of Michigan Press, 1988), describes radical feminism—also termed cultural feminism—as the attempt to "reverse the gender hierarchy by theorizing female values as superior to male. . . . The revelation of women's experience and intuitive, spiritual connection with each other and the natural world is idealized as the basis of cultural feminist knowledge" (6–7).

9. Such works as Simone de Beauvoir's *The Second Sex* (New York: Knopf, 1953) and Claude Lévi-Strauss's study *The Elementary Structures of Kinship* (Boston: Beacon Press, 1959) encouraged women to delve more deeply into their own sex's attempts to explore and control the natural world around them. *Woman, Culture, and Society* (Stanford: Stanford University Press, 1974), edited by Michelle Zimbalist Rosaldo and Louise Lamphere, Mary Daly's *Beyond God the Father: Toward a Philosophy of Women's Liberation* (Boston: Beacon Press, 1973) and *Gyn/Ecology: The Metaethics of Radical Feminism* (Boston: Beacon Press, 1978), as well as Susan Griffin's *Woman and Nature: The Roaring Inside Her* (New York: Harper & Row, 1978) and Charlene Spretnak's *The Politics of Women's Spirituality* (Garden City, N.J.: Anchor Press, 1982), are just a few of the books that investigated ancient spirituality and woman's relationship to nature, even suggesting that in mythic and prehistoric times, women (often symbolized by a "Great Goddess" figure) dominated. They inspired the development of new women's rituals that were designed to create and maintain a feminist culture.

10. Other feminist performances located in nature include M. L. Sowers's *Protective Coloring* (1973), Mary Beth Edelson's *See For Yourself* (1977), Donna Henes's *Cocoon Ceremony* (1979), and the Mt. Tamalpais rituals of 1980.

11. Other feminist performances located on the street include the Feminist Art Workers's *Traffic in Women: A Feminist Vehicle* (1978) and Lacy's *Three Weeks in May* (1976). Protests such as the N.O.W. Abortion Rights March in Washington, D.C., on April 9, 1989, could be considered a part of these "performances" as well.

12. Lucy R. Lippard, *The Pink Glass Swan: Selected Essays on Feminist Art* (New York: New Press, 1995), 215.

13. Lucy R. Lippard, "Lacy: Some of Her Own Medicine," *TDR* 32.1 (1988), 73.

14. Josephine Withers, "Feminist Performance Art: Performing, Discovering, Transforming Ourselves" in *The Power of Feminist Art: The American Movement of the 1970s, History and Impact,* ed. Norma Broude and Mary D. Garrard (New York: Abrams, 1994), 170.

15. Suzanne Lacy and Lucy R. Lippard, "Political Performance Art," *Heresies* 5.1 (1984), 24.

16. Stephanie Arnold, "Theatre Reports: Suzanne Lacy's *Whisper, the Waves, the Wind*," *TDR* 29.1 (1985), 130.

17. Lippard, *Pink Glass Swan*, 219.

18. Ibid.

19. Lacy and Lippard, "Political," 29.

20. Diane Rothenberg, "Social Art/Social Action," *TDR* 32.1 (1988), 62.

21. Lippard, *Pink Glass Swan*, 218–219.

22. Rothenberg, 65.

23. Leslie Labowitz-Starus and Suzanne Lacy, "In Mourning and In Rage," *Frontiers* 3.1 (1978), 54.

24. Suzanne Lacy, "In Mourning and in Rage (with Analysis Aforethought)," *Femicide: The Politics of Woman Killing,* ed. Jill Radford and Diana E. H. Russell (New York: Twayne, 1992), 321.

25. Yolanda M. Lopez and Moira Roth, "Social Protest: Racism and Sexism," *The Power of Feminist Art: The American Movement of the 1970s, History and Impact,* ed. Norma Broude and Mary D. Garrard, (New York: Abrams, 1994), 149.

26. Henry Lesnick, ed., *Guerrilla Street Theater.* (New York: Avon, 1973), 12.

27. Ibid., 13.

28. Leslie Kanes Weisman, *Discrimination by Design: A Feminist Critique of the Man-Made Environment,* (Chicago: University of Illinois Press, 1992), 7.

29. Leslie Labowitz's 1980 *Sproutime* fits within the rubric of "domestic" feminist performance; in it, audiences moved through Labowitz's house as she told stories about the benefits of sprouts, simultaneously serving samples. Other examples of feminist performances in the "workplace" in its various forms include the work of the Women's Guerilla Theater and the Omaha Magic Theatre.

30. It was the Victorian era and its cult of female domesticity that intensified the notion of the private house as a place of sanctuary and renewal. Although home and work had been virtually inseparable up to the nineteenth century, the Industrial Revolution forced a split between the two, and the home provided a safe haven from the ruthless economic ambition and individualism of industrialized society. This idealized view of the home, typically single-family and suburban, has continued until today. See Weisman for an analysis of this phenomenon.

31. Moira Roth, "Interview with Barbara Smith," Exhibit Catalogue, *Barbara Smith.* La Jolla, Calif.: San Diego Art Gallery, 1974. Rpt. in *Performance Anthology: Sourcebook of California Performance Art,* eds. Carl E. Loeffler and Darlene Tong, (San Francisco: Contemporary Arts Press, 1989), 118.

32. Jeanie Forte, "Women's Performance Art: Feminism and Postmodernism," *Performing Feminisms: Feminist Critical Theory and Theatre* (Baltimore, Md.: Johns Hopkins University Press, 1990), 262.

33. Roth, "Interview," 118. Smith claims that she accepted "affection" from her guests/audience, but it is unclear as to whether or not this included any sexual acts.

34. Generally, "women's" jobs, including administrative support, private household workers, and service workers, pay less and offer fewer benefits than occupations, such as management, that are considered "men's" jobs. Daphne Spain, in her *Gendered Spaces* (Chapel Hill: University of North Carolina Press, 1992), offers one explanation for the "wage gap"—Mincer and Polachek's "human capitol theory":

> They argue that women invest less than men in acquiring labor-market skills because they expect to work less than men throughout their lives. According to this theory, women anticipate family-related absences from the labor force and choose occupations that can be easily entered and left. These occupations offer little on-the-job training or potential wage growth because employers will invest less in a transitory labor force. (226)

35. Jan Alexander-Leitz, "Serving Up Food For Thought," *Ms.* (March 1980), 19.

36. Forte, 252–3.

37. Moira Roth, ed., *The Amazing Decade: Women and Performance Art in America,* (Los Angeles: Astro Artz, 1983), 142.

38. Alexander-Leitz, 19.

39. Ibid. Although not the inventor of "invisible theatre," Augusto Boal has become the main disseminator of this form in the late-twentieth century, particularly as it relates to addressing forms of aggression central to the capitalist system. Many theorists consider invisible theatre related to, or even the same as, guerilla theatre, mentioned earlier in the essay. For more information on Boal's theories on invisible theatre, see his *Theatre of the Oppressed,* trans. Charles A. and Maria-Odilia Leal McBride (New York: TCG, 1979).

40. Rothenberg, 62.

41. Ibid., 70.

42. Lippard, "Lacy," 74.

12

"WALKING IN THE STEPS OF YOUR FOREFATHERS": LOCATING THE ACTOR AND THE AUDIENCE IN DERRY'S SIEGE PAGEANT

Patrick Tuite

Since 1997, the Crimson Players Drama Group has staged an annual pageant to commemorate Derry's successful defense during the Jacobite siege of 1688–89.[1] The Crimson Players perform their pageant outdoors during the city's Maiden City Festival. The Apprentice Boys of Derry organize the festival and its various events in the first week of August. The Apprentice Boys are a unionist marching institution with strong links to Northern Ireland's loyalist organizations, and their festival reaches its climax with a parade of over ten thousand Apprentice Boys and flute bands on the final day.[2] Scholars representing a variety of disciplines have described the dramatic aspects of Northern Ireland's most contentious parades.[3] This chapter examines the Siege Pageant alone, identifying the importance of its audience and the changing contexts in which its organizers stage the outdoor performance. The pageant's stylistic elements and historical content offer answers to questions regarding the role of the audience in similar productions.

This chapter investigates the Crimson Players' annual pageant in order to answer the following questions: If Northern Ireland's most contentious parades and Derry's Siege Pageant commemorate the same historical events, why do bystanders react differently to each? Who actually attends the pageant, and what does a sympathetic audience member expect of the performance? How does the environment in which the Crimson Players stage their pageant shape the audience's response to it? How and when do audience members interact with the performance? Finally, Derry City constitutes a deeply divided community. Given these political and religious divisions, what do the pageant's actors and patrons hope their performances will do to or for their audience?

THE SIEGE AND ITS REENACTMENT

No outside observer can understand Derry's Siege Pageant or the audience's reaction to it without first knowing the history that the pageant dramatizes. I will reduce that history to its bare essentials, but even the barest essentials, or reconstituted versions of them, still dominate Northern Ireland's politics and culture today. Three wars between mainly Catholic Irish and Protestant English forces raged across the island during the seventeenth century. In 1603, the end of the Nine Years' War resulted in the defeat of rebellious Gaelic Chieftains and their Spanish allies, the confiscation of their land, and the plantation of English and Scottish settlers in Ulster. In 1641, a confederation of Catholic forces, including Gaelic Chieftains and Old English Royalists, rebelled, claiming to fight in defense of Charles I in Ireland against English Puritans. Many Protestants who had settled in Ulster after the Nine Years War lost their lives in the 1641 uprising. Oliver Cromwell crushed the Gaelic Irish and Old English lords and his forces confiscated even more property. In 1660, the English Parliament restored Charles II to the throne. However, Charles II died in 1685, and his brother James II accessed to the throne. James was a Catholic, and when he baptized his son a Catholic, the English Parliament moved against him. They asked the husband of James' daughter, the Protestant William of Orange, to be their king. Most of the war that followed took place in Ireland, and one of the war's most important battles happened around the walled city of Derry.[4] In fact, Derry suffered three serious attacks in the seventeenth century, but the city's most popular unionist commemoration glorifies its longest siege.[5]

Both the Apprentice Boys' parades and the pageant remember the events surrounding the 1688–89 siege. In 1688, forces supporting James II marched to Derry in order to occupy the stronghold for their King. Derry's apprentices refused to open the city's gates for the approaching Jacobite forces. The city's inhabitants rallied in support of William of Orange and refused the orders of James' Catholic officers. The ensuing siege lasted from December 1688 to August 1689, during which thousands of the city's inhabitants died. The Apprentice Boys' parades mark the beginning and end of the siege every December and August, while the pageant reenacts the last days of the siege with dramatic action, authentic weapons, and taped music.

DIRECT THEATRE VERSUS THEATRICAL REPRESENTATION

The Apprentice Boys support the pageant by providing the Crimson Players with actors and financial backing, and the Crimson Players strive to authenticate the same unionist version of Derry's history that the Apprentice Boys' parades commemorate. Protestant gentry created the modern version of the Apprentice Boys of Derry in 1813.[6] To this day, the organization professes that its mission is: "The purpose of celebrating the Anniversaries of the Shutting of the Gates and the relief of Derry, and thus handing down to posterity the memorable events of the years 1688 and 1689 connected with this City."[7]

The parades and the Siege Pageant recall the same history. Yet, in the mid 1990s, the Apprentice Boys' parade inspired violent reactions among Derry's Catholic and Protestant citizens, while the pageant has not. Why do these acts of commemoration generate different responses among the city's various political and religious communities? To be brief, the crowds react to the events differently because the parades represent a form of direct theatre, while the pageant narrates past events using the conventions we normally associate with theatrical representation. According to Richard Schechner, in a more institutional piece of theatre, the actions within a performance are given, and their outcome known. In direct theatre, the outcome of the event is not known. In most theatrical productions, the audience understands that the identities of the character and the actor are distinct and separate. In direct theatre, the actor does not perform as a character. In other words, direct theatre demands that a real person performs real actions for an audience, and both the actor and the audience do not know what the consequences of those actions will be.[8]

Certain clubs and bands that participate in the Apprentice Boys' parades have used the historical events they commemorate to fuel existing hatreds. The parades glorify a unionist version of history, and many of Derry's nationalists contest that history. Some Catholic communities in Northern Ireland no longer tolerate how militant loyalists announce their culture and history through the region's most contentious parades. Nationalists in Derry view the parades as a form of triumphalism.[9] The marchers assemble in rank and file and present themselves to their fellow loyalists and to the larger unionist community as the latest incarnation of Derry's Protestant defenders. In this way, the marchers relive old conflicts, not as characters, but as themselves. According to this argument, the Apprentice Boys metaphorically march from the past into the present, reliving the events of the 1688–89 siege in contemporary Ulster. Performing this rite before a hostile audience opens the Apprentice Boys' carefully selected narrative to resistance and possible revisions. Staging this form of direct theatre in such circumstances often leads to violence.[10]

Although the "Siege Pageant" recounts the events in 1688–89 from a unionist perspective, it has not inspired the kind of violence that plagues the parades. Eamonn Deane, who lives and works in Derry, explained how the pageant avoids a similarly aggressive reaction: "Once they began to move the situation from merely marching and began to engage in theatre it took a lot sting out of it. I don't know how to express it properly, but there is the real life theatre of them marching on the walls. That is the real theatre that engages people. But then to make a piece of theatre, a piece of drama, it takes a lot of sting out of it for both sides. We recognize this as a piece of theatre.

This may cause you to feel a lot of different things, but it's only a piece of theatre. Whereas just marching, it is real. It is theatrical, but it is real. It is everyday; it is our lives; it is our position."[11]

From a sociological and political perspective, the decision to create and promote the Siege Pageant represents a very important shift in the way that the Apprentice Boys conceive their mission. Staging the pageant demonstrates that the leaders of the Apprentice Boys are to find new and less divisive ways to disseminate their history. Three important developments helped clear a space for the outdoor performance. First, in 1998, the signing of the Good Friday Agreement ushered in a period of peace and calm after nearly thirty years of sporadic violence in Derry.[12] Second, the Apprentice Boys did not want to participate in the same kind of confrontational behavior that the members of the Orange Order engaged in at Portadown. In 1995, nationalists outside Portadown attempted to stop the Orange Order's Portadown Lodge from marching along the Garvaghy Road. The Orange Order asserted its right to march down the road, which runs through a predominantly Catholic housing estate. The British government has blocked the route, and the stalemate has produced riots every summer since 1995. The leaders of the Apprentice Boys have been much more pragmatic than the Orange Order. The leaders of the Apprentice Boys have met with representatives of the local nationalist groups, and these relationships have recently improved. This pragmatic stance opened the door for the third development, which put the city and its business leaders behind the continued growth of the Maiden City Festival.

The changes described earlier have allowed the Apprentice Boys to experiment with new methods in order to accomplish their mission. None of these developments would have amounted to any significant change within the Apprentice Boys organization without leaders who were willing to take risks. The Governor and Secretary General, Alistair Simpson and William Moore, have opened the doors of their Memorial Hall and welcomed tourists, politicians, journalists, and academics from a diverse political spectrum. According to Norman Rosborough, the director of the Crimson Players, these men had to reinvent the image of the Apprentice Boys. They had to demonstrate that their institution was not as intransigent or aggressive as the Orange Order. Simpson and Moore live in Derry, and they worked with local merchants, city officials, and artists to promote the establishment of a new festival, which would be staged during the height of Derry's marching season. The Apprentice Boys still maintain that the parades are essential to the organization's relevance and continued existence. However, in 1997, the leaders of the Apprentice Boys believed that a pageant provided the best means to promote the organization's progressive image and educate the general public about Derry's history.

SETTING, PERCEPTION, AND THE AUDIENCE'S COMPOSITION

Between 1998 and 2001, I documented four different performances of the Siege Pageant. The Crimson Players first staged the Siege Pageant outside of the Apprentice Boys' Memorial Hall the morning before the main parade in 1997. I attended the pageant at the same site in 1998. In 2000, Rosborough and his actors moved the pageant to the Guildhall Square, and I witnessed the event in that space in 2001. A close reading of these performances demonstrates that the pageant's setting has a direct impact on the composition of its audience, and the two spaces shape audience's response to the production in different ways.

In 1998, the crowd that attended the pageant outside the Memorial Hall on the day of the Apprentice Boys parade was almost entirely Protestant.[13] Of those groups attending the pageant, the Apprentice Boys were foremost in their identifiable allegiance to the production. They normally walk to and from the Memorial Hall on the day of the parade, and attending the pageant before the march allows them to socialize with friends and family and support the mission of their organization at the same time. In 1998, they provided a significant portion of the pageant's audience, watching the play from the doorways and windows of the Memorial Hall or moving through the crowd with their collarettes, bowler hats, dark suits, and blue windbreakers. The symbols that they wear or carry separate the marchers from the rest of the audience. The presence and bearing of the marchers at the event announced that they would accept nothing less than an appropriate response to the pageant. Therefore, when the Crimson Players performed before the Memorial Hall, friends and families of the Apprentice Boys provided the largest portion of their audience. These people come to Derry to enjoy both the pageant and the parade, and they showed their support for the Crimson Players by packing themselves into the small street and parking lot adjacent to the Memorial Hall before the performance began.

The pageant's audience does not represent a unified whole. In 1998 and 2001, four distinct groups constituted the pageant's audience. Of those, I have already described the largest and most influential two, the Apprentice Boys and their supporters. Members of the Royal Ulster Constabulary (RUC) and visiting journalists supply the remaining two distinct groups that attend any of the Crimson Player's performances, and their relationship with the pageant's actors and audience is complicated. The RUC is Northern Ireland's police force. Over 90 percent of its twelve thousand officers are Protestant, and nationalist politicians hope to change both its demographic and its royal title.[14] These forces appear to share the interests of Northern Ireland's unionist marchers. However, since the 1980s, officials within the British government have ordered the RUC to block or reroute the most contentious and openly loyalist parades.[15] From 1969 to 1994, the British government blocked the Apprentice Boys from marching along Derry's walls, and when they returned to the walls in 1995, the marchers clashed with nationalists and the RUC.[16] In December 2000 and August 2001, I watched members of the Apprentice Boys and the RUC collaborate in a friendly manner to move the parade along peacefully. I also witnessed marchers and police in riot gear clash violently at the end of the parade in December 2000. As a consequence, the relationship that the Apprentice Boys and the RUC share is an ambivalent one at best. The RUC attend the pageant with as much discretion as possible. They hover at the pageant's periphery with their weapons and armored trucks, watching the crowd more than the pageant.

In 1998 and 2001, representatives of the media attended the Siege Pageant in force, and, if the pageant's sympathetic audience members have ambivalent feelings regarding the RUC, they openly dislike the visiting reporters and their camera crews. Many unionist marchers believe that journalists are their enemies. Regarding the negative portrayal of loyalist parading institutions in the papers and on television, many Apprentice Boys agree with Governor Simpson, who claims, "It was the media [that] caused the problem. Because they were so negative in their reports. It gave the people the wrong idea."[17] These beliefs explain the deeply felt animosities that the unionist marchers and their loyalist allies direct toward the media. At the pageant, journalists and their equipment take a great deal of space, and they secure the best possible places to view the performance. In 1998, the Apprentice Boys and the RUC corralled a large group of reporters and cameramen and placed them on the city's walls next to the performers. This placement isolated the media from an audience that already viewed them as suspect. Moreover, when the rest of the audience watched the performance from the small street and parking lot outside the Memorial Hall, they saw the performers in the street and the press above them on the wall. In this way, the tight group of journalists resembled a Greek chorus, appearing in the performance like an assembly of skeptical actors.

In the spring of 2000, William Moore suggested that the Crimson Players move the pageant to the Guildhall Square. Rosborough and his actors were anxious. The area outside the Memorial Hall offered greater security for the children performing in the show and for the families attending the production. In a deeply divided terrain, Derry's citizens identify the parking lot and small street adjacent to the Memorial Hall as unionist territory. The city's western wall, the Memorial Hall, and a nearby RUC post offer protection to the people performing in and attending the Siege Pageant. A performance in the Guildhall Square would move the production outside of the old city's walls and place the pageant within a nationalist domain. However, Governor Simpson and other Apprentice Boys wanted to create a new image for their organization, and they decided that it was the right time to perform the pageant in a, "nationalist situation."[18] Rosborough argued that staging the pageant in the Guildhall Square exposed the Crimson Players and their audience to the possibility of violent attacks, but he finally agreed that recent political changes indicated that the time was right.

I was a bit apprehensive until things settled down politically after the Good Friday Agreement. Then Billy Moore said, we're thinking about doing it in the Guildhall Square this year. It wasn't quite the jump I wanted to do. It was a big jump, but we went with it. The climate was right; the mood was right, and atmosphere was good. So we said, "Let's do it. Let's not be ashamed anymore." The only way we could have lost was if we made a complete and utter mess of the pageant. If we went down there and got stones and bottles thrown at us and jeered, we were still the winners. If we went down there and started a riot we were still the winners. We were saying, "Here we are; this is it. If you want to watch, you're welcome. If you don't want to watch, I won't be offended."

Governor Simpson believed that the new space would invite a more diverse audience. In August 2000, the move to the Guildhall Square produced the results he had hoped for. John Hume, the leader of Northern Ireland's largest nationalist political party, attended the event. Simpson argued later that moving the pageant's location was instrumental in opening the production to a new audience, and Rosborough was equally pleased by the crowd's diversity and the pageant's polite reception in the Guildhall Square. According to Rosborough, the audience attending the performance at the Guildhall Square was, "completely different," when compared to the mostly Protestant attendees at the Memorial Hall production. Catholic nationalists and Protestant unionists joined the RUC and the media to quietly watch the pageant without any serious disturbances.

The different reactions to the Apprentice Boys' parades and the Crimson Player's pageant indicate that Northern Ireland's contested history is not the sole cause of the region's conflicts. A small number of contentious parades, including the Apprentice Boys' march through Derry, can trigger riots. The pageant reenacts the same unionist version of history that the parades commemorate, but the pageant does not inspire an immediate and violent reaction. The problem is not the history that each event memorializes. The real problem is how certain groups articulate that history. In this respect, the pageant's form, style, and setting appear to be important factors, which contribute to its wide appeal. If the pageant is as popular as its patrons claim, what do its different audience members expect of the production?

HORIZON OF EXPECTATIONS

What do spectators hope to see and experience when they attend the Crimson Player's Siege Pageant, and what are the conventions and cultural codes that people use to judge its performance? The group that produces the event, and where they stage the event are important factors that Derry's citizens use to appraise any cultural production. For example, in 1989, the Derry City Council staged an outdoor pageant without the assistance of the Crimson Players or the Apprentice Boys to celebrate the tercentenary of the 1688–89 siege. The City Council created a lavish spectacle, and it enjoyed an audience, whose members represented a plurality of interests. However, many Protestants living in the Waterside, an area with a large loyalist population across the River Foyle, perceived the City Council's pageant as a nationalist event. As a consequence, many Protestants feared to venture across the river to attend the 1989 performance in the Guildhall Square.[19]

Perceptions concerning ownership are very powerful in Northern Ireland, especially now that recent changes have challenged the power of the city's unionist political parties. From a unionist perspective, it appears that a nationalist-dominated City Council now controls the arts in Derry. From the same perspective, the city's unionist community believes it owns Northern Ireland's history, and the Apprentice Boys have nominated themselves as the protectors of that history. The director of the Crimson Players explains this territorial approach to Derry's culture and popular memory: "We talk about our culture here, and, unfortunately, there are two cultures. There is the Unionist culture, and there is the Nationalist culture, and the Nationalist culture focuses on a mysticism that doesn't exist and never did. We have a Unionist culture, which is: the Derry walls, the Cathedral, Governor Walker. The walls are there for you to see and walk upon. When was the last time you saw a Leprechaun?"

How does Rosborough's statement apply to an audience member's assessment of the pageant? Susan Bennett uses a two-frame model to interpret how an audience decodes a particular performance, and her model helps identify the different expectations that the pageants' audience inherits. According to Bennett, the outer frame consists of, "all the cultural elements which create and inform the theatrical event." The performance itself and the playing space that houses it constitute the inner frame. The audience works where these two frames intersect. Bennett explains this process best when she states, "The spectator comes to the theatre as a member of an already constituted interpretive community and also brings a horizon of expectations shaped by preperformance elements." Together these preconceived notions of what is an appropriate performance create commonly acknowledged theatre conventions.[20]

In Derry, employing Bennett's terminology, the Protestant and unionist persons constitute a distinct interpretive community, and they concentrate more on the ways in which the play correctly recounts their history than they criticize its production values. In Derry, unionist history provides a powerful outer frame that contains the Crimson Players' performance, and, in the case of the pageant, a strong outer frame composed of a shared unionist history supports a weaker inner frame, the performance itself. In other words, Derry's unionist community cares more about the pageant's history than they care about the productions' artistic qualities. When I asked Rosborough about the expectations of the spectators watching the pageant outside the Memorial Hall, he said that he could do almost anything and they would cheer him on. According to Rosborough, the expectations of his unionist audience revolve around a shared sense of history and identity. By attending the pageant, the audience can affirm that, "This is our day; these are our people; this is our history." These deeply held feelings privilege the pageant's narrative. The audience does not wait outside in the rain to watch great theatre; they support the pageant in order to preserve its history. In this respect, the pageant's sympathetic unionist audience, including the family, friends, and Apprentice Boys attending the event, do not concern themselves with the professionalism of its actors or the quality of their costumes. As Rosborough said, "The pageant is not so much entertaining as it is educational."[21]

OPPORTUNITIES FOR AUDIENCE INTERACTION

The success of any theatrical performance depends on the presence and participation of an audience. Derry's Siege Pageant raises the importance of the audience to an even higher and more urgent level, and the pageant invites the people watching it to be more than spectators. For Northern Ireland's unionist community, the pageant provides a unique opportunity to participate in the collective production of meaning, and individual audience members can actively shape the performance by doing the following: interacting with other audience members, interacting with the pageant's actors, and by engaging with, or becoming a part of the performance's environment. I will explain the first two sites in this section of the chapter and explain the last opportunity for audience interaction in the following section.

Susan Bennett rightly argues that the "communication between spectators" has a serious impact on an audience member's response to a performance. Despite the religious, political, or ideological perspectives an individual brings to an event, a crowd's reactions to a performance often limit an individual's response to it.[22] Moreover, Northern Ireland's sectarian divide has fueled thirty years of violence, and, despite the latest peace initiative, a tense atmosphere further circumscribes the pageant and restricts the audience's possible reactions to the performance and to one another. These real and tangible factors shape the expectations of the various groups attending the pageant and, depending on a particular audience member's political or religious position; these factors also create different approaches to the performance.

The RUC come to the pageant prepared for trouble, and they are well aware of their difficult situation. The nationalists identify them as enemies, and unionists no longer see them as their allies. On Easter Monday, 1986, the RUC stopped an Apprentice Boys' parade in Portadown. The police fired 148 plastic bullets at the marchers and killed one of the Apprentice Boys.[23] In 1996, the RUC attacked an Apprentice Boys Branch Club from Belfast in riot gear and beat the marchers with batons.[24] In 1995, 1997, and 1999, the

RUC battled with marchers and protestors from both the unionist and nationalist communities in Derry's streets.[25]

In 1998, the police gathered next to the wall outside the Apprentice Boys' Memorial Hall and waited quietly for the pageant. The officers carried weapons and wore bulletproof jackets, but they were careful not to disrupt the performance. They discreetly placed their armored vehicles in the back of the parking lot outside the Memorial Hall, and they did not interact with individual audience members or actors unless someone addressed them. In 2001, the police adopted the same tactics. They parked their armored vehicles in nearby alleys and under the city's stone arches, but even the most naive audience member could not miss their presence. The RUC remained an important part of the pageant's performance text. The RUC's armed presence at the pageant highlights how the much the present looks like the past, and, in such moments, the audience recognizes that a siege mentality still shapes policy in Northern Ireland.

The pageant's unionist audience members distance themselves from the representatives of the media. The journalists who watch and record the pageant contribute to the pageant's tense atmosphere. Although the Apprentice Boys welcome the presence of the journalists and use the media to promote their new and more progressive persona, many unionists regard journalists as intruders. The police offer the media the best places to view and document the event, and the press often displace families and friends who had waited for the performance. Worse still, in 1998 and 2001, I found that certain journalists talked among themselves and disregarded the performance. Like the members of the RUC, the journalists do not attend the pageant in order to enjoy its narrative or critique its form and style. They come to Derry on the day of the Apprentice Boys' parade in search of an exciting story, and, according to unionists and nationalists with whom I have spoken, certain journalists are notorious for engineering such excitement.

While examining the ways in which different groups attending the pageant interact with one another, it is apparent that the Apprentice Boys constitute the most powerful group within the pageant's audience. The presence of the Apprentice Boys does more to discipline the crowd than the RUC could ever hope to achieve on its own. Just as a more institutional theatre space has its rules, so does the Crimson Player's Siege Pageant, and the members of the Apprentice Boys enforce those unwritten rules. The Siege Pageant glorifies their past, and during its performance the Apprentice Boys serve as the pageant's unofficial ushers. The Apprentice Boys perceive themselves to be the "guardians of an incredible social history," and they are prepared to defend it.[26] The Apprentice Boys' parades have met with resistance in the past. Most recently, in 1995, 1997, and 1999 the Apprentice Boys' parades and their opposition in Derry's mostly Catholic neighborhoods triggered violent confrontations. These confrontations followed a pattern of resistance, opposition, and violence involving both sides of Derry's sectarian divide. During these confrontations, the Apprentice Boys felt that they were under attack yet again, and many of the marchers defended their history aggressively. Because of this recent history, individual audience members attending the pageant know that they risk a stern if not angry response if they react to the pageant in a way that the Apprentice Boys and their allies find offensive.

However heated the political climate may be in Northern Ireland, the Maiden City Festival and its pageant still provide people with a colorful and exciting moment of theatre. Instead of trying to further divide Derry's citizens, the pageant encourages both an historical and an interpersonal connectivity. The performance attempts to bind its audience to one another and to its players. The pageant's setting provides its mostly Protestant audience with a direct connection to Derry's glorious history, and the performance itself blurs the boundaries that normally separate a production's actors and audience. The spaces in which the Crimson Players perform encourage free movement among its audience members and between the pageant's actors and audience. During the performance of the pageant, audience members freely interact with one another. They talk to one another and move along the edges of the performance space without violating behavioral codes that limit movement and noise in a traditional theatre. In the open spaces that the Crimson Players utilize there is no proscenium, fixed seating, lighting, or stage machinery that could separate an actor or audience member. Therefore, the pageant's actors and audience members mingle freely before and after the performance. Mothers and fathers primp and prod their costumed children, while friends enjoy a quiet chat or a smoke with one of the actors before the show begins. In 2001, during the performance in the Guildhall Square, strolling shoppers came and went without disturbing the show. Friends and family members talked to one another, took pictures, waved to and cheered on the actors. Afterward, the RUC, journalists, costumed actors, and onlookers mixed with one another in the open square in a visibly relaxed mood. The pageant's setting encourages such interaction, but what does a performance within such a space do for its audience?

SIGNS, SYMBOLS, AND THE PERFORMANCE TEXT

The Crimson Players' Siege Pageant celebrates Derry's walls as much as it memorializes the city's seventeenth-century heroes. The Apprentice Boys' annual parades and pageants make the walled city a stage. Both forms of performance incorporate the city's historically significant walls, buildings, and memorials as part of their spectacle. The Crimson Players in particular utilize what Richard Schechner calls a "theatrical environment," an outdoor space with great dramatic potential. According to Schechner's terms, the Crimson Players astutely selected large public spaces and transformed them into theatres.[27] In their outdoor performances, the Crimson Players use existing architectural elements as narrative devices and symbolically laden backdrops.

When asked about the importance of the walls and ramparts on which the Crimson Players perform, Rosborough stated, "you couldn't build a theatre backdrop like that. There are 400 years worth of history cemented together there. I wrote the pageant specifically for that area." The signs and symbols that Derry's defenses offer make each environment in which the Crimson Players stage their performances vital in the expression of their narrative.

Within Derry's walls, the city's authorities have memorialized the Jacobite siege in one form or another since 1718, and, except for the most recent troubles, these commemorations employed Derry's famous defenses.[28] During the eighteenth and nineteenth centuries, colonial authorities modified Derry's walls to exploit their dramatic potential.[29] Both the Crimson Players and the Apprentice Boys occupy these spaces in order to educate, consolidate, and mobilize their audience. Today each gate, bastion, and any other significant feature along the city's seventeenth-century walls has an historical marker that explains the site's importance for uninitiated visitors, and these gates still frame the dramatic display of power during the Crimson Players' Siege Pageant and the Apprentice Boys' parades.

Derry's Siege Pageant utilizes the same walls and many of the same streets and buildings that colonial authorities used in the eighteenth and nineteenth centuries. In the pageant's 1998 production, the Memorial Hall, with its heavy iron doors and stone façade provided retiring rooms and storage spaces for the Crimson Players, their costumes, and numerous props. Rosborough stated that the Memorial Hall's Scottish baronial architecture adds to the pageant's atmosphere. Together, the Memorial Hall and the city's walls supplied an impressive setting for the pageant's historic content. Through the day, the Apprentice Boys' crimson flag waved defiantly over the Memorial Hall, and the Crimson Players used the ramparts inside the wall as a stage. The walls are an integral part of both productions. Eamonn Deane explains that, "As an architectural piece of theatre the walls are amazing, and they continue to be a powerful symbol for unionism."[30] In 1998, the pageant's costumed performers mimed actions around artillery pieces that fired on Jacobite positions over three hundred years ago. In 2001, the performance in the Guildhall Square used the city's walls and their cannon as an impressive backdrop, which loomed over the actors and audience alike.

What effect do these historical markers have on the Crimson Players' Siege Pageant, and how do they shape the audiences' response to the performance? The pageant reenacts the last days of the 1688–89 siege and ends with the citizens' deliverance. All of the actors dress in period costumes. The important male characters wear wigs, gowns, feathered hats, and carry swords. These characters represent Derry's Protestant heroes, including Governor Walker, Captain Ash, and Colonel Mitchelburne. Rosborough performs in the pageant as Colonel Mitchelburne, and his character functions as the pageant's narrator. This is appropriate; Mitchelburne did much to preserve the memory of Derry's defenders, and he wrote two plays about the siege in the early eighteenth century.[31]

The walls and the cannons mounted on them lend the pageant a sense of authenticity and authority, and, in terms of the audience's culturally constituted horizon of expectations, these architectural elements signify the importance of the pageant's historical content. Moreover, the walls provide an interface, a nexus where people connect with one another and their history. Thus, the pageant's setting offers the third site for audience interaction. Through the setting, the audience works with the actors to collectively re-create their cherished and closely guarded history. The Crimson Players perform in the same spaces in which Derry's original defenders fought and died. The Apprentice Boys claim that the city's ramparts are, "soaked with the lifeblood of the defenders."[32] According to unionist mythology, this blood has fortified Derry's walls, made them impregnable, and has rendered them sacred for succeeding generations of Protestant Ulstermen. The conflation of historical and sacramental images and themes lends the pageant great emotional power. Rosborough incorporates the walls in order to invoke the emotional intensity of their history. He claims that when the Crimson Players perform on the walls, "the ghosts come back to haunt you."

Rosborough compares the significance of Derry's walls to Mecca. Just as Mecca unites all Muslims, Derry's walls bind all loyal Protestants to a common history and purpose.[33] All pious Muslims must travel to Mecca, and many unionists undertake a pilgrimage Derry and its walls. All Protestant men who hope to join the Apprentice Boys must go to Derry for their rite of initiation, and the Apprentice Boys use their Maiden City Festival to bring as many people as possible to Derry's walls and introduce them to the dramatic history they signify. In this respect, the Crimson Players perform outdoors in spaces that are available to the general public at most times, and, as a result, the audience attending the pageant can interact with its setting before or after the show. For the Siege Pageant's audience, the performance is available only for a limited time, but the history it recounts lives on in the pageant's environment.

In Derry, the historical significance of the pageant's setting and the narrative that the Crimson Players perform attempt to unite the interests of the pageant's audience with the Apprentice Boys' loyalist ideology, which more deeply connects the individual audience members to the pageant's actors. In order to do this, the pageant conflates the fears of Derry's heroic defenders with the anxieties of its contemporary audience. The pageant reenacts a moment of desperate struggle, when Derry's Protestants were literally under siege, and, in this powerfully emotional narrative, the pageant relies less on words than it relies on the power of performing specific actions before carefully selected signs and symbols existing in the pageant's environment in order to instill the same sense of urgency in the pageant's audience. The signs found in and around the pageant emphasize that what was vital, what was at stake

in the 1688–89 siege, is still vital and at risk today. The Crimson Players'
pageant and the Apprentice Boys' parades link Northern Ireland's present
troubles with the city's valiant defense in 1688–89. The pageant connects
the siege's heroes with those who have assumed their defensive posture, the
Apprentice Boys. In 1998, following the pageant, the members of the Apprentice Boys Parent Clubs assembled on the city's walls. A flute band and
the Crimson Players joined the Apprentice Boys, and together they paraded
along Derry's ramparts with the costumed Crimson Players leading the
march. The Crimson Players continue to lead the Apprentice Boys' main
parade through Derry's streets each summer, and their message is clear: the
siege has never really ended.

Nationalists and republicans have blocked a small number of Northern
Ireland's unionist marches, and riots have plagued a few contentious parades.
As a result, the RUC erect tall fences along Derry's western walls before the
Crimson Players perform outside the Memorial Hall. The fences prevent republican youths from throwing rocks, bottles, or bombs into the performance
space from the Catholic neighborhood below. The police also place strong
metal barriers along the perimeter of the performance. The barriers help define the pageant's playing space, and the same barriers line certain sections
of the Apprentice Boys' parade route. Because of the presence of metal barriers, the RUC, and army helicopters floating above these spectacles, the
pageant and the parades share a disturbing tension and sense of urgency. The
signs and supplementary characters that surround the pageant strongly suggest that recent events directly connect Derry's violent past with the present,
making the pageant's environment a very powerful part of the spectacle for
any audience member.

EDUCATION, CONSOLIDATION, AND MOBILIZATION

The Crimson Players provide Derry's citizens with a living connection,
linking them to their history and one another, but the actors cannot maintain
these bonds without an enthusiastic audience. The actors perform within
historically significant spaces, whose signs and symbols lend the pageant emotional power, but performing in these spaces would lack meaning without an
active and informed audience. The pageant performed within the city's walls
in 1998 consolidated and mobilized its primarily Protestant audience. The
people attending that pageant demonstrated their determination and loyalty
by waiting for the performance in the rain on a cold and dreary day. The
audience's resolve clearly inspired the actors, who offered the crowd outside
the Memorial Hall an emotional performance. At the end of the pageant,
when Norman Rosborough proclaimed that the defenders' rallying cry was
"No Surrender," the audience loudly responded with the same slogan. The
patterned call and response between the pageant's narrator and its energetic

audience highlights the importance of the audience for this particular form of public performance.

Derry's Siege Pageant utilizes living actors, who attempt to achieve two important goals for Protestant Ulster. First, they hope to educate a diverse audience about the Maiden City's heroic past, albeit a selective and openly unionist version of that history. Second, in an effort to preserve their way of life both the Apprentice Boys and the Crimson Players use the pageant to summon individual audience members to become the custodians of Ulster's Protestant history and culture. Joseph Roach argues that certain performed behaviors function as vehicles of cultural transmission.[34] The pageant identifies the Apprentice Boys and their allies as the successors to Derry's former Protestant defenders. According to Roach, a community reproduces its culture by a process of surrogation. He claims that in certain performances alternates fill the positions of missing leaders.[35] On the walls outside the Memorial Hall, the Crimson Players rally the crowd to defend Northern Ireland's Protestant history. In this respect, they ask the audience to join them as substitutes for Derry's dead heroes. Norman Rosborough detailed how he links his actors with the audience and unifies both groups with figures from Derry's past. He argues that when an actor performs in the pageant, he becomes the character. "I am Colonel Mitchelburne. I am Governor Walker. This is the way I would have done things." Rosborough explained to me how he extends his passionate identification with the past to his audience: "[I tell them] "'You are walking in the steps of your forefathers.' I finished [the pageant] outside there last year by saying to the crowd, 'so when you walk upon this righteous ground, give pause, and think of those who walked before you and cleared a righteous path. Keep them in your hearts and remember them forever. Remember their watch cry, which was, No Surrender.'"

At the end of the 1998 pageant, the crowd outside the Memorial Hall joined Rosborough and loudly repeated his cry with the rest of the Crimson Players. In that moment the difference between the actor and spectator disappeared. The pageant's simple props, costumes, taped music, and relatively amateurish production qualities offer the audience a certain distance. These elements reveal that the production offers a mediated form of instruction. However, the production's setting is very real, and it underscores the harsh reality of the pageant's narrative. This makes the performance both distant and very close. The show is more than spectacle. For its unionist actors and audience the pageant is intensely personal. The audience members know and care for its actors, and they identify with the characters their friends represent. When the Crimson Players join the Apprentice Boys and parade along Derry's walls, the actors further blur the boundaries that normally separate the actor and the audience. These actions strongly suggest that the Apprentice Boys are also players within a highly stylized performance. In this respect, the two sets of costumed characters revert to a form of direct theatre, the dangers of which I have already described. Within the context of the unionist calendar of commemorations, such interconnected events mobilize Northern Ireland's Protestant populace with drums, music, costumes, flags, and dramatic action. On these special occasions, the actors and audience establish an imaginary community through performances of loyalty at strategically located sites of memory. In other words, these events invite the audience to become actors in a very real drama. Therefore, a loyal and energetic audience is essential for the success of the pageant in both its performance and its continued relevance. At the simplest level, the pageant's creators need to recruit new actors, and these recruits come from its spectators. The words and actions of one proud father support my claim. While moving his little boys through the crowd waiting in the rain outside the Memorial Hall in 1998, he asked people to make room for his children, stating, "These are our future."

Bennett argues that an individual's reaction to a performance is the "core of the spectator's pleasure."[36] Bennett describes what an audience member hopes to experience when he or she attends a theatrical event that obeys the conventions we normally associate with a modern proscenium style production. This does not describe the experience of a sympathetic audience member attending Derry's Siege Pageant. The spectator's pleasure also can come from his or her participation in a larger collective experience. The unionist audience member who witnesses the pageant and supports its actors and patrons can say, through the vicarious pleasure of witnessing Derry's siege, "I have also participated in the city's defense." Thus, the performance within Derry's walls provides a uniquely collective pleasure, one that binds the pageant's Protestant audience and actors to the city's heroic defenders.

If the Crimson Players only performed their pageant inside Derry's walled city, the performance would appear to buttress the city's defenses and build even larger divisions within the community. Fortunately, the Apprentice Boys and the Crimson Players have decided to move beyond the city's walls, and that move has changed the performance and its reception. Instead of reconstructing Derry's defenses, the performance in the Guildhall Square provides new portals through which the city's larger community can learn about Derry's past. Ironically, the pageant highlights Derry's impregnability in the past, while also promoting greater accessibility to that history in the present. By relocating the pageant outside its usual frame of unionist commemoration, the public performance invites people of all backgrounds to participate in a theatrical event and interact with its players. As a result, the latest version of the Siege Pageant allows people from many different communities to approach the city's walls and their history in a new way, a way that promotes openness rather than reinforcing existing divisions.

NOTES

1. In Northern Ireland, Protestant unionists and Catholic nationalists argue over the city's name. Certain unionists refer to the walled city as Londonderry, while na-

tionalists call it Derry. I use the latter term because the city council adopted it and the Apprentice Boys use the title in their literature. This chapter uses two other important terms: loyalist and republican. Whereas unionists strive to maintain Northern Ireland's political and cultural link to the United Kingdom through political means, loyalist paramilitaries, such as the UVF (Ulster Volunteer Force) and the UDA (Ulster Defense Association), are prepared to defend that status through violence. Republican organizations, such as the IRA (Irish Republican Army), INLA (Irish National Liberation Army), and the RIRA (Real Irish Republican Army), hope to unite Northern Ireland's six counties with the larger Irish Republic in the south and, despite recent changes, some of these clandestine organizations have not abandoned their campaign of shooting and bombing.

2. The Apprentice Boys is a unionist organization, whose members are exclusively Protestant and believe that Northern Ireland should remain within the United Kingdom. They have a Governor, Secretary General, and a governing committee. Eight Parent Clubs exist within Derry itself, and many other Branch Clubs have been formed in Northern Ireland, England, Scotland, Canada, and America. The Apprentice Boys also have strong links to Northern Ireland's loyalist organizations.

3. See particularly Dominic Bryan, "Drumcree and 'the Right to March:' Orangeism, Ritual, and Politics in Northern Ireland." In *Following the Drum: The Irish Parading Tradition,* ed. Tom Fraser (London: Macmillan Press, Ltd., 2000), 191–207; Tom Fraser, "The Apprentice Boys and the Relief of Derry Parades." In *Following the Drum,* ed. Fraser, 173–89; Neil Jarman, *Material Conflicts: Parade and Visual Displays in Northern Ireland* (Oxford: Berg, 1997); Patrick Tuite, "The Biomechanics of Aggression: Psychophysiological Conditioning in Ulster's Loyalist Parades," *The Drama Review* 44.4 (2000), 9–30; and Tuite, "Performative Mnemonics and the Construction of Myth: An Historical and Textual Analysis of Ulster's Loyalist Parades," *Theatre Insight* 10.2 (1999), 3–13.

4. Liam De Paor, *The Peoples of Ireland: From Prehistory to Modern Times* (Notre Dame, Ind.: University of Notre Dame Press, 1986), 144–67.

5. Brian Lacy, *Siege City: the Story of Derry and Londonderry* (Belfast: Blackstaff Press, 1990), 78–139.

6. Ian McBride, *The Siege of Derry in Ulster Protestant Mythology* (Dublin: Four Courts Press, 1997), 47.

7. Fraser, "Apprentice Boys," 175.

8. Richard Schechner, "Invasions Friendly and Unfriendly: The Dramaturgy of Direct Theatre," in *Critical Theory and Performance,* ed. Janelle Reinelt and Joseph Roach (Ann Arbor: Michigan University Press, 1992), 98.

9. Eamonn Deane, Personal interview with the author, November 29, 2000.

10. Tuite, "Biomechanics," 10.

11. Deane, interview.

12. Norman Rosborough, Personal interview with the author, December 2, 2000. All subsequent Rosborough quotes refer to this interview.

13. The majority of the audience indicated their association with the Pageant, its members or its history, symbolically or physically. Many children and young men wore clothes whose colors or ornamentation signaled their allegiance to Protestant Ulster, while many older women and other less conspicuous bystanders positioned themselves as close to the performance, the members of the RUC, or Apprentice Boys as possible. In addition to these indices, I asked colleagues who live in Derry and attended the

same performance about this point, and they supported my assessment. At this stage, few Catholics attend the Pageant, and those that do, unless they hold a political office, remain along the margins of the performance, or only watch part of it while passing through the Guildhall Square.

14. Tuite, "Performance," 7; Suzanne Breen, "Unionists angered as Adams rejects policing Bill," *The Irish Times,* May 22, 2000 (located at http://www.ireland.com/newspaper/front/2000/0522/fro1.htm).

15. Tuite, "Biomechanics," 10.

16. Fraser, "Apprentice Boys," 183–85; Maeve Quigley, "Move to avoid the Derry clash," *Belfast Telegraph,* April 8, 1996, A6.

17. Alistair Simpson, Personal interview with the author, November 30, 2000.

18. Ibid.

19. Deane, interview.

20. Susan Bennett, *Theatre Audiences: A Theory of Production and Reception* (London: Routledge, 1997), 139–40.

21. Rosborough, interview.

22. Bennett, *Theatre Audiences,* 153.

23. Tuite, "Performance," 7.

24. Paul Connolly, "Blood and batons at battle of the bridge," *Belfast Telegraph,* April 9, 1996, A5.

25. Quigley, "Move to avoid;" Gerry Moriarty, "Violence erupts despite best efforts," *The Irish Times,* August 11, 1997 (located at http://www.ireland.com/newspaper/home/1997/0811/home1.htm); Suzanne Breen, "RUC rejects criticism after weekend clashes," *The Irish Times,* August 16, 1999 (located at http://www.ireland.com/newspaper/front/1999/0816/north6.htm).

26. David Hoey, Personal interview with the author, December 2, 2000.

27. Schechner, "Invasions," 102.

28. Fraser, "Apprentice Boys," 183–85; McBride, *Siege of Derry,* 36.

29. Derek Miller, *Still Under Siege* (Lurgan, Co. Armagh: Ulster Society [Publications] Limited, 1989), 19.

30. Deane, interview.

31. McBride, *Seige of Derry,* 36.

32. Miller, *Still Under Siege,* 9.

33. Rosborough, interview.

34. Joseph Roach, *Cities of the Dead: Circum-Atlantic Performance* (New York: Columbia University Press, 1996), 13.

35. Ibid. 2.

36. Bennett, *Theatre Audiences,* 155.

13

COMMUNITY-BASED THEATRE: A PARTICIPATORY MODEL FOR SOCIAL TRANSFORMATION

Mark S. Weinberg

All theatre, by virtue of its being a cultural construct, and therefore ideologically inscribed, is political. The operative definition I will use of *political theatre* in this chapter, however, is narrower. By political theatre I mean theatre that overtly, through its creation and/or performance, seeks social change rather than stasis, transformation rather than consolidation of power. It is political in that it operates, as Janelle Reinelt puts it, under the "assumption that the optimal relationship between theater and society is one in which theater, as a cultural practice, has an active role to play in the discovery, construction, maintenance, and critique of forms of sociality appropriate to that society."[1]

In the introduction to their anthology *Staging Resistance: Essays on Political Theatre,* Jeanne Colleran and Jenny Spencer list three types of political theater: "[1] theater as an act of political intervention taken *on behalf of* a designated population and having a specific political agenda; [2] theater that *offers itself* as a public forum through plays with overtly political content; [3] theater whose politics are covertly, or unwittingly, *on display,* inviting an actively critical stance from its audience." (emphasis mine)[2] Although this taxonomy covers most political theatre, it is limited to theatre *for* an audience, observed theatre.

But after I had done such theatre for many years on university campuses,

Portions of this chapter were taken from my article of the same title previously published by the University of Alabama Press in the *Theatre Symposium,* volume 8, *Theatre at the Margins: The Political, the Popular, the Personal, the Profane,* 2000.

as a member of a collective, in alternative restaurants and labor temples, and for various social and activist organizations, "I came," as Jan Cohen-Cruz simply put it, "to believe that change was brought on more by people making theatre than by watching it."[3] This chapter, therefore, will focus on political (or transformative) *participatory* theatre, in particular community-based theatre, and on the internationally practiced and highly effective techniques of Augusto Boal's *Theatre of the Oppressed* (*TO* subsequently) as they contribute to community-based theatre development. By community-based theatre, I mean theatre that closely allies itself with a particular community, develops performances about that community's concerns, and involves some level of participation by community members, ranging from simply being interview subjects for story gathering to performing on stage. As an illustration of a community-based theatre project using *TO* techniques, I will describe a project I facilitated in the winter of 1999 with University of Wisconsin-Milwaukee students, members of the Milwaukee Public Theatre, and participants in Project Q, a support group for youth connected to the Lesbian/Gay/Bi-sexual/Trans-gendered Community Center in Milwaukee, Wisconsin.

Why my belief in and focus on community-based theatre? Obviously, history proves that politically charged theatre offers much of great value for spectators. I do not deny that, but, while observed political theatre functions very well as an agenda-setting tool, it also may function inadvertently as a tool of hegemony and stasis because it seems to promote the delegation of work toward social change to the players. Participatory theatre unseats the spectator and then embodies the subject position in the spectator-as-actor and her or his relationship to the audience and broader society. It recognizes and uses the voices of those silenced in the oppressive monologues of dominant power structures and provides an arena in which those voices can be raised. Also, it seems to me that at some point we must evaluate political theatre by its impact and efficacy—and I believe that community-based theatre far surpasses observed theatre in both.

I cannot make this claim without expressing some concerns. Bruce McConachie examines the nature of community and its relationship to community-based theatre, and concludes that although community-based theatre does lead to citizenship in terms of identification and participation, it does not necessarily lead to progressive change, regardless of the intent and (in the performers' minds) clarity of presentation.[4] I would also note that, as significant as identity formation and community definition in the face of cultural homogenization are for empowerment, the results can be isolationist and there is often a very conservative edge to a community's desire for self-determination. I would maintain, however, that the following logic holds:

- If citizens are participants in the art making, then the process will help guide their thinking in and out of the theatre.

- The process in which they are involved reveals social systems and the images of such systems as constructs.
- The process thereby empowers.
- The strength of *TO* is that it is grounded in trusting those it empowers.

Theatre, as bell hooks put it, "can be an agent for change . . . in liberatory ways, only if we start with a mind-set and a progressive politics that is fundamentally anticolonialist, that negates cultural imperialism in all its manifestations. . . . The fierce willingness to repudiate domination in a holistic manner is the starting point for progressive cultural revolution."[5] Community-based and participatory theatre is in some ways a repudiation of claims of superiority in aesthetic judgment and artistic virtuosity, political astuteness, and so forth. It may be difficult for those of us who spent so many years training to let go of our mantle of expertise, but if we see collaboration of this kind as an expansion of the experiential base of the activist artist we can gain a great deal.[6]

During a recent project in Milwaukee, Wisconsin, I tried to both use and critique *TO* as a liberatory methodology and as a viable educational and creative tool for community-based theatre making. I taught a course called "Performance Workshop: A Community-Based Theatre Project" as part of the BA program of the UW-Milwaukee Theatre Department. From the get-go, the course was designed to conclude in a public performance. I chose Theatre of the Oppressed as a working methodology for two major reasons. First, *TO* is closely connected to Paulo Freire's pedagogical approach, which is predicated on the belief that problem-posing is the most significant activity of critical or liberatory pedagogy. "In problem-posing education, people develop their power to perceive critically *the way they exist* in the world *with which* and *in which* they find themselves. They come to see the world not as a static reality, but as a reality in process, in transformation."[7] The process of liberatory education is dialogic, active, and co-intentional, and to me it is related in goal and action to community-based theatre. Both are engaged in the de-colonization of the imagination, thereby giving back to the student/audience/participants the sense of choice, a reminder of the constructed nature of their agreed-on reality, and of their ability to choose and change, to manufacture a culture that is their own. Also, *TO* provides what I consider a set of achievable goals and noncoercive "rules" for reaching them. The work begins with what the participants know, provides various ways of examining knowledge, and promotes the raising of risky questions, all parts of a sound pedagogy and creative methodology.

This venture was, at first blush, a class. The students[8] and I spent seven weeks in the classroom examining the nature of community-based theatre and practicing the *TO* techniques of *Image* and *Forum* Theatre. (Image Theatre is done in silence and uses a series of progressively more complex body sculpting exercises to examine topics. Forum Theatre develops plays in which the audience intervenes. It is explained in more detail later.) The focus of this early work was to give the students an opportunity to use *TO* to explore some issues with which they were concerned, and to examine simultaneously the role of the techniques and of the outsider/facilitator/"joker" (Boal's term for the facilitator/director). We met in the performance space given to BA students, a place of which they took a certain ownership, but in which they were used to being watched and evaluated. Because I do not teach on the Milwaukee campus regularly, I was treated at first as a guest, and acknowledged as an "expert." One of my first tasks was to disabuse the students of the notion that I was the source of what they were to learn.

The early exercises and games were devoted to personal discovery and "demechanization," the breaking of habits of movement and thought. We did a number of the image exercises described in Boal's *Games for Actors and Non-Actors* and used a variety of other exploratory approaches.[9] One of the strengths of *TO* is that the techniques can be modified to suit the nature of the situation, the make-up of the participant group, and the rhythm and methods of the joker. I found that I came to every class with a plan, based on what seemed to me to be discoveries made in the last session, and then modified the agenda as that day's work unfolded.

I approached the class members as representatives of the student community, brought together both to accomplish a performance task and to explore a method of doing that. They were both excited and skeptical. I claimed to them, and still do, that community-based participatory theatre can do four things that allow it to be efficacious, without denying that there are dangers in noncritical acceptance of such claims. First, I assert that community-based theatre, often performed in venues primarily devoted to other activities, provides a reclamation of space. Dominant groups have always represented their dominance in the most accessible spaces—in parades on public streets, on billboards, in theme parks, and so forth. Community-based theatre reasserts the power of communal over commercial spaces.

Frederic Jameson writes that "the new political art [will require] some as yet unimaginable mode of representing . . . in which we may again begin to grasp our positioning as individual and collective subjects and regain a capacity to act and struggle which is at present neutralized by our spatial as well as our social confusion."[10] Community-based theatre is necessarily local. It is, therefore, theatre that reasserts and constructs physical and social place, thereby providing grounds from which to struggle.

In successful community-based performances, then, "ideally, the semiotics of location, space, and architecture work together to invite and include resident audience members as they reinforce ownership and frame elements of the community's identity."[11] Our performances in the same building as, but in a large room next to, the LGBT Community Center, meant that the performers and much of the audience was simultaneously home and away—an interesting development.

Second, I claim that community-based theatre supports and perhaps even helps to create, a sense of community in which people may participate as agents of change. Bruce McConachie notes:

As real communities—cohesive social groups engaged in sustaining their members' identities through face-to-face interactions—dwindle in significance in people's everyday lives, the imaginative construction of "community" assumes greater importance . . . Surely part of the reason for the success of grassroots theatres is that they provide images for their audiences that help them to do the symbolic work of including and excluding that constitutes community. No performance itself can alter the routines of everyday life, but community-based theatre can provide "what if" images of potential community, sparking the kind of imaginative work that must precede substantial changes in customary habits.[12]

Although I assert a more direct pressure toward change, especially when *TO* is used in the developmental and performance process, I harbor many doubts. We must certainly "scrutinize community-based theatre and the ways in which the collaborative process helps to build, perform, and destabilize community."[13] For example, Kuftinec's study of the work of Cornerstone Theatre reminds us that "production work demonstrates the difficulty of using the term 'community' to imply stability or permanence. Thus, when [speaking] of the work as celebrating community or unifying the community, it is essential to bear in mind the unstable and temporary nature of this community [and not to operate] with a certain idealism and mythology about the purpose and affective impact of the work."[14] Whereas the groups with which I worked came together first to create, and then with a larger group to share a performance event, it would be foolish to think that we had established a long-lasting communal bond. What we hoped for was a long-lasting community impact.

I would maintain, however, that in the creation of a community-based performance, the structuring of the work reminds those involved that their everyday culture is a construct, full of difference and contestation, and changeable without demanding homogeneity. The communal celebration of such local agency mitigates against the assumption that one permanently holds victim status in an unalterable social structure and disavows an unalterable monolithic oppressor.

Third, I maintain that community-based theatre uses representation to challenge representation and narrativity. It raises the simple questions of who gets to make art and why. In community-based theatre, community members construct the representation of the community's own stories. Participants, in the midst of a most intimate connection to events, gain a distance from which to question narrative as an "inevitable series" and culture as "the way it is." Creative collaboration with others whose views of events differ reveals much about the force of social circumstances. Because the participant "is engaged fundamentally in the active construction of meaning as the performance event [which includes its development] proceeds" then the performance is, in a sense, "'about' the production of meaning."[15] Unlike observed theatre, community-based theatre is resistant, not transgressive; rather than presenting counter-representations, it investigates the processes and apparatuses that control representation itself.

This is not to say that community-based theatre work will lead to intentional clarity and representational accuracy. I maintain that community-based theatre, particularly that informed by techniques of *TO*, celebrates the uncertainty of the signifier and in so doing asserts the centrality of dialogue and the power of participation, which actively construct not only meaning, but the event itself. It empowers and reveals. The empowerment and revelation, in turn, invigorate the creative community, which may be heterogeneous and competitive, but is clearly productive and self-determined (at least within certain boundaries of influence). Participation promotes agency through ownership of the work, demystification of artistic creation and "talent," awareness of the construction of culture, and reassertion of contextualized identity.

In the Milwaukee project, after workshop sessions on Image Theatre, the class developed images of oppressions they suffered or in which they were complicit—financial, lack of respect in education for the arts, and idealization of images of beauty. The process was most revealing. After the theatre students let go of the feeling that they were expected to "be on," the work progressed rapidly. Often discussions turned to personal responses to the work or to questions about its practicality in other performance venues. Groups were formed around topics with which individuals most resonated, and the explorations led to a series of rather striking pictures and personal discoveries. The difficult task for me was to balance use of and training in the techniques; for the students it was to let go of the narrative of rehearsal and product. When we worked with the members of Project Q, the freedom provided by imagery without "captions," and without narrative and behavioral expectations, led to a rapid expansion of creative energy. It also provided a way for those reticent to speak to contribute to the silent dialogue and impact the work.

I justified spending a great deal of time in physical exploration by my fourth and final claim about what makes community-based theatre efficacious: that embodied participation in the process of theatre making—performance itself—is the most subversive element in participatory community-based theatre. Participatory theatre mobilizes all resources—experiential and embodied, as well as intellectual—in the construction of meaning rather than in merely finding an index to it. Community-based theatre is a cultural construct and a means of cultural production.

The performative "acts out" (i.e., is, lives and relives, embodies) learning, which I see as reintegrative. By that I mean first, the performative act itself attacks the dualism that is at the heart of hegemonic practices in mass-mediated culture. Second, it attacks a repressive educational process that compartmentalizes not only knowledges but also ways of knowing. On the one hand, the system of doers and watchers privileges certain epistemological pairings and insists on a hierarchy of value for each; it also dispossesses both integrative choices and the crossing of boundaries that such choices entail. On the other hand, performative exploration is a way of achieving a sense of self as a subject among many—confused and contested perhaps, but still subject. It is a radical democratization of cultural creation and allows theatre to be a rehearsal for and imagining of the same in the broader society.

Put another way, all theatre is not only political but also potentially subversive (or at least resistant) because it is integrative and embodied. Moreover, theatre that allows all participants (or at least those who become designated representatives of others temporarily waiting or watching), allows the performance of integration and construction—that is, of power and possibility. In the theatre class, for example, everyone eagerly participated in the next step—improvisations that led to the development of Forum Theatre.

The last three sessions on campus were devoted to Forum Theatre. Several students told stories of times in which they felt "un-voiced" and oppressed, and groups were formed to develop pieces that used the stories, but were not necessarily retellings of the specifics. In each case the protagonist and the situation were clearly defined before improvisatory work began. One play focused on the refusal of school officials to acknowledge homophobia in an elementary school, a second dealt with abuse of a waitress by customers and co-workers, and the third was about a woman who was sexually harassed because she stopped into a bar for a drink on the way home from work. The class eventually chose to develop the last, in part because it provided a sharp illustration of a Forum play and invited interventions easily. In addition, we did not want to take a play about a gay/lesbian issue to Project Q and thereby imply that we knew in advance what problems they had and needed to solve. We constantly reminded ourselves during the class that we must enter any community as co-learners and co-creators, not as experts and problem solvers.

We were, however, outsiders. But, even if one maintains that there is still an initial separation of facilitator-from-community, of performer-from-the-community, or of performer-from-spectator,

performers and audience members enjoy the dynamic oscillation between corporeality and signification in the embodied images they have constructed together in the theatre. . . . [It] is possible to hypothesize that audiences use the symbolic exchange of theatrical experience to make judgments about the kinds of images to include or exclude from their ideal community. Community-based theatre, then, is less about representing the realities of actual or historic communities—although markers of these realities need to be present to "authenticate" the experience—and more about imagining and constructing the relationships of an ethical community for the future.[16]

If this is so, how much more efficacious, how much more fraught with possibility, is the tension when the subjects are the bodies—when the imagined possibility is (re)presented by, acted out by, the body/person for whom it is imagined? If (put simply) the "we" is on stage? Theatre that puts community onstage, as does Theatre of the Oppressed, has the potential for the greatest impact and is, in my estimation, the core of today's most exciting socially active theatre.

TO provides for me a particularly attractive method for approaching community participants and for developing, even if only initially, a collaboration with performers. Augusto Boal's theory is based in part on the simple definition of oppression as having lost one's voice. To him monologue is oppressive; dialogue is liberating and productive. *TO* is transformative, dialogic, participatory. *TO* is best known for the *Forum Theatre* technique, in which a play developed in response to a particular community problem is performed for an audience which is then invited to intervene in a second performance of the same play to change the course of the action.

In her book *Theatricality* Elizabeth Burns discusses the notion of the audience's "horizon of expectations."[17] This set of performative conventions—rhetorical conventions (the interaction between the performers and the spectators) and actualizing conventions (interaction between the characters, which implies a connection to the "real world" of the audience)—creates the framework within which observed theatre needs to stay in order to be successful. *TO* challenges, yet uses, the framework within which performance is understood by blending conventions. It supports a structure in which the community can explore situations and responses to them in a space that is simultaneously a part of their real world and *not* the real world. Spectators become "spect-actors" and the performance becomes a rehearsal for transformation outside the theatre.[18]

In the classroom portion of the project, each piece was rehearsed using methods suggested in *Games,* and other approaches, the most fruitful of which was reducing each character's dialogue to a single line and then trying to make the entire scene work. During development of the sexual harassment scene, an interesting discovery was made by the student participants about how difficult, and how revealing, it was to play an antagonist. Several students performed the piece for the other class members who intervened as would happen in any Forum performance. The difficulty of maintaining an oppressive stance and staying in character while responding to unexpected actions by spect-actors who replaced the protagonist became very clear. I would have liked to spend much more time training actors to improvise as Forum performers, but the next phase of the project had to begin. Nevertheless, we decided that we would share this piece with the Project Q members as an illustration of the work we had done (not as a model of what we hoped they would create), and as an invitation for them to intervene in our work.

During the eighth week of the semester, the entire class joined members of Project Q, a youth support group, at the LGBT Community Center in Milwaukee. Even though the class and I had discussed our position as co-creators with the Project Q members, and had repeatedly discussed how foolish it would be to assume that we were there to "help," knew what had to be said or done, or what problems had to be solved, I anticipated two impediments to getting the two groups to function as a unit. The first was level and amount of performance experience. I assumed that my theatre students would dominate improvisational work. The second was the fact that each group had worked together for quite awhile, and that ties had been formed that would keep each group in its own clique. I was wrong on both counts.

The space we used in the community center building was not officially Project Q's. It was in some ways a foreign, yet public, arena for all participants, and as we claimed the space together, a sense of communal ownership of place and event was established. Another mitigating factor was the desire of Project Q members to voice themselves. This provided such motivation that improvisations, either with Images or in Forum development, were quite balanced. Finally, the *TO* techniques themselves provided so much and encouraged such rapid sharing and discovery that the groups were quickly united.[19]

As in the class, early work was devoted to demechanization and habit breaking. We moved rapidly to Image work. The willingness of the Project Q youth to take risks to secure their right to speak and to stand in the subject position was quite powerful. The group images of oppression were so striking that we included ten of them in the public performance. The topics included oppression by religion, because of age, and because of stereotyping and expectations. It is important to note that, in spite of the seriousness of the investigations and the tension associated with the topics, the constant in all rehearsals was energy that often erupted in laughter. The process provided participants with release and, I would maintain, deep and abiding pleasure.

As part of the transition from Image to Forum Theatre, class members performed the sexual harassment piece for the entire group. In some ways it was a most uncomfortable time. While we tried to make it clear that this was a sharing of work and an illustration of a product, it felt like we were showing, or showing *off*, our creative output *for* the Project Q participants. The interventions were few and half-hearted, and the communal sense disrupted. However, students and Project Q members quickly connected again in the story-telling circles during which each person in a focus group related a personal incident of oppression, danger, or loss.

After story-telling sessions in focus groups, Forum Theatre pieces were developed improvisationally around several stories, each of which pointed to a number of problems faced by LGBT youth. Each cast included UW students and Project Q members. The group chose two pieces—one about a gay couple being forced to leave their senior prom and one about a lesbian coming out when she and her partner came home for Christmas—because they found them most provocative. As the holidays approached their pressure began to inform the second piece. The fact that it included multiple oppressions kept it growing in immediacy and intensity.

The scenes were rehearsed separately and then in front of the entire group, which made script and directorial suggestions. Once again, we found that it was difficult to play the antagonist, but also most instructive. We had some trouble getting cast members to say with conviction the very things they would hate to hear, but the pieces came together at the last moment. I think that with more rehearsal time they might have developed a performative punch that they did not quite reach, but I think that such polish might have inhibited audience intervention. I do know that the appropriate evaluative standards for participatory theatre must focus on audience activity or response, and the amount and intensity of involvement by the one hundred-plus audience members was, to the cast members and I, most rewarding.

The performance was part of the weeklong anniversary celebration of the LGBT Community Center. The night we performed, a new mural was unveiled, the coffee bar was opened, and a photo display of our rehearsal process was exhibited. A full-page article in the weekly arts-oriented Milwaukee paper asked "Is this theatre liberatory?" and described our rehearsal process, its energy and joy, and the goals of the performance. The space was jammed. Audience members were invited to a pre-show reception, heard ten minutes of welcoming and thank you speeches, and were treated to a delightful drag, lip-synch performance. I did a brief introduction to our performance, noting that we would begin with a series of tableaux, both realistic and abstract, about pressures the cast felt. I announced each topic and sculptor's name and the groups rapidly produced the images. Each was held for about twenty seconds, although some generated such sharp responses that I let them remain visible for far longer. Everyone who had been a regular participant performed in this segment.

As soon as the images were completed, I got the audience on its feet, doing the Circle and the Cross and Writing in the Air, TO exercises described in Boal's *Games*. These games ask the audience members to perform different tasks, first with their hands and then with one hand and one foot, simultaneously. Everyone "fails" because of our own habits. The activities generated a great deal of laughter, as they always do, and indicated a willingness on the audience's part to be active. Boal's Handshake game, in which a person must constantly be shaking hands with at least one other person, provided a concrete way of practicing audience cooperation and got everyone circulating around the room. By the time people returned to their seats, the energy level in the room was quite high.

I used another handshake activity (that I had seen Boal do in New York a few months earlier) to illustrate how Forum Theatre works. I invited an audience member to shake my hand, but when she got to me, I folded my arms and turned away. When I asked people what they might do in that situation, several spectators came up to respond to my actions.

Once the audience understood the invitation to replace the protagonist, we moved immediately into the prom piece, and the audience watched with rapt attention. During the scene a gay couple danced together, was hassled by others at the prom, and forced to leave by the chaperones, ostensibly "for their own safety." At the end there was applause, but also signs of distress in the audience. However, when I asked for someone to replace the protagonist (noting that the person would get to wear a fabulous tuxedo as enticement) no one moved. Fortunately, one of the UW students not in the scene stepped in as one of the protagonists. She chose the worst possible option—to say that dancing with her partner was a joke and deny his sexual identity. When I asked the audience members what they had seen, there was rapid description of and disagreement with the choice. Someone during the brief discussion began his comment with, "What he should—" but I cut the person off and asked him to come on stage and *show* us what he was going to suggest. I did not have to prod anyone again. What was significant about the suggestions that generated the most support from the spectators was that they were all confrontational. All tried to force the chaperones/antagonists to admit either the legal or social irresponsibility, or the homophobic and discriminatory basis, of their decision to make the men leave. Only once did someone confront the other couples at the prom who had taunted the couple.

The second piece generated a far more empathetic response. In it a daughter comes home for Christmas with her partner. Her two younger siblings, dominated mother, narrow-minded and bigoted father, Bible-toting minister, minister's wife, and their son (who is hoping to get a New Year's Eve date with the protagonist) are all there. During the first performance, she was verbally abused by the young man, threatened with hell fires and damned by the minister, taunted by the siblings, and disowned by the parents. She and her partner were forced to leave the home in which she wanted to be accepted and loved. The applause at the end of the scene capped off frequent verbal responses from the audience, and many instances of nodding in recognition.

The interventions came quickly, and, during the brief discussions that followed each intervention, the audience was extremely astute in describing the action that spect-actors chose, what was really behind it, and what result it had. Various attempts were made at confrontation or logical argument with, and appeals for support from, those gathered for the Christmas celebration. While each generated momentary success, the end result was always the same. After more than thirty minutes a man from the audience replaced the protagonist, managed to get everyone except the father, the chief antagonist, to leave the room under pretense of giving them a great surprise, and then appealed to her father's sense of fairness and justice, his previous love, and his moral lessons to her, before she told him the nature of her relationship with the woman she brought home. The father, and the audience, fell silent under the power of the choice.

I cannot, of course, say that the world or even the lives of the audience members will be made better by the work, but I can without reservation say that there are choices that they are aware of that they might not have known before. I can say without reservation that the voices of the participants were raised, and heard, and responded to in a public forum. And I can say without reservation that as participants explored the variety of choices and performed, themselves, the ways in which antagonistic forces try to build obstacles and boundaries that limit possibilities, they gained insight into the constructed nature of their culture and into the way in which their identities develop in compliance with and in response to that culture.

The week after the performance I met with the students to do an evaluation of the class and to get their advice about future projects. One member of Project Q attended, and several more joined us at a postclass celebration. We may not be a community—university students, LGBT youth, and a professor from another city—but as a group we had the power to create something challenging and moving about and with a community. Project Q's director, class members, and audience letters and e-mails convinced me that the work had been successful, but the nature of that success is not sharply defined.

I am not certain that this description of this project is sufficient to convince readers about the claims I made earlier in this chapter. But I am certain that the Milwaukee project provided an experience with value beyond what might have accrued to an audience who merely watched someone else's play. In any event, I don't wish to make my claims easy to swallow. "The process of theatre, how the authority of the word, the presence of the performer, and the complicity of the silent spectator articulate dramatic play," must be thoroughly explored in political and community-based theatre.[20] I urge constructive and critical confrontation with the process and products and rigorous theorizing about the work. Otherwise community-based theatre-making methods will be relegated to the quaint, will reproduce the very hierarchies they are designed to challenge or transform, or will become static and self-congratulatory.[21]

NOTES

1. Janelle Reinelt, "Notes for a Radical Democratic Theater: Productive Crises and the Challenge of Indeterminacy," in *Staging Resistance: Essays on Political Theatre,* ed. Jeanne Colleran and Jenny Spencer (Ann Arbor: University of Michigan Press, 1998), 283.

2. Jeanne Colleran and Jenny S. Spencer, Introduction to *Staging Resistance: Essays on Political Theatre,* ed. Jeanne Colleran and Jenny Spencer (Ann Arbor: University of Michigan Press, 1998), 1.

3. Jan Cohen-Cruz, Introduction to *Radical Street Performance: An International Anthology,* ed. Jan Cohen-Cruz (New York: Routledge, 1998), 5.

4. See Bruce McConachie, "Approaching the 'Structures of Feeling' in Grassroots Theatre," *Theatre Topics* 8 (March): 33–53.

5. bell hooks, Introduction to *Outlaw Culture: Resisting Representations,* ed. bell hooks (New York: Routledge, 1994), 6. Although hooks was writing about cultural criticism, not theatre directly, this quotation applies equally to the theatre.

6. Political theatre has often been marginalized by activists as separate from the ebb and flow of life, and therefore ineffective, or by theatre professionals and scholars as just an aspect of "real" life apart from the art of the theatre. The separation of ideology and aesthetics, on which these dismissals are based, has remained operative since the eighteenth century. Participatory, particularly community-based theatre, continues to be devalued today using the same labels. And yet I would maintain, again, that it is through this kind of theatre work, *central* to the lives of those it touches, that the goal of political theatre—the transformation of society—is most likely to begin.

7. Paulo Freire, *Pedagogy of the Oppressed* (New York: Continuum, 1995), 64.

8. There were initially twenty-two members of the class; nineteen finished the course. Fifteen of them were theatre majors, one was a film studies major, and the other three worked in various capacities with Milwaukee Public Theatre, a group that has been doing community-based work for many years using a variety of techniques that they have developed.

9. See Augusto Boal, *Games for Actors and Non-Actors* (New York: Routledge, 1992).

10. Fredric Jameson, *Postmodernism, or, The Cultural Logic of Late Capitalism* (Durham, N.C.: Duke University Press, 1991), 54.

11. Sonja Kuftinec, "A Cornerstone for Rethinking Community Theatre," *Theatre Topics* 6 (March 1996): 100.

12. McConachie, "Structures of Feeling," 37–38.

13. Kuftinec, "Cornerstone," 91.

14. Ibid., 98.

15. Baz Kershaw, *The Politics of Performance: Radical Theatre as Cultural Intervention* (New York: Routledge, 1991), 16.

16. McConachie, "Structures of Feeling," 40–41.

17. Elizabeth Burns, *Theatricality: A Study of Convention in the Theatre and in Social Life* (White Plains, N.Y.: Longman, 1972).

18. See Augusto Boal, *Theatre of the Oppressed* (New York: Urizen Books, 1979).

19. It is important to note that the one difference between the groups was that the students, because they had a regular class schedule, were there essentially all of the time. Project Q participants often had work or personal conflicts, and some were not able to come consistently enough to be part of the final performance. Everyone who showed up on any night was welcomed to do warm-ups and contribute ideas. The scenes grew with contributions from more than twenty Project Q members, though only about half that number came to every session or were in the final performance.

20. W. B. Worthen, "*Still Playing Games:* Ideology and Performance in the Theatre of Irene Fornes," in *Feminine Focus: The New Women Playwrights,* ed. Enoch Brader (Oxford: Oxford University Press, 1989), 167.

21. The project has produced some unexpected results. Project Q is attempting to organize its own theatre company to explore and develop performances about issues

of concern to its members. The Center for Applied Theatre (under whose auspices I do similar work outside of the University) and Milwaukee Public Theatre will be working together on a project focusing on alcohol and drug abuse with community and school leaders. The UW-M class was repeated in Fall 2001 with a smaller number of college students and a large number of participants from the Lighted Schoolhouse, an at-risk program in the Milwaukee Public Schools. I will be doing ongoing work with that program. And, while not simply the result of the course, UW-Milwaukee has added a "Theatre in Society" track to its BA program and is including "Participatory Theatre Techniques" as a required class for all majors.

14

THE (OC)CULT OF PERSONALITY: INITIATING THE AUDIENCE INTO *THE EDWARDIAN MYSTERIES*

J. Lawton Winslade

Ritual involvement reveals the audience.
—Pat McDermott, quoted in Sainer, *Radical Theatre Notebook* (74)

Since most people believe what everybody else believes, the creation of a group of implicate practitioners creates its own conditions for success . . . A passive audience could be recruited (temporarily, at least) by a powerful spell; active participation is far stronger . . . Also, if everybody does it, it doesn't look as silly.
—Jeff Grygny, "De Nostrum Verum Magikum"
("Of Our True Magik")[1]

As I entered the theatrical space at the Performance Loft in the Second Unitarian Church of Chicago in October 1998, I was greeted by a woman dressed in a ceremonial robe and a small moon-shaped headdress. She held in her hands the notorious Thoth deck, a popular set of tarot cards attributed to the nineteenth-century magician and self-proclaimed Antichrist Aleister Crowley. She pulled a card for me. It was the Knight of Wands. The fortune-teller (Robyn Tisch) told me that I would be starting a creative project by the beginning of November. She was right, as I was in the planning stages of directing a production. A bit taken aback by this momentous greeting, I hesitantly took my seat in the small auditorium. The audience was then subjected to an over-the-top and extremely campy sample of pseudo-classical melodrama, with a fainting damsel and a hero with stuffed tights, all speaking bad classical language. Thankfully, this sketch was interrupted by an announcer who informed the audience that they were already playing a game, in which the rules were unknown and had to be discovered. We were then escorted outside the theatre, around the front of the building, where we glimpsed a nightclub-like performance by "Persephone" and "Hades," well-dressed party-goers in grotesque masks. The implication was that we were actually being taken through the land of the dead, a journey to the underworld, albeit an elegant one. In order to reemerge into the theatrical space, the audience was required to come up with a secret password that we chanted three times before we could enter. The space had been transformed into a ceremonial drawing room with chairs on either side of the floor, decorated on all sides with altars, candles, and party tables. Thus, the phantasmagoria began.

This experience was an evening with *The Edwardian Mysteries: a phantasmagoria,* presented by the Mystery Caravan during the early autumn of 1998, on the north side of Chicago. The brainchild of theatre artist Jeff Grygny, *The Edwardian Mysteries* attempted to emulate the social gathering of a late-Victorian and Edwardian-style secret society. Influenced by Grygny's work with Tibetan Buddhism, the performance carried the idea of audience interaction, inherent to events like murder mysteries, to another level. The characters in the drama were all real historical figures, all odd in their own way based on their somewhat radical views about transforming society. Most were active from the late 19th century into the 1930s and early 1940s, and many actually knew each other and worked together (or against each other).

Though experimental audience participation in the mold of The Performance Group or Living Theatre is rare these days, the Chicago theatre scene, known for its tradition of improv comedy, has become the site for much of what can be called "interactive." The long-running spoof *Tony n' Tina's Wedding,* in which the audience is treated as guests to the title wedding, provides a popular model for such works. Indeed, productions that feature murder mysteries and courtroom dramas, for instance, seem to be the current trend for commercially successful theatre, encouraging the audience to participate in social contexts (the party, the dinner, the courtroom) only slightly more staged than "real" situations. Audiences flock to these hyper-real events, perhaps merely to experience drama with more immediate consequences than reality. Whatever the reason, this kind of dinner theatre, often quite banal in its slapstick-y offerings, draws crowds. *The Edwardian Mysteries* may have its roots in such interactive theatre, but in terms of both its performance and its driving social theory, it is quite a different animal.

Grygny's Mystery Caravan, which his Web site describes as a timeless troupe of mystics, scholars, and travelers carrying and exchanging "living wisdom," are based on real historical characters who were involved to varying degrees in what could be called a Western mystery tradition. They were all, in a sense, occult initiates, practicing eclectic forms of mysticism, spiritualism and ceremonial magic popular at the turn of the century. The key here is that each one of these characters is a flamboyant individual who produced writing, performances, and artwork rife with lofty ideals about humanity. In the performance space, these ideals often come in conflict with each other, even while maintaining a common thread that points to the spiritual evolution of hu-mankind. These characters, both in monologues and in audience interaction, reach out to audience members, expecting the audience to emulate their example of the enlightened individual. Here, content and method are inex-tricable, for these traditions of mysticism and magic, as they were practiced in the early twentieth century, were based on personal development. Thus, *The Edwardian Mysteries* illuminates for its audiences the possibility that, through magical (or theatrical) means, the individual can create a persona worthy of participating in an elite party, and worthy of initiating into the secret society to end all secret societies.

Because these characters are colorful historical figures rather than fictional characters, the audiences may have felt more compelled to socially interact with them, especially if an audience member was familiar with that person's life or work, like I was. Here, we seem to be crossing over into the territory of so-called living historians, actors who research and characterize a historical figure, often for historical reenactments, restored villages, or other theme sites that make up much of what Richard Schechner called "restored behavior" in *Between Theater and Anthropology*.[2] Though these sorts of performance con-texts often involve tourist audiences asking questions of the "characters" about their life and environment, the opportunity for interaction between audience and performer is still somewhat limited. With the Mystery Caravan, the setting was unmistakably and intentionally a theatrical space. Yet, the politics of the Edwardian encounter are also markedly different from the experiments of the 1960s and 1970s, in which theater companies attempted to educate and involve certain kinds of spectators who were not unwilling to take matters into their own hands, as in Schechner's *Dionysus in 69*, when audience members effectively ended the play by carrying off Pentheus.[3]

First it is necessary to meet the Edwardians. These figures seemed to fall into three groups. The leader of the entire crowd was Madame Helena Blavatsky, the psychic spiritualist and Orientalist founder of the Theosophical Society in England, and her cronies, Anna Kingsford and Alice Bailey. The mystic Krishnamurti, frequent speaker at the Theosophical Society, was also characterized. The second group included members of the Hermetic Order of the Golden Dawn, a secret society of artists and Freemasons formed in England roughly the same time as the Theosophical Society. They were represented by rivals Aleister Crowley and William Butler Yeats, along with Dion Fortune (played by the same actress who told the fortunes) who was active in an off-shoot of the Dawn in its later years. The third was literally the wildcard group: the Dadaists Tristan Tzara and Jean Arp, along with Arp's dancer wife, Sophie Tauber, Cabaret Voltaire singer Emmy Hennings, and the painter Kandinsky. The fictional society that the Mystery Caravan creates has echoes of The Golden Dawn, The Rosicrucians, the Theosophical Society, the Freemasons, and many other European societies of the late nineteenth and early twentieth century. Although a good deal of these characters did actually know each other in their physical lives, the situation of their coming together is fictional, and indeed, many of them were not contemporaries at all.

The frame of the production was simple: scenes of instruction and presentation by the members were interspersed between moments of social interaction between audience members and actors over wine and cheese. In preparation for the first scene, the audience was divided by gender, a move that often broke up couples who attended together. This crucial removal of a safety factor prepared the audience for what was ahead. The first scene was a "séance," invoking the historical figures that the actors would portray. After the spirits were made present, each actor gave a short speech, culled from that figure's body of writing, followed by the mantra-like phrase, "Let there be no misunderstanding," and an accompanying ceremonial gesture: a handclap followed by waving the right hand in an arc. Scenes throughout the evening included mystical instruction by Yeats, a *Star Wars*-style light-saber battle between Yeats and Crowley, a tea party of theosophists, a masked dance tableau performance complete with smoke machine, gong, and large doors, a chaotic sound poem by the Dadaists, involving audience members throwing balled up bits of paper at the performers, and a lecture by Krishnamurti on the nature of freedom. In the midst of all of this, the audience was receiving esoteric lessons while witnessing both ritual and dialogue. During the well-timed breaks, audience members could observe, interact, and even be initiated.

Despite the simplicity of the frame, the experience of *The Edwardian Mysteries* was complex. Although the nature of the presentational scenes was unmistakably didactic—the adapted texts were generally presented as instructional lectures—the overall atmosphere of the proceedings was one of both ceremony and play. It is this tension between solemn ceremony and raucous play that ultimately worked for the *Mysteries*. Grygny, who, in an apt bit of self-casting, also portrayed Crowley, is quite aware of the density of the material he is adapting for performance. However, he transformed what could have been an extremely dry evening of meaning-of-life contemplation into an entertaining party, with equal parts witty banter, formal dance, wine and cheese, and Ouija board. The genius of this particular production was that despite the irony and humor of the situation, Grygny subtly slipped in complex mystical and philosophical concepts. Grygny fed the postmodern individual's innate hunger for a transcendent experience that can still entertain. The concepts discussed in the piece encompassed a wide range of issues important to these people who hoped to somehow change the world through spiritual means. Concepts like free will, love, power, dreams, chaos and order, self-control and discipline, and the individual's place in the cosmos, do not fall on deaf ears. As the production occurred in 1998, a particular resonance was possible between turn of the century characters and turn of the millennium audiences.

Besides appealing to the individual's thirst for knowledge, the Mystery Caravan employs many savvy moves to bring audience members fully into the experience. One method Grygny employed to help people feel at home concerned actors serving wine, cheese and hors d'oeuvres to audience members. Though sharing food with the audience is certainly nothing new—The Performance Group's production of *Mother Courage* is one notable example—there is something to the serving.[4] Rather than emphasize merely an egalitarian sense of community, the Edwardian food sharing had its class issues intact. In correspondence, Grygny describes the intent to create a "grand function," a cocktail party where the audience member is being treated like nobility, and comfort is created through dignity, decorum, and ceremony. One of Grygny's primary intentions was to convey an air of elegance: in the proceedings, in the characters, in the treatment of the audience, and even in physical exercises for the actors to inhabit particularly turn-of-the-century European bodies.[5]

The most prominent audience interaction took place in a short initiation ceremony that two or three audience members were taken through at the end of each of the social breaks. The initiation ceremony itself comes out of social interaction with the performers. My own experience began when Crowley whisked my friend, who had accompanied me to the performance, away in a dance, leaving me holding the rose that Krishnamurti (David Hawkins) had given her. She was then passed on to Alice Bailey (Jeanine Caughlin), who later recommended her initiation. I put the rose in my teeth and began to dance with Crowley. We engaged in the classic dialogic tango, exchanging witticisms, volleying esoteric wisdom through the rose in our teeth. This interesting conversation, based on my particular knowledge of Crowley's writings, would lead to the creation of my initiatory title, "Lord of the Dance." We bandied about Crowley's famous aphorisms (such as "Do what thou wilt shall be the whole of the law") until the character Crowley posed the inevitable question: "Do you wish to know the Mystery?" Such exchanges were common between actors and audience participants, along with the question "Have we met before?" which was usually directed at repeat audience members (who, as we'll see, were not uncommon). However, in this particular spiritualist atmosphere, the implication is always that you, the audience member, had known these people in a past life, thus saying "you are (or were) one of us," a member of this secret society that stretches through time.

After exchanges like this, one of the characters would briefly instruct the audience member and lead the initiate through a gauntlet of chanting and gesticulating performers, behind the large doors. A gong was then struck, and the doors were opened amid large quantities of smoke, the participant emerged, and would speak the magic phrase "Let there be no misunderstanding," and its accompanying gesture, while Grygny as Crowley endowed the initiate with a title, and Dion Fortune presented the participant with a handmade talisman. Both the title and the talisman would become things that were uniquely the participant's. I'm not sure if everyone experienced this, but I was taken to an altar hidden from general view and asked to place my hand in a bowl of sand, from which I pulled an aquamarine gemstone. This "secret" part of the initiation, an intimate scene between Crowley and me, further developed my sense of participation in the mystery.

In essence, like a secret society that simultaneously separates and integrates its initiates, the Edwardians both individualize audience members—giving them a name and an actual thing to take home—and welcome them into the fold. Lynda Daniels, who portrayed Emmy Hennings, later revealed to me the techniques used in choosing the initiates: "We were supposed to make the audience want to be involved in the secrets . . . and he [Grygny] wanted us to do it in a way that had them actually doing something, as opposed to just conversing with us, because we felt that if we had them do things, they would be far more willing to interact."[6] For instance, I was informed that my task of giving the juggling ball to Emma was a common signal that the Dadaists had worked out between themselves. It certainly speaks to the skill of the cast, or to my willingness to immerse myself in the Edwardian world, that I had no idea I was being tested. So these challenges—often simple, mundane tasks—would indicate to the actors that an audience member would be willing to interact, and even get on stage for an initiation.

Daniels divulged other techniques for spotting initiates that might include, for instance, a code phrase that an audience member would be asked to repeat. Or a request for initiation could result from a successful attempt to involve an audience member in an impromptu debate between two characters (she spoke of how this often worked well between her and Yeats). Sometimes these codes were set up beforehand—Daniels called them "haphazard deals"—and other times they were spontaneous, and these techniques evolved throughout the run of the show. Therefore, when the audience member would repeat the correct phrase or complete a task, he or she would be sent on for further challenges or for initiation, which was usually overseen by Grygny as Crowley. So here we have levels of initiation, with different social groups performing different roles in the hierarchy of initiation. For instance, the Dadaists often acted as catalysts, encouraging people to get involved in the action, whereas the Theosophists often announced an audience member's candidacy for initiation and Crowley and Fortune performed the final honors.

Each initiate would lend to the proceedings his or her own sense of theatricality and play, so that each initiation had its own particular character. I tried to wrest from Daniels some colorful stories about initiates and their performances, but she claimed that audience members were more interesting in moments of subtle engagement, especially when audience members understood Grygny's game and how to play, which they apparently often did. "It wasn't that they would do something fascinating but that they were present in the moment," she insisted. In our conversation, Daniels seemed genuinely surprised at both audience members' knowledge of the content of the *Mysteries,* as well as their savvy ability to catch on quickly. Of course, there were those who came to the show looking for escape, or a chance to act out and garner attention, and the production certainly did not disappoint those expectations. Daniels spoke of one gentleman who, donned in cape and sword, used his initiation as an opportunity to make a speech. Yet, she claimed that "even though he was living in a different world than us, he was finding what he needed in what we were offering."

In the midst of a "secret," elitist society, *The Edwardian Mysteries* gave its audience the opportunity and the access to full participation, and to know the mystery: "Let there be no misunderstanding." Essentially, Grygny and his Mystery Caravan were educating and initiating their audience, creating their own elite secret society. Repeat audience members were indeed welcomed warmly, and actors often made use of the initiate's experience in order to garner other initiates. "They understand the mysteries," according to Daniels, "and so we played on that . . . I think that's why people came back three or four times, after they realized the second time that they were actually part of it, it was a place they could come to belong." She further describes how she'd often witness the transformation of meek and quiet audience members: "They started warming up and became a part of it. And I saw this happen again and again. I couldn't believe how people opened up."

Besides elegance, humor was also a major factor in reaching the audience. Yet, this is not merely slapstick but a sort of humor intended to reveal spiritual truth. Grygny also mentioned his intent to offer the play as a ludibrium, a technique not unknown in the history of Western (and Eastern, to a degree) esotericism, in which a fine line exists between charlatan and guru.[7] Accordingly, higher wisdom can often come from a so-called laughing master, a concept not foreign to Tibetan Buddhism, one of Grygny's acknowledged influences. In an adept move, Grygny decided to include the Cabaret Voltaire Dadaists as the tools for this humor. Even though one does not generally associate the Dadaists with millenarian movements, their inclusion makes sense as a group that raised itself to elite status based on its own absurdity. Their presence within the performance is crucial to the piece's overall sense of humor. One of the first secrets whispered to me by Alice Bailey as I entered the space was "Tristan Tzara is not to be trusted." Tzara and his extremely physical sidekick, Jean Arp, were literally all over the place, as they drew audience members into their discordian antics. Amid the seriousness of the others, the Dadaists offered the necessary perspective that such a thing as a secret society of extreme eccentrics can be very ironic and humorous. In an interview, Grygny denies that he mocks the characters, stating "We have fun *with* these people." Furthermore, he acknowledges that enlightenment often involves "lightening up."[8]

I would agree with Grygny, however, that these characters are more than simply entertaining. In fact, Grygny's choice to portray these particular figures is essential to the socio-political scene he is creating. These historical characters are indeed presented to the audience as models for a certain kind of identity. First, we must place them in the context of the elite secret society.

The Edwardian Mysteries not only points to the secret society as a problematic, yet intriguing social structure, but to that society's hidden performances as constitutive of the politics of exclusion and secrecy. Defining what could easily be the secret society's place in culture, Joseph Roach claims that New Orleans Mardi Gras clubs, "with their continuously renegotiated boundaries of exclusion, exemplify the smaller atoms of affiliation through which larger societies may be constructed."[9] He later describes Mardi Gras funerals, and I would add séances, as indicative of the role of performance in general, in that "they make visible through symbolic action both the tangible existence of social boundaries and, at the same time, the contingency of these boundaries on fictions of identity."[10] After all, these groups are made of individuals who see themselves as separate from the world at large and on a level with each other. Some of these individuals imagined themselves controlling or influencing that world from behind closed doors, while some simply practiced isolation in order to develop themselves more spiritually. Often, the two types existed in the same group, a fact that accounts for many of the conflicts in the Golden Dawn, for example.

Like many other occult groups, the Golden Dawn was historically plagued with personal conflicts, power struggles, and psychodramas. Writing about the Golden Dawn as a former member in the early 1930s, Israel Regardie describes the society as a product of its time: "Having been founded just prior to the [18]90's, it incorporated within itself all the inherent faults and vices of that period. The fact that it admitted numerous theatrical people to the ranks of its membership indicates the presence of superficiality and self-satisfaction . . . and many of its members were incurable poseur."[11] Regardie goes on to tell of a person of high ranking who wore her full ceremonial regalia, something only members were allowed to see, to a costume ball. These people, often leaders of occult and spiritualist movements, some outrageous, like Crowley who thrived on his over-the-top tabloid persona, some more reserved, who were content to work silently in the shadows, all form what I would call the "occult of personality." These individuals walked a thin line between personal spiritual development and a public persona often at odds with that development.

With practices such as taking on a new name or motto, like Crowley's "Perdurabo" (I will endure to the end), in the secret society, individual identity becomes fluid and changing ethnicity is as simple as donning a new costume. Identity changing becomes, in essence, a magical act. Robert Anton Wilson, in an introduction to Regardie's biography of Crowley, describes the magician's recommendation that an individual "adopt two 'opposite' personalities, such as a vegetarian pacifist and a chauvinistic militarist, key each one to a different piece of jewelry (a talisman or a ring) and change his verbal opinions, his outer behavior, and his more subtle inner responses, depending on which piece of jewelry he was wearing."[12] Crowley often went native when he traveled, while still maintaining his elitism by creating elaborate and absurd

names and titles for himself. Although the goal of Crowley's individual magical work was ostensibly the removal of ego, the success of this venture is
certainly debatable. In describing his training, Crowley borrows from the
alchemists the term "Great Work." He also calls it the "Knowledge and Conversation with the Holy Guardian Angel," in which the angel is the higher,
true self.[13] Crowley's goal, however, should not be confused with a New Age
style of self-actualization. David Halperin, in outlining Foucault's project in
The Care of the Self, delineates the development of the self in classical Greek
culture from the self-absorption of current trends: "In the classical Greek
world, after all, the purpose of self-fashioning was not to discover one's "true
self" but to work on one's self so as to transform it into a vehicle of personal
autonomy and social preeminence. Self-regulation was a specific strategy for
gaining power over oneself and over others; it was not an ancient forerunner
of New Age mysticism."[14] I don't necessarily want to claim that Aleister
Crowley and Michel Foucault were soul brothers, but Crowley remains the
prime example of the individual member of the secret society working on the
self as a socio-political strategy.

In the case of Aleister Crowley, naming becomes a method for assuming a
false identity based on both classist and colonialist pretensions, as well as
delusions of grandeur. Yet, naming can be at once a personal, political, and
performative act. This strategy continues in current neopagan practices, in
which individuals take on mythic names. In her groundbreaking ethnography,
Persuasions of the Witch's Craft, Tanya Luhrmann describes the practice of
magical naming: "The crucial feature of the secret name is that it not only
separates two 'worlds' but allows magicians to move between them with ease.
The straddled separation makes the magicians feel special. They acquire identities more dramatic than those of their daily lives, identities in which they
have great power and influence."[15] Yet these names are more than just comic
book "secret identities." In many cases they become psychological and archetypal templates. Neopaganism and Wicca, like many alternative religions,
are religions based on self-transformation and healing. Helen Berger, in her
ethnography, *A Community of Witches,* informs us that the main forum for
this work is in ritual practice: "Rituals are in part organized around changing
the self, in relationship to changes that are occurring in the individual's life
trajectory and in terms of changes within the larger society."[16] Thus, audiences attending *The Edwardian Mysteries* find the opportunity to expand their
personality, to believe in their personal transformation, without committing
themselves to a particular path or method. A person who may be unwilling
to involve herself in religious ritual may be more willing to participate in a
theatre piece.

Yet, in order for the audience to be initiated, the actors in the production
have to take on elevated roles as priests and initiators. Despite Grygny's description of his actors as "modern day shamans" who invoke historical figures
through séance, the more appropriate term would be medium, with all the

historical, cultural, and class context that term implies. This is, after all, about genteel possession. Like the spiritualist trance speakers, whose spirits afforded women the power and status to speak in public, these voices are very much a product of a finely tuned style.[17] Despite the wide differences in cultural context, Michael Taussig's work in *Magic of the State* reminds us "how laden with possibilities for stately representation is spirit possession."[18] The possession of Chicago actors by the spirits of privileged turn-of-the-century European occultists, Edwardian orishas, exposes a more familiar power structure of class politics and spiritual philosophy.[19]

Michael Lambek's description of possession, although applied to African possession performances, also has a curious resonance here: "Possession demands both reflexivity and the engagement of onlookers [. . .]. Not intrinsically functional, possession is simply a discursive practice. With its open-endedness, the unexpected outcome, the continuing conversation, the discourse operates in the personal, interpersonal, and public domains, constructing a multiplicity of ongoing, overlapping, emergent "objects." [. . .] [P]ossession provides means and procedures that contribute to an ongoing, historically located process constituting the self and subjectivity."[20] The controlled chaos of the Edwardian experiment echoes these kinds of social negotiations, but within an American theatrical frame. Lambek further reminds us that possession is not only a text, but a culture-constructing performance. In many cases, "possession is a kind of serious parody of orthodox religion, social convention, or the accepted language of power relations. Possession may even be self-parodic."[21] The possession of the Mystery Caravan, then, points to both a celebration and a critique of the dominant culture. The secret society is parodied through the ridiculous behavior of the Dadaists and the camp of overexaggerated magical characters. Yet, it is also genuinely offered as a method for enlightenment. Again, the ludibrium.

Indeed, ritual possession as both a framing device and as a model for behavior is essential in *The Edwardian Mysteries*. From the very beginning, the audience is subjected to levels of initiation. They enter the theatre expecting to see a play and are confronted with a piece intended to make them feel somewhat uncomfortable because it is so bad. Their expectations are further subverted when they have to physically leave the theatre, process outside (the underworld) and reemerge into the space as a new community after speaking the magic password. But even here, they are faced with the gender separation, which Lynda Daniels describes as a technique for "restructuring you . . . you're forced to be something different or new, to look at the séance from your own personal point of view."[22] Thus, the spectator cannot ignore the paradigmatic nature of the séance scene, because the actors do not begin as their characters; they *invoke* them. It is only once the initial initiations are passed, the invocations are complete, and the characters are present (invoked), can the audience come back together as a community.

The further lesson is that only by imitating the Mystery Caravan, the taking on of the fantastic persona (such as "Lord of the Dance"), playing the game and joining the group (being initiated) can the individual truly belong. Playing the game may lead to enlightenment, and it is not insignificant that requirements for initiation are often based on simple challenges. In essence, the Mystery Caravan is subtly teaching its audience the rules of a much larger social and magical game. These are indeed a certain form of "making do" described by Michel de Certeau in *The Practice of Everyday Life*. In both games and stories "[m]oves not truths are recounted" and these structures "offer their audience a repertory of tactics for future use."[23] The training of the spectator, both social and spiritual, then, is what really takes center stage in *The Edwardian Mysteries*. Of course, this "new" spectator is not that new at all. But the Edwardian spectator may be just a little different.

Writing in the early 1970s, Arthur Sainer describes the savvy spectator who may acknowledge the ludibrium: "He has been given the chance to physically test out the illusory figures performing for him and to discover that these figure may be no more illusory than he himself is, may be realer than he, may be part of a trick being played on him, may in fact be fraudulent, may be neither be illusory or symbolic at all but nervous, vibrating, questioning creatures who, like himself—the spectator—are trying to find their way in the play."[24] But unlike many of the avant-garde experiments of the 1960s and 1970s, this is no worker's theatre or theatre of the oppressed. There is no illusion that the actors are, like the spectators, "trying to find their way in the play." Not at first, anyway. It is clear who is the initiate and who is the initiator, even though once an initiate, the spectator may change his or her status. So, rather than the actors pretending to be "common people" just like the audience in some show of communal and political solidarity, the audience of *The Edwardian Mysteries* is raised to an elite status. Even though elitism is the name of the game, the opportunity for initiation offers a possibility to "reform the boundaries of culture" because, as Susan Bennett suggests, the audience's "role no longer maintains the fixity that dominant cultural practice assumes."[25] Thus, the production plays back and forth with notions of elitism and egalitarianism, proposing a model for interrogating, promoting, or even parodying the structures of belief while still offering the possibility for secret and mystery.

Perhaps this speaks to a different urge in audiences today based on a vastly different political situation than thirty years ago. Again, referring to Tibetan Buddhism—this time in terms of its levels of development—Grygny ponders, "Being an American, you know, we live in a very un-hierarchical society—so to go into a situation where it's very normal for some people to know the secrets and other people to be the initiates, the seekers, creates a very unusual social dynamic."[26] Yet, it is that very desire for initiation and the ghostly presence in everyday life of secrecy and hidden knowledge (look at your average corporation) that makes such a work appealing to today's audiences. Most of all, *The Edwardian Mysteries* appeals to the individual's need to be initiated, to feel a part of something larger and more powerful, the need to actually be elite, to obtain knowledge that others do not have. In a society that has given hierarchy a bad name by abolishing systems that have oppressed and wielded power over individuals, Grygny's production argues that we also have destroyed an essential part of human development along with it: initiation and the ritualization of being welcomed into the fold. What sets *The Edwardian Mysteries* apart from other interactive works is that social and theatrical conventions are revealed as exactly that: contrived conventions that only have meaning if they are given meaning, that acting, especially "is playful illusion—as is the world itself."[27] In this, Grygny and the Mystery Caravan display a profound grasp of a postmodernist occultism. The search for spiritual truth is very appropriately presented as a game. The irony of the experience is encapsulated in a trope common to occultism throughout history: the mystery is that there is no mystery beyond what is revealed to the individual, and this mystery is accessible to anyone who has the will and the determination to seek and find. Let there be no misunderstanding, indeed.

NOTES

1. From the "magik" section of Grygny's Web site for "The World-Wide Federation of Wizards and Witches for a Free World," http://www.wwfwwffw.net. The Web site cleverly describes Grygny's theatrical actions and the spiritual and political philosophy behind them, complete with hidden (occult) links.

2. See Richard Schechner, *Between Theater and Anthropology* (Philadelphia: University of Pennsylvania Press, 1985).

3. Arthur Sainer, *The Radical Theatre Notebook* (New York: Discus Books, 1975), 74.

4. Richard Schechner, *The End of Humanism: Writings on Performance* (New York: Performing Arts Journal Publications, 1982), 28.

5. Personal correspondence, July 15, 1999.

6. My dissertation topic heavily involved the social politics of occultism, so a significant amount of research was autoethnographic, based on my experiences with esoteric groups in Chicago. Ironically, about two years after the production, Ms. Daniels became involved with the group I was most associated with: the Hermetic Order of Chicago. We became friends and it was not until after an early draft of this chapter had been written did we discover that she had indeed acted in the show. It was out of this that my interview with her emerged.

7. The term *ludibrium* means a practical joke or hoax, and is associated with the Lutheran author, Johann Valentin Andreae, who used the term to describe his novel "Chemical Wedding" (1616), one of the foundational mythical works of Rosicrucianism (*The Chemical Wedding of Christian Rosenkreutz* (1616), trans. Jocelyn Godwin, Introduction and Commentary by Adam McLean [Grand Rapids, Mich.: Phanes Press. 1991]). In *The Rosicrucians: The History, Mythology, and Rituals of an Esoteric Order,* Christopher McIntosh interprets "ludibrium" as "an act of playfulness in the spirit of homo ludens" (3rd ed. [York Beach, Me.: Samuel Weiser, Inc., 1997], 138).

8. "A Conversation with Jeff Grygny." *The Monthly Aspectarian* (September 1998), 26.

9. Joseph Roach, *Cities of the Dead: Circum-Atlantic Performance* (New York: Columbia University Press, 1996), 18.

10. Ibid., 39.

11. Israel Regardie, *What You Should Know About the Golden Dawn*, 1936, 6th ed., (Phoenix, Az.: New Falcon Publications, 1993), 39. Indeed, one of the leaders of the order in later years was Florence Farr, the famous actress and companion to George Bernard Shaw.

12. Robert Anton Wilson, Introduction to Israel Regardie's *The Eye in The Triangle: An Interpretation of Aleister Crowley*, 1970, 5th ed. (Phoenix, Az.: New Falcon Publications, 1993), xii.

13. Accordingly, Grygny has made a connection in his work between Crowley's "Conversation with the Holy Guardian Angel," and the Tibetan Buddhist's mandala principle, which, according to Grygny, allows one to develop the "personality as deity in the midst of a sacred world, allowing the yogin to manifest as a distinctive, even quirky, personality while remaining egoless" (Personal e-mail, 7/15/99).

14. David M. Halperin, *Saint Foucault: Towards a Gay Hagiography* (Oxford: Oxford University Press, 1995) 74.

15. T.M. Luhrmann, Persuasions *of the Witch's Craft: Ritual Magic in Contemporary England* (Cambridge, Mass.: Harvard University Press, 1989), 230.

16. Helen Berger, *A Community of Witches: Contemporary Neo-Paganism and Witchcraft in the United States* (Columbia: University of South Carolina Press, 1999), 29.

17. See Alex Owen, *The Darkened Room: Women, Power and Spiritualism in Late Victorian England* (Philadelphia: University of Pennsylvania Press, 1990), and Anne Braude, *Radical Spirits: Spiritualism and Women's Rights in Nineteenth-Century America* (Boston: Beacon Press, 1989).

18. Michael Taussig, *The Magic of the State* (New York: Routledge, 1997), 78.

19. In a conversation with Janice Pope of Penn State, who organized performances by actors who portrayed colonial figures at local theme sites in Virginia, we talked about "living historians" who sometimes used vaguely spiritualist language to describe their experience of "channeling" historical persona (2000 ATHE Conference in Washington, D.C.). In similar spiritualist language, Civil War reenactors have spoken of "the veil disappearing" when they enter into simulated battle (Randel Allred, "Catharsis, Revision and Re-Enactment: Negotiating the Meaning of the American Civil War," *Journal of American Culture*, 18.4 [1996], 7).

20. Quoted in Robert I. Levy, Jeannette Marie Mageo, and Alan Howard, "Gods, Spirits, and History: A Theoretical Perspective," in *Spirits in Culture, History, and Mind*, eds. Jeannette Marie Mageo and Alan Howard (New York: Routledge, 1996), 26.

21. Ibid., 25.

22. Daniels also indicated that there were esoteric reasons for the gender separation. According to her, Grygny described this as "harnessing the energies of polarity."

23. Michel de Certeau, *The Practice of Everyday Life* (Berkeley: University of California Press, 1984), 23.

24. Sainer, *Radical Theatre,* 79.

25. Susan Bennett, *Theatre Audiences: A Theory of Production and Reception* (New York: Routledge, 1990), 180.

26. "Conversation," 25.

27. Schechner, *Between Theater,* 97.

INDEX

ABOUT THE AUTHORS

Joshua Abrams is adjunct assistant professor of liberal studies at the New School University and a doctoral candidate in theater at the City University of New York Graduate Center, where he is completing his dissertation, "Staging Alterity: The Ethics of Performing Difference(s)." His essays and reviews have appeared in publications including *Theatre Journal, TDR, Slavic and East European Performance,* and *Didaskalia.* Joshua is the former managing editor of *Western European Stages.*

Katherine Adamenko is a performance/installation artist, poet, curator, and teacher. A trained dancer, actress, and singer, she generates work that is a pastiche of artistic styles and disciplines from Cabaret to Butoh, informed by feminist and performance theory. Her work has been presented at galleries, theaters, museums, and clubs throughout the United States and Europe. Original works include two full-length one-woman shows, *The Story of a Phallus Woman* and *Ladies Who Go Bump in the Night,* the intimate *Salon Apartment Series,* and *CENSORED.* Katherine holds a BA in dance and joint political science/history from Rutgers University and received her MA in contemporary theatre practice (distinction) from the University of Essex in England.

David Callaghan has an MFA in directing from Western Illinois University and received his PhD in theatre from the CUNY Graduate Center in 1998.

He has taught a wide variety of theatre courses at AMDA in New York City, Illinois Wesleyan University, and at the University of Montevallo in Alabama, where he is currently an assistant professor of Theatre. David has previously written about The Living Theatre and 1960s performance in *Theatre Journal, Viet Nam Generation, Journal of Dramatic Theory and Criticism,* and *Theatre Symposium.* His most recent conference paper was presented on "Brecht and The Living Theatre's Plays of the 1990s" at the 2002 Twentieth Century Literature Conference. David also has directed many plays in academia and around the country, and worked on the casting of new plays and several TV projects in New York City and Los Angeles.

Uttara Asha Coorlawala teaches in the dance programs of Long Island University's C.W. Post Campus, Barnard College (Columbia University) and Princeton, N.J. She served as editor for *The Newsletter of the Congress of Research in Dance.* Her articles have been published in *Dance Chronicle, Dance Research Journal, Sangeet Natak Akademi Journal* and included in anthologies on Indian and intercultural dance. As a dancer-choreographer, Coorlawala pioneered what is now a growing trend on the Indian dance scene toward innovation. Her choreographic style and performances brought her three disciplines—modern dance, Bharata Natyam and yoga—to the dance stage. She danced throughout India, in Europe, East Europe, Japan, and the United States, and as a designated cultural representative of India and the U.S. Information service.

Judith W. Fisher is an associate professor in the Department of Drama, Queen's University, Canada, where she teaches acting, directing, and theatre history. She received her PhD from the University of Alberta and she also trained at the Bristol Old Vic Theatre School and continues a professional acting career, begun in England in the early 1960s as a dancer and choreographer. Publications include dramatic adaptations of *A Christmas Carol, The Legend of Sleepy Hollow* (produced with Bunraku puppets), and *The Lion, the Witch, and the Wardrobe,* all produced at the Citadel Theatre, Alberta, Canada; chapters in books and articles in journals on eighteenth-century drama, fiction (particularly Samuel Richardson and Jane Austen), and theatre history. She is currently working on a book on the working lives of eighteenth-century actresses.

Susan C. Haedicke currently teaches drama at The George Washington University and has taught theatre history and dramaturgy at University of Maryland, University of Massachusetts/Amherst and Mount Holyoke College. She is the Director of Inside French Theatre, an annual summer program giving

American students the opportunity to work with French theatre professionals and produce a show in Paris. Dr. Haedicke has published several essays and presented numerous papers on community-based theatre and she has coedited a book, *Performing Democracy: International Perspectives on Community-Based Performance* (2001). Her current research interest focuses on the work of contemporary Algerian dramatists living in exile in France whose plays explore the complex postcolonial relationship between the two countries. In addition, Dr. Haedicke currently works as a professional dramaturg in Paris, France and has worked professionally in Washington, D.C.

Susan Kattwinkel is associate professor of theatre history at the College of Charleston in Charleston, South Carolina. She is the editor for *Theatre Symposium: A Publication of the Southeastern Theatre Conference*, vols. 12 and 13, and edited the book *Sketches and Afterpieces from the Vaudeville Theatre of Tony Pastor* for Greenwood Press in 1998. Dr. Kattwinkel presents papers on vaudeville theatre and contemporary variety theatre regularly at academic conferences and has published in the *New England Theatre Journal* and *Theatre Symposium*. She is currently a primary investigator on an NSF grant project to create a live performance simulation system that is based at the University of Georgia.

Joanne Klein is professor of dramatic arts and the coordinator of women, gender, and sexuality studies at St. Mary's College of Maryland. She has published in *Journal of Dramatic Theory and Criticism, Theatre Journal,* and *The Chelsea House Library of Literary Criticism.* Dr. Klein's book, *Making Pictures: The Pinter Screenplays,* was published by Ohio State University Press. Currently, she is researching the relationship between postmodern mediations and spectating both as a scholar and as a director.

Nina LeNoir is assistant professor in the Department of Theatre Arts at Minnesota State University, Mankato. She received her PhD and MFA in directing from the University of Texas at Austin. Dr. LeNoir teaches classes in directing, acting, theatre history, and theory, and directs in academia and professionally. She has published in *Theatre Symposium* and has presented papers at ATHE, NCA, MATC, and Theatre Symposium conferences.

Dawn Lewcock was an associate of the (now defunct) Drama Board (1973), and has a teaching Diploma in Speech and Drama from the London Guildhall School of Music and Drama (1976). She was awarded a BEd (Hons Cantab) in 1982 as a mature student followed by a PhD in 1987. She directs Diploma and Certificate courses in drama and theatre history for the Cambridge University Institute of Continuing Education. She continues to research theatre history, has published in several journals, contributed to *Aphra Behn Studies* (CUP, 1996) and provided entries on *Aphra Behn, Alan Ayckbourn, Richard Brinsley Sheridan, Restoration Drama, English Verse Forms,* and *Art and Literature* for the *Continuum Encyclopedia of Literature* (2003). A book on classical art and the god Dionysus is in progress.

Judith Sebesta is assistant professor of theatre history and director of graduate studies at the University of Arizona. She has served as editor of ATHENews, the newsletter of the Association for Theatre in Higher Education, and has published on performance space and musical theatre in *Theatre Journal, On-Stage Studies,* and *The Sondheim Review.* Additionally, she has worked extensively as a dramaturg and is coediting an anthology on women and musical theatre.

Patrick Tuite earned a PhD in theatre history at the University of Wisconsin. He now serves as the head of the MA program in theater history at the Catholic University of America, where he also teaches courses for the Center for Irish Studies. He has recently completed a manuscript that examines the role of theatrical practices in seventeenth-century Ireland. The text identifies the relationship between the pageants and processions that early modern settlers performed in Ireland's walled cities and Northern Ireland's current parading institutions. He continues his performance studies research in Northern Ireland and hopes to complete a documentary that details the apparent success of cross-community productions staged during Derry's Maiden City Festival. Grants from the Catholic University of America, the Joan B. Kroc Institute for International Peace Studies, and the Keough Institute for Irish Studies at the University of Notre Dame have made this research possible. Patrick would like to thank the faculty at these institutions for their support.

Mark S. Weinberg, professor of theatre at the UW-Rock County and UW-Milwaukee, has studied with Boal in Atlanta, Omaha, Toronto, and New York and with Boal practitioners Douglas Paterson, David Diamond, Marc Weinblat, and Michael Rohd, among others. Professor Weinberg teaches and uses TO techniques on his campus with students and faculty. He has lectured widely on Boal and Community-Based Theatre and has conducted workshops for educators, administrators, students, children, social activists, community groups, and others in the United States, Australia, and Canada, including the Eighth International Theatre of the Oppressed Festival in Toronto, where he also performed with OPTION: CTO Omaha. He has written about activist